The History of Christianity in the Reformation Era
Part I

Professor Brad S. Gregory

THE TEACHING COMPANY ®

PUBLISHED BY:

THE TEACHING COMPANY
4840 Westfields Boulevard, Suite 500
Chantilly, Virginia 20151-2299
1-800-TEACH-12
Fax—703-378-3819
www.teach12.com

ISBN 1-56585-797-6

Brad S. Gregory, Ph.D.

Assistant Professor of History, Stanford University

Brad S. Gregory holds five university degrees, including undergraduate and advanced degrees in both History and Philosophy. He received a B.S. in History from Utah State University (1985); B.A. and Licentiate degrees in Philosophy from the Institute of Philosophy of the Catholic University of Louvain, Belgium (1984, 1987); an M.A. in History from the University of Arizona (1989); and a Ph.D. in History from Princeton University (1996). From 1994–1996, he was a Junior Fellow in the Harvard Society of Fellows. In 1996, he joined the history faculty as an assistant professor at Stanford University, where he has since taught courses on late medieval and early modern Christianity, early modern Europe, and historical methodology, in addition to directing the history department's honors program. His scholarly interests range widely over the long-term transition from the Middle Ages to the modern era.

Professor Gregory has received numerous awards and fellowships, including the Walter J. Gores Award, Stanford's highest teaching honor, after just his second year of university teaching (1998), and the Dean's Award for Distinguished Teaching in the School of Humanities and Sciences at Stanford (2000). In 1999–2000, he was a faculty research fellow at the Stanford Humanities Center. The author of numerous scholarly articles, Professor Gregory's first book, *Salvation at Stake: Christian Martyrdom in Early Modern Europe*, was published in 1999 by Harvard University Press, from which it received the Thomas J. Wilson Prize as the best first book published by the press during the calendar year. The book has also received the 2000 John Gilmary Shea Prize of the American Catholic Historical Association, the 2000 Phi Alpha Theta Book Award, the 2000 California Book Award silver medal for nonfiction, and second place in the 2000 Catholic Press Association Book Awards.

Table of Contents

The History of Christianity in the Reformation Era
Part I

The History of Christianity in the Reformation Era

Scope:

The century and a half from about 1500 to about 1650 is among the most tumultuous and consequential periods in all of European history. At the center of the upheaval stands religion, particularly the disagreements and divisions in Western Christianity. This course presents an analytical narrative of the religious developments of the Reformation era in their political, cultural, and social contexts, emphasizing the embeddedness of Christian beliefs and practices in the institutional and intellectual life of the period. It treats not only the Protestant Reformation and state-supported Protestantism but also the radical Reformation and varieties of Anabaptism, as well as the persistence and transformation of Roman Catholicism. The overall goal will be to understand historically the theological and devotional aspects of each of these three broad traditions on its own terms and to grasp the overall ramifications of religious conflict for the subsequent course of modern Western history. Geographically, the course ranges across Western Europe, with most attention devoted to England, France, Germany, the Low Countries, Italy, and Spain.

The first six lectures discuss the late Middle Ages and the late medieval Church as the matrix out of which Reformation-era Christianity emerged. After an introductory lecture that provides an overview of the entire course, a second lecture surveys some of the basic demographic, political, and social realities common in this distant, pre-industrial, hierarchical world. The third and fourth lectures discuss some of the most important, interwoven beliefs, practices, and institutions of Latin Christendom on the eve of the Reformation. The countervailing signs of corruption and vitality in the late medieval Church are addressed in Lecture Five, while Lecture Six explores an important strand of reform that would influence sixteenth-century developments in significant ways, namely Christian humanism, above all in the person of Erasmus of Rotterdam.

From here, in Lectures Seven through Twelve, we enter the world of the early Reformation in Germany and Switzerland. Two lectures are devoted to the most important of the Protestant reformers, Martin Luther. The first of these discusses his trajectory from an obscure

Augustinian monk and university professor in 1517 to an international figure who defied pope and emperor by 1521. The next lecture addresses the meaning and implications of his basic theological convictions. Lecture Nine looks at Huldrych Zwingli, the Protestant preacher and leader of the Reformation in Zurich, in the broader context of the Swiss Confederation. The spread of the early evangelical movement in the towns of Germany during the early 1520s is the subject of Lecture Ten. Lectures Eleven and Twelve are the first devoted to the Radical Reformation, considering, in turn, the "social Gospel" and revolutionary demands of the "Common Man" during the Peasants' War of 1524–1525 and the emergence of early Anabaptist separatist groups in Germanic lands after the suppression of the peasants.

Looking beyond central Europe, the next four lectures explore further key developments during the crucial decades of the 1520s and 1530s among Protestants, Catholics, and Anabaptists. Lecture Thirteen discusses the similarities and differences in the spread of early Protestantism to England, France, and the Low Countries. The fourteenth lecture considers Henry VIII's Reformation in England, an ecclesio-political development that severed the country's longstanding ecclesiastical ties to Rome. The theological and institutional Catholic reaction to the early Reformation is the subject of Lecture Fifteen; it treats the counter-arguments marshaled against Protestantism and radical Protestantism. Lecture Sixteen tells the remarkable story of early Dutch Anabaptism and the rise and fall of the Kingdom of Münster in 1534–1535; the practices of this group under the radical, violent Anabaptist leader Jan van Leiden reinforced authorities' suspicion of all forms of religious radicalism.

In Lectures Seventeen through Twenty-Two, we move through the middle decades of the sixteenth century, again by looking at all three traditions but especially Protestantism and the emergence of Calvinism. Lecture Seventeen is devoted to John Calvin himself, including his life, some key emphases in his theology, and the chief Reformation institutions in his adopted city, Geneva. In the following lecture, we move south, to Italy, and discuss aspects of Catholic reform before the Council of Trent, including the founding of the Society of Jesus by Ignatius Loyola. Lecture Nineteen considers the growth and embattlement of Protestantism in Germany, France, England, and the Low Countries during the 1540s and the first part of the 1550s. This theme is pursued in more detail in

Lecture Twenty, which considers the rapid growth of Calvinism in France and the Netherlands in the late 1550s and early 1560s, and in Lecture Twenty-One, devoted to John Knox and the adoption of Calvinism in Scotland in 1559–1560. Lecture Twenty-Two tells the story of Menno Simons and the difficulties faced by persecuted Mennonites in the Low Countries in the decades following the collapse of the Kingdom of Münster.

The next three lectures are devoted to fundamental developments in Roman Catholicism. The doctrinal and disciplinary aspects of the Council of Trent (1545–1563) are the subject of Lecture Twenty-Three, while Lecture Twenty-Four treats the efforts made to implement the council's prescriptions among the Catholic clergy and laity. Lecture Twenty-Five discusses the vast missionary efforts that accompanied European trade and conquest both before and after the Council of Trent, in both Asia and the Americas, noting parallels to concurrent efforts made in Catholic Europe.

Lectures Twenty-Six through Twenty-Nine focus on the conflicts and coexistence of Catholics and Protestants in the later sixteenth century in four different countries or regions. The French Wars of Religion (1562–1598) from the Massacre of Vassy to the Edict of Nantes are treated in Lecture Twenty-Six. Next, we turn to the Low Countries and the Dutch Revolt against Spain, chronicling the emergence of an independent United Provinces of the Netherlands and the foundations of a Calvinist Netherlands and a Catholic Belgium in the modern era. Lecture Twenty-Eight examines the religious spectrum of Elizabethan England, including conformist Protestants of the Church of England, godly Puritans who wanted a Christianity more in the continental Calvinist mold, and dissenting Catholics who were loyal to Rome. Moving to central Europe after the Peace of Augsburg (1555), Lecture Twenty-Nine discusses confessionalization, the cooperative efforts between churches and states, whether Lutheran, Catholic, or Calvinist, in the territorial states of the Holy Roman Empire.

The next three lectures pursue these national narratives through the first half of the seventeenth century. Lecture Thirty contrasts the trend toward anti-Calvinist Catholic uniformity in France and the southern Netherlands with the religious pluralism and comparatively broad de facto religious toleration in the United Provinces, noting too the continuing theological debates about grace in Protestant

Arminianism, as well as Catholic Jansenism. Lecture Thirty-One chronicles the bloodiest of all the era's wars of religion, the Thirty Years' War (1618–1648), which was fought largely in central Europe but involved nearly every European country at one point or another. The religious tensions in early seventeenth-century England, the English Revolution, and the Restoration of 1660 are treated in Lecture Thirty-Two.

The final four lectures address wide-ranging, comparative, analytical questions about the nature, influence, and legacy of Christianity during the era. The thirty-third lecture attempts to assess the impact of the religious transformations on different aspects of early modern society and culture, including the family and marriage, religious art, and literacy and education. Lecture Thirty-Four seeks to evaluate whether and in what senses the Reformations can be said to have been successful and whether certain traditions were more successful than others. The penultimate lecture offers reflections on large-scale changes in European Christianity, including the era's volatile combination of shared and incompatible beliefs across distinct communities of faith. The final lecture notes the supreme irony by which the religious commitments and conflicts of the era helped contribute to the rise of secular institutions and ideas, to a world in which Christianity was eventually marginalized but not replaced.

Lecture One
Early Modern Christianity—A Larger View

Scope:

In the period from c. 1500 to c. 1650, modern Christian pluralism took shape in Western Europe. Catholicism persisted and was renewed; various forms of Protestantism were born and institutionalized; and a wide range of radical forms of Protestantism emerged. This course seeks a contextual understanding of all three of these traditions on their own terms and in conflict with one another. Its overriding purpose is to provide an international perspective on early modern Protestantism, radical Protestantism, and Roman Catholicism in their complex social, political, and cultural contexts. We will then discern how their differences and conflicts contributed decisively to the emergence of modern ideas and institutions.

Outline

I. "The Protestant Reformation" is an insufficiently broad category to encompass early modern Christianity, which includes Protestantism, radical Protestantism, and Roman Catholicism in Western Europe from c. 1500 to c. 1650.

   A. "The Protestant Reformation" as a category reflects the legacy of Protestant confessional history. Implicitly or explicitly, it pays less attention to, and judges as inferior, the radical Protestant and Catholic traditions.

   B. The approach in this course will be comparative and cross-confessional; our main goal will be to understand Protestants, radical Protestants, and Catholics on their own terms, as well as in relationship with one another.

II. The attempt to understand historically these distinct and often mutually hostile Christian traditions presents at least four major challenges.

   A. Many of the beliefs and values of early modern Christians are alien or offensive to modern moral and political views, whether the latter are religious or secular.

   B. Religion was deeply embedded in human life in this era, which necessitates familiarity with other early modern institutions, assumptions, and customs.

C. The political reception of a given form of Christianity varied dramatically in both national and local contexts and changed, sometimes drastically, over time.
   1. Our geographical focus must shift depending on the particular issue in hand.
   2. Rulers' decisions enormously affected Christians' experience.

D. The ways in which people responded to the various traditions differed radically and were shaped by a host of social and cultural variables.
   1. Recent scholarship has greatly extended our knowledge of how religion was received, understood, and practiced.
   2. It is important to integrate new knowledge without losing sight of what we already know.

III. Three fundamental themes throughout the course include the character of religiosity, the relationship between ecclesiastical and political authorities, and the socially embedded spectrum of religious engagement.

A. The course aims to provide a sympathetic presentation of Protestantism, radical Protestantism, and Catholicism in early modern Europe, exploring religious beliefs and behaviors, doctrines and devotion. This exploration includes the disagreements and conflicts of these traditions with one another.

B. The course emphasizes the ever-present, extremely important relationship between ecclesiastical authorities and political authorities for the experience of early modern Christians.

C. The course aims never to lose sight of the wide-ranging spectrum of religious commitment, from fervent devotion to indifference and hostility, set in the concreteness of early modern European life.

IV. The course is structured as an analytical narrative that starts around 1500 and ends around 1650.

A. The presentation combines a largely chronological ordering with analysis and organization that shifts depending on the subject matter of each lecture.

B. As a narrative, the course has a beginning and an end, each of which was deliberately chosen.

   1. The course starts on the eve of the Reformation, because without some understanding of late medieval Christianity, it is impossible to grasp the nature or significance of what followed.

   2. The course ends in the mid-seventeenth century, because that time marks a watershed in the relationship between religion and politics in European history.

Questions to Consider:

1. How do the choices of approach and subject matter that historians make influence the nature of the stories they tell and the analyses they provide?

2. What do we lose if we impose modern values and concepts on pre-modern people?

Lecture One—Transcript
Early Modern Christianity—A Larger View

Hello. Welcome to this lecture course on the history of Christianity in the Reformation era. My name is Brad Gregory. I'm a professor of European history at Stanford University, and I'll be your director, your tour guide, as it were, for this lecture course consisting of 36 half-hour lectures.

I specialize in the early modern period at Stanford, the sixteenth and seventeenth centuries, a period of tremendous tumult, marked by upheavals in virtually every area of life; these upheavals had religion at their centers, however. This is also an extraordinarily influential period for understanding the modern world, and a great deal of the modern assumptions—the ways in which we think, the ways in which we deal with our everyday lives. Part of the course, then, will be to show, over the course of the 36 lectures, the ways in which this distant world has impinged on our own.

The purpose of today's lecture is to provide an overview of the scope and the objectives of the course, to lay out several of the fundamental challenges we face in approaching our subject matter, to introduce some of the fundamental themes that will run throughout the lectures, and to explain the course's chronological span. First things first, then; the scope of the course. We will cover Christianity in Western Europe from about 1500 to about 1650, part of which is called, and which I will often refer to, as the "early modern period," between the Middle Ages and the modern era. The fundamental subject matter for the course are the three main traditions that either emerged or persisted during this era, namely, Protestantism, radical Protestantism, and Roman Catholicism.

Right off the bat, there are a couple of points of clarification. The distinction between Protestantism and radical Protestantism, as I will use the terms, is the distinction between the Protestantism that supported, and was supported by, political authorities, and the Protestantism that in principle rejected alliances with political authorities, and was often opposed by them. A second point of clarification is that both Protestantism and radical Protestantism are wide umbrella categories, comprising numerous groups in each. There are specific traditions, each of which is comprised by the two terms as I use them. The most important tradition within radical Protestantism was Anabaptism, which was itself composed of different subtraditions; these subtraditions will become clear as the course proceeds. I simply want to make clear the terms I'm using as I introduce them.

This, then, is not a course on just the Protestant Reformation, if by "Reformation" you simply mean "Protestantism." Hence, the title of the course, "The History of Christianity in the Reformation Era." We'll take here a broader view of the phenomenon, and a different view of its legacy and influence, than was often traditionally the case. We're not studying just one broad tradition, but three; these are three traditions in relation to one another. To understand the significance of this shift in approach, we have to know something about traditional confessional, or church, history of the Reformation.

Until recent decades, this was the dominant way of approaching subject matter in this country as well as in the Protestant areas of Europe. According to this view, the key development within early modern Christianity in the sixteenth and seventeenth centuries was the emergence of Protestantism as a purer and truer, better form of Christianity, as compared to the corruption and superstitions of late medieval Catholicism. The Reformation was fundamentally about the liberation of individuals to believe as they pleased, at least over the long term. This was in contrast to the authoritarianism of the medieval church. It was the high road to modern religious toleration and individual freedom of belief. Indeed, the very term "Reformation," within this approach, implies that a good form of Christianity reformed and replaced a bad one. In Protestant confessional history, then, radical Protestantism and Catholicism were treated almost as afterthoughts, and with either explicit or implicit criticism.

In short, Protestant confessional or church history was the history of modern Christianity, written on the basis of Protestant conviction; this had a built-in Protestant bias, and made Protestantism the center of the story. An important point to make is that it was paralleled by lesser-known, Catholic confessional historical approaches, or radical Protestant confessional histories. In the latter case, this was most often Mennonite confessional history. Both of these were minority strands among American and European scholars of early modern Christianity. They essentially take the same approach, but simply write on the basis of either Catholic or radical Protestantism convictions.

In this course, by contrast, I will trace the principal developments in all three of these traditions within an inclusive rubric, early modern Christianity. In comparison to confessional history, about which I've just said a few words, the approach here differs in the following three ways. First of all, I will give substantial coverage to all three traditions, not letting one dominate and the others be marginalized. Secondly, I will separate the attempts to understand and analyze each of the three traditions from any present-day value judgments about them, either about the truth of their teachings or the worth of their practices. Thirdly, I will strive to understand and present the protagonists of each of the three traditions on their own terms, such that they themselves would recognize themselves in my own account.

The approach in this course, then, will be deliberately cross-confessional and comparative. It will attempt to understand the men and women within each of these three traditions on their own terms, and in relationship to, and conflict with, each other. This will enable us to grasp the significance of early modern Christianity as a whole, in ways that I do not think will be possible if we focus primarily on one tradition, or if we favor one of the three traditions over the other two. The long-term payoff, and the payoff at the end of this course of lectures, will be a better understanding between the world of early modern Europe, and the modern world to which it gave rise.

This objective, as I've laid it out—understanding different traditions on their own terms, and in conflict with one another—is more challenging than it sounds at first. I'd like to mention four important ways as to why it's so challenging, which will also serve to introduce some elements of our subject matter.

First of all, the first challenge to be faced is the simple fact that we are dealing in this course with people who lived four and five centuries ago. They are from a word and a culture drastically different from our own, that of pre-modern Europe. Not only are there all of the obvious material and technological differences from a time pre-dating the Industrial Revolution, but there are also perhaps even greater cultural, moral, and political differences; these are differences in values and convictions that separate us from them.

The fact is that the beliefs and values of the late medieval and early modern people are not only often alien, but also often profoundly offensive, to modern Western sensibilities, whether they concern assumptions about social privilege and hierarchy, about the relationships between men and women, about conceptions of God and religion, religious freedom, the relationship between public and private, or the relationship of individuals to society as a whole. The list goes on and on. If we want to understand these past people, then, rather than simply judging them on the basis of our own modern beliefs and values, we must strive to bracket our own convictions. Otherwise, we will only, and can only, see them on our terms, and will be unable to grasp not only them, but how their world gave rise to ours.

The problem, as I stated it here, that of the "otherness" of the past, is intensified for our purposes insofar as it relates to our efforts to understand not simply "a" past culture and society, but three broad and complex Christian traditions that were in sharp and often violent conflict with one another, those of the Protestants, radical Protestants, and Roman Catholics. If we simply condemn them from the outset, we'll never understand them, nor will we understand at all if we happen to sympathize strongly with one to the exclusion of the others. The first challenge we face, then, in the course is that of dealing sympathetically and empathetically with the "otherness" of the men and women whom we'll meet.

The second challenge we'll face in the course is that, very much unlike religion in the modern Western world, Christianity in the early modern period was deeply imbedded in the public institution, wider cultural assumptions, social relationships, and political activities of Europeans in the sixteenth and seventeenth centuries. This means that in order to understand religion in the period, we have no choice but to understand a great deal more about the early modern world as well; its political institutions and social order, the wider culture, and so forth.

For example, among Protestants, radical Protestants, and Catholics, religion was inextricably social. It involved certain kinds of social obligations, certain forms of association and exhortation. Conversely, it's difficult to imagine social relationships among earlier modern Europeans, of whatever Christian persuasion, that were not in some way religiously significant. This is to be expected, perhaps, when dealing with a religion that stressed "Love thy neighbor" as a good thing to do. That, of course, implied that a failure to love one's neighbor was a bad thing, and so forth. Certain kinds of social obligations and relationships were implied in Christianity per se. In short, to reiterate this point, if we tried to pursue Christianity alone in early modern Europe, whatever that would mean, and left out the social relationships and the political entanglements, we would get a deeply distorted view. It would take us far away from our goal of trying to understand early modern Christians in our three broad traditions on their own terms. In short, if they didn't separate religion from their political engagements, familial relationships, views on education, and so forth, then neither should we, we who want to understand those people.

The "otherness" of the past and the deep embeddedness of religion are two fundamental challenges that we'll face throughout the course. The third major challenge, and obstacle to our major goal, is that the political context for the reception of, or the resistance to, the various forms of early modern Christianity varied radically at both the national and local levels. Reception, or resistance, changed dramatically over time. This means that we have to distinguish among, and be sensitive to, the differences among Protestants, radical Protestants, and Catholics, but we also have to differentiate our analysis, and to tell our story, wherever appropriate, with national and/or regional frameworks in mind, so as to give examples, and make the abstractions I've just articulated somewhat more concrete.

The early Reformation spread rapidly in southern Germany, but it was suppressed in England and France. The Catholic reforms of the Council of Trent were received relatively quickly in Spain and Italy, and received more slowly in the southern Netherlands and in France. Baptism gained a following in Germanic lands, in Switzerland, and in the Low Countries, but almost none in France, very little in England, and so forth.

Another example. The changes over time in particular countries, and rulers' decisions, affected religion enormously. England between the years 1530 and 1560 is perhaps the most dramatic example, with its successive official shifts from Roman Catholicism to Henrician Catholicism under Henry VIII, to reformed Protestantism under Edward VI, back to Roman Catholicism under Mary Tudor, and finally to a more moderate Protestantism under Elizabeth, after Mary. A great deal of recent scholarship on early modern Christianity has discovered how important local particularities were in the course of religious development. For example, local political realities within a given region hugely affected the receptiveness to early Protestantism.

In our lectures, I will make reference to these sorts of differences at various times; it's always important to bear them in mind with whatever I say in the course. However, I will not dwell on these local particularities and differences, in a course that seeks to be a comprehensive overview. If this were a course on just one tradition in one country, for example, just English Protestantism, then a fine-grained approach emphasizing local differences between different towns and regions in that particular country would be both possible and appropriate. Geographically, the course will concentrate on the German-speaking areas of central Europe, France, England, and the Low Countries—the modern-day Netherlands—and Belgium. There will also be attention given to Switzerland, Scotland, Italy, and Spain.

The final, fourth challenge that we'll face throughout the course is that the reception by men and women across the social spectrum of the various Christian traditions we'll be dealing with varied enormously, depending on a wide range of factors. These included social background, education, occupation, age, sex, family position, and personal decision-making. Perhaps the biggest single development in the last generation of scholarship on the Reformation has been the emergence of questions concerning the reception of, and resistance to, religion and religious change across the full social spectrum. They are sensitive to these factors I've just mentioned, in what is often referred to as "the social history of the Reformation." It involves more than just the emphasis on major theologians and pivotal events that tended to be characteristic of confessional history, regardless of its particular doctrinal stripe.

Without question, this recent social history of the Reformation has added enormously to our understanding of early modern Christianity. We've seen crucial differences that weren't apparent before; for example, between urban and rural contexts, men and women in certain situations, or learned and unlearned Christians. These factors impacted how a given form of Christianity was experienced, adopted, adapted, or rejected. This approach has also reinforced our appreciation of the importance of local contexts. For example, it sometimes made all the difference in the world if one had a local village pastor who was conscientious rather than lazy. That could make an enormous difference in how people learned, or failed to learn, their Christianity.

At the same time, while acknowledging the importance and undeniable significance of these advances in our knowledge and research in terms of the Reformation's social history, it's possible to go too far; for example, emphasizing ordinary people at the expense of the major reformers and political decision-makers whose influence was enormous and undeniable. It's also possible to emphasize social and cultural factors so much that one almost loses sight of religion altogether, or subsumes religion under reductionist explanations that, in fact, do not succeed in understanding early modern people on their own terms; rather, their views are merely filtered through modern sociological or anthropological theories, in which early modern people would never have recognized themselves.

The endeavor to understand Protestants, radical Protestants, and Catholics in the Reformation era, then, presents considerable challenges: The challenge of understanding across a chasm of half a millennium, of grasping the embeddedness of religion in life, of sensitivity to variations in political context, and finally, to variations in the practice of religion across the social spectrum. All this being said, I'd now like to note three major themes that run throughout the lectures. I'll bear in mind both our goal to understand Protestantism, radical Protestantism, and Catholicism, and to understand them historically, meaning contextually, in the world of early modern Europe.

The first theme. My concern in the lectures will be to penetrate and present fairly the religious convictions, sensibilities, and practices for Protestants, radical Protestants, and Catholics alike. This is true not only for their religious doctrines, but in regard to what those who articulated those doctrines thought about them, and what they themselves said about what they believed. It means that we must not only pay attention to the religious beliefs, but the religious practices, and to the relationship between these two components. It means that we must plunge ourselves into the world of their devotion, theology, and worship. We must sympathetically try to understand the appeal of their respective versions of Christianity.

Again, we'll be trying to do this for each of the three main traditions; these traditions did not agree with one another, and often came into violent conflict with each other. To be consistent with our original objective, I will not shy away from, or try to sugar-coat, the often bitter religious controversies of the era, or the disputes among Protestants, radical Protestants, and Catholics in their various combinations; nor will I do so with the disputes in Protestantism itself. I will let the various sides have their say. Accordingly, we'll try to understand the controversies and what they held at stake for the respective protagonists. These controversies are part of the respective traditions. We would paint a grossly impoverished picture of early modern Christianity if we were to pay them little attention. Literally thousands of works devoted to denouncing and undermining specific religious adversaries were published in the sixteenth and seventeenth centuries. This began immediately with the start of the Reformation, in the early 1520s.

That's the first major theme, to penetrate and fairly present the views of each of the three main practices. The second major theme is the relationship between ecclesiastical and political authorities; to put it in more modern shorthand, of churches to states. This is an ever-present reality that affects the three main traditions in early modern Christianity. Sometimes, I will refer to "secular authorities" in the lectures; these are political magistrates or authorities. This should not be confused with modern secularism, however. All early modern Christian authorities practiced some kind of Christianity. They were not ecclesiastical or church authorities. This is an institutional distinction, rather than a comparative one of "religion" versus "non-religion."

A great many issues would arise in the sixteenth century, that were concerned with the proper relationships between ecclesiastical and political authorities. Who had jurisdiction over what? Should civic magistrates make decisions that bear on true doctrine and proper moral behavior? Should dissident groups be permitted, or suppressed? What would the likely costs be in either case? Do political authorities have a duty to promote true Christianity? Do conscientious Christian subjects have the right, or even duty, to rebel against a ruler imposing a false Christianity, as they see it? With few exceptions, sixteenth-century rulers believed that religious uniformity within their territories or countries was a political, social, and spiritual ideal. Whether a particular group was either protected, or prosecuted, at a given time and place, is perhaps the most dramatic example of how important the decisions and policies of secular authorities were to Christians' experiences in early modern Europe.

Thus, we'll try to penetrate the religious views and practices, bear in mind the relationships between churches and states, and finally, that men and women within and across these beliefs and practices reveal a spectrum of religious commitment. They run the gamut from most fervent, to basic conformity, to shoulder-shrugging indifference, to foot-dragging noncompliance. This spectrum also cannot be coordinated within a grid of social status, in that those who were well-educated were devout, while the illiterate majority was indifferent, or vice versa. There were devout, conformist, and indifferent Christians among social and cultural elites, and among humble artisans and peasants. This theme underscores our required attempt to always be alert to the cultural embeddedness of early modern Protestants, radical Protestants, and Catholics. Early modern Christianity unfolded within a real world, rather than in an abstract, abstruse realm of ideas per se.

As I've outlined the presentation here, the obstacles, challenges, and major themes throughout the course will take the form of an analytical narrative across our 36 lectures. I'll explain what I mean by that. It's a narrative because it tells a story. It moves more or less chronologically from the late Middle Ages, when the eve of the Reformation began in the early sixteenth century, through the sixteenth century, and ending in the middle of the seventeenth century, around 1650. It's analytical because it shifts emphasis and pursues different objectives in different lectures, depending on the subject matter at hand. For example, a lecture on Luther's theology will not have the same structure or purpose as does a lecture on the Council of Trent, on Catholic missions, or on the Anabaptist kingdom of Muenster.

The lectures are deliberately and carefully designed so that you can follow a particular subnarrative through a selection of the lectures, if you wish. For example, you can pursue the development of one of the three traditions, such as radical Protestantism, throughout the various lectures that deal with it. You may also deal with the story of early modern Christianity within a particular national context, a particular country. For example, you may trace England's progression through several different lectures. I've done it this way because I imagined that people might have certain particular interests in one of the three main traditions, or in particular countries.

Narratives or stories have a beginning and an end. As a concluding note to this introductory lecture, I'd like to tell you why the course begins around 1500 and ends around 1650. In logical terms, one must start prior to the beginning of the Reformation, with late medieval Christianity, in order to know how and why early Protestantism and radical Protestantism were challenging what came before them. How was the Reformation different than what had preceded it? What was objectionable in Protestantism and radical Protestantism to Catholic authorities? Unless we have some sense of what late medieval Christianity was, we can't get any real purchase on the differences that arose in the early years of the Reformation. Therefore, we must begin with late medieval Christianity, in order to understand the early Reformation, and what came afterwards.

The ending of the story is less obvious. It concerns the importance of the relationship religion and politics, between churches and states, by the middle of the seventeenth century. Specifically, it involves the end of the Thirty Years' War on the continent in 1648, and the English Restoration following the English Revolution in 1660. Many of the long-term processes that we'll discuss in the course continue long beyond the middle of the seventeenth century. In terms of the relationship between churches and states, however, the middle of the seventeenth century marks an important watershed.

This brings our first lecture to a close. I've explained the subject matter of the course, my approach to the material, and have articulated the four major challenges or obstacles that we must overcome in order to achieve the goals that we have for the course. I've laid out three major themes to be woven throughout our analytical narrative, and have explained the chronological scope of the course as I've laid it out, from the early sixteenth century, the late Middle Ages, up to the middle of the seventeenth century. In the second lecture, we'll look at some of the fundamental demographic, social, and political aspects of late medieval Europe, as we start to set the stage for our main story.

Lecture Two
The Landscape of Late Medieval Life

Scope:

To understand Christianity in the era we are examining, one must have some sense of the broad demographic, material, social, and political contours of Europe at the time. High infant mortality and the constant threat of infectious disease contributed to lower life expectancy and general uncertainty about life. The large majority of the population worked the land directly in an agricultural capacity and was illiterate. From the family through larger institutions in both rural and town settings, hierarchy was a social reality, as well as a habit of thought. In the political sphere, local urban institutions included craft guilds and town councils, while rural lands were typically subject to the control of secular or ecclesiastical nobles and worked by peasants or small-scale farmers. Europe's two basic patterns of large-scale political organization were monarchies and independent or semi-independent territories or city-states.

Outline

I. Demographically, early modern Europe was a fairly thinly populated, predominantly agricultural world, subject to high infant mortality, waves of epidemic disease, and agricultural subsistence crises.

   A. Seen broadly and in the long term, the demographic recovery from the Black Death started in the mid-fifteenth century and continued throughout the sixteenth century.

   B. The majority of the population worked the land in some agricultural capacity, although towns were disproportionately important politically, economically, and socially.

      1. Depending on the region, 65 to 90 percent of the people were peasants or small farmers.

      2. The most densely populated and urbanized areas of Europe were northern Italy, the southern Low Countries (modern-day Belgium), and southern Germany.

      3. Based on population, very few true cities existed in Europe.

C. In concrete terms, physical suffering and death were pervasive elements of life from the cradle to the grave.

> **1.** Between 15 and 35 percent of infants died before their first birthday; another 10 to 20 percent of children died before they reached 10 years.

> **2.** Lacking effective medical care and exposed to famine, epidemic disease, the ravages of war, and more, the vast majority of the population found life hard.

II. Socially, in rural areas, as well as in towns and cities, in social units from the family through the nation or empire, early modern Europe was fundamentally a society of ranks and hierarchy with limited social mobility.

> **A.** Stratification and hierarchy were social realities, as well as ingrained habits of thought. Socially, most people would remain in the status to which they were born.

> **B.** In rural areas, the fundamental divide was between peasants and lords, although many variations existed, depending on the country and region.

>> **1.** For those who survived the plague, the century after the Black Death (1350–1450) was probably the best of times in material terms for medieval peasants.

>> **2.** The Black Death had made agricultural labor scarcer, resulting in opportunities for higher wages and more work for surviving peasants.

>> **3.** Landlords commuted traditional feudal dues to rents, which afforded them more liquid capital, because they were paid rents in coin, rather than traditional payments in kind.

> **C.** After about 1450, with population growth and other pressures, relationships between peasants and lords grew more strained, especially in central Europe.

> **D.** Towns were socially stratified by status and occupation linked to wealth.

>> **1.** At the top of urban hierarchies stood wealthy patricians and merchants, followed by urban professionals, members of craft guilds, and domestic servants and wage laborers, with the indigent poor at the bottom.

>> **2.** Towns were characterized by extreme disparities in the distribution of wealth.

3. Towns were disproportionately important as centers of economic exchange, education, the circulation of ideas, and relative social mobility.

E. Throughout society, a mutually reinforcing relationship of paternalism and obedient deference, combined with appeal to the "common good," helped maintain basic order.

III. Politically, structures varied in different regions and countries but always involved some sort of local institutions, relationships between local and central institutions, and some form of large-scale organization.

A. Local political institutions often included some form of city council, along with merchant and craft guilds, which frequently conflicted with one another.
   1. With rare exceptions, only male heads of households could participate in civic government.
   2. For the most part, clergy were exempt from civic obligations.
   3. In city councils, urban tensions came to the fore and political decisions were made.

B. In rural areas, peasants were politically dominated by the nobility and monasteries. In some areas, this domination was greater by 1500 than it had been in the previous century.

C. Relations between local and central political authorities were delicate and precarious, dependent on cooperation more than coercion.
   1. Towns fiercely guarded whatever independence and privileges they enjoyed. Dozens of "free imperial cities" in central Europe owed their allegiance directly to the emperor and were essentially self-governing.
   2. Central authorities sought to extend their authority and control at the expense of local urban privileges.

D. The largest political institutions were monarchies and territorial conglomerates.
   1. The slowly centralizing, bureaucratizing monarchies included Tudor England, Valois France, and Habsburg Spain.
   2. Italy, Switzerland, and the Holy Roman Empire (in central Europe) were the most important territorial conglomerates.

E. Internationally, the most important political rivalry in Europe in the early sixteenth century was between the Holy Roman Empire and France.

IV. The basic social and political realities of early modern Europe are profoundly important to the developments in Christianity during the period.

Supplementary Reading:

George Huppert, *After the Black Death: A Social History of Early Modern Europe.*

Thomas Robisheaux, "The World of the Village," in *Handbook of European History, 1400–1600,* ed. Thomas A. Brady, Jr., et al., vol. 1.

Steven Rowan, "Urban Communities: The Rulers and the Ruled," in *Handbook*, vol. 1.

Jan de Vries, "Population," in *Handbook*, vol. 1.

Questions to Consider:

1. How might particular religious teachings strike different chords in a pre-modern society than in a modern one?

2. In what ways might religious changes upset the tenuous political relationships that existed locally, and between local and central authorities, in early modern Europe?

Lecture Two—Transcript
The Landscape of Late Medieval Life

Welcome to Lecture Two, entitled "Structures of Life in Late Medieval Europe: Demography, Society, and Politics." I stressed in the introductory lecture the social and political embeddedness of early modern Christianity. I emphasized that it unfolded in a real, concrete world, not a world of abstract ideas divorced from life. Having articulated the principal goals, obstacles, themes, and chronology of the course in Lecture One, it's now time to explore some of the basic contours of life in this distant world. This is very important, to give us a sense of the context, parameters, framework, within which our main story unfolds.

This lecture has three main sections. They address, in turn, some of the most important demographic realities of late medieval and early modern Europe, the basic social structure within which early modern Christians lived their lives, and finally, some of the most important political institutions and arrangements, from local urban and rural environments to international political rivalries. Just a reminder before we start with the body of the lecture, that the broad generalizations demanded in this sort of an overview should be tempered by awareness of local variations and particularities, as I pointed out in the opening lecture.

We'll begin with demographic realities. The demographics define the basic features, conditions of the material life, and life-cycle of the population, as they were experienced in this time. The big picture in late medieval Europe's demography was of a predominantly rural, agricultural society. It was fairly thinly populated, highly vulnerable to the ravages of disease and to agricultural subsistence crises. A poor harvest meant that people went hungry or faced starvation, in some cases. The great demographic story of the late Middle Ages is the Black Death, the massive epidemic of bubonic plague that wiped out roughly 25 of the estimated 80 million Europeans in three short years, between 1347 and 1350. The devastation was so great that it took a century and a half, until about 1500, for most areas of Western Europe to reach the levels of population present in the 1330s and 1340s. After about 1450, most areas began to experience a steady but slow population growth that continued throughout the sixteenth century. The period that we're focusing on, primarily the sixteenth and early seventeenth centuries, is a period of general demographic growth. As we look at it, we already see a real contrast to the modern world; since the late eighteenth century, we've experienced largely steady demographic growth. We are now more than six billion in total planetary population.

In the world of the sixteenth and early seventeenth centuries, the majority of the people, from two-thirds to up to 90 percent or greater, worked the land in some agricultural capacity of one sort or another. The most densely populated areas of Western Europe were the southern part of the Low Countries, such as modern-day Belgium, a region known as Flanders; northern Italy; and southwestern Germany. There were very few cities, when judged by the modern criterion of population, rather than by the certain jurisdiction and legal privileges that defined cities at the time. By around 1500, the largest city in Europe was probably Naples, with about 150,000 people, or a bit bigger. To further indicate how thinly populated this world was, in the entire area of the vast Holy Roman Empire, all of modern-day Germany, Austria, Bohemia, and the Netherlands, the entire region had only ten cities with as many as 20,000 people. Luther's Wittenberg was a town of 4000 to 5000 people. Calvin's Geneva, the icon of the Reformation era, had 10,000 people.

We're talking about small, intimate, face-to-face societies, with wooden buildings, for the most part, clustered within stone walls that can still be seen surviving in many European areas. It's not the stone of the churches and town halls that people see today, that characterize most medieval towns. Almost all of the buildings were built of wood. The mortality rates and the physical vulnerabilities of this world are often stunning to modern Americans. Late medieval and early modern Europe knew extremely high rates of infant mortality. Between 15 and 35 percent of all children died before they reached the age of one. Between one-sixth and one-third of people died before their first birthdays. Another 10 to 20 percent perished before they reached age ten. Thus, anywhere between 40 and 50 percent, or a bit more, of the population never made it to their tenth birthday. It was a result of the combination of undernourishment, disease, and lack of any kind of effective medical care.

After this point, though, past age ten, people remained subject to famine, epidemic disease, and to the ravages and dislocations of war, endemic in the era, throughout their lives. This was a hard life, in material terms, for the vast majority of the population. They were surrounded by, and constantly exposed to, death, illness, and physical suffering in a way that is known to virtually no one in the United States. Even in good times, it was a life of hard agricultural labor, one of following the seasonality; winter, spring, summer, fall. It was an era, in other words, that aptly merits Hobbes' famous quip, "Life is nasty, brutish, and short." The supreme irony that it was uttered by a man who lived to be more than 90 years old is often not noted, but I note it here.

Moving from demographic realities to the social order, it, too, differed dramatically from modern-day democracies with their considerable social mobility, their large middle class, the ideal of equality for all citizens under the law, and the emphasis on individual freedom, choice, striving for fulfillment. Late medieval and early modern Europe, by contrast, was fundamentally a society of ranks and hierarchy, with widespread acceptance throughout the society that one was born into a certain rank and remained there. Peasants would remain peasants. Nobles would remain nobles. Artisans would remain artisans. In the family, husbands would always wield authority over their wives, and parents over their children, just like kings over their subjects.

Social status was enforced through sumptuary laws that made it illegal, for example, for ordinary citizens to wear certain fabrics or certain clothing, lest they be seen as usurping the privileges of higher rank. I might not be able to wear a jacket like this among my senior colleagues at Stanford. At the same time, this wasn't a socially static society. There was limited social mobility, both upward and downward. For example, urban merchants could, through the accumulation of wealth, buy their way into the nobility, as they often did.

Let's look a little more closely at the way the social hierarchy of ranks was typically organized in rural areas and in towns and cities. We'll take each one in turn, beginning with rural areas. Here, the fundamental split was between the vast majority of peasants, who lived in small villages and worked the land, and the members of the nobility, whose lands the peasants worked. The nobility possessed legal rights over both the land and the peasants. There were further important gradations, both within the peasants and the nobles. For example, some well-to-do peasants held their own land outright, and were able to produce some agricultural goods to sell directly in the local market. Other peasants were, for practical purposes, little more than slaves. There were huge differences in wealth and status as well between the wealthiest and most powerful nobles, and those who possessed noble status, but little more, really, than a title.

Certain regions, too, were more differentiated than this. They had a significant number of independent farmers. They were higher than the levels of the peasantry, but did not possess noble, or "gentle," status. For example, England was known for having a considerable number of yeomen, independent farmers in this era.

Broadly speaking, the century or so after the Black Death, from about 1350 to the middle of the fifteenth century, around 1450, was probably the best of times for the medieval peasantry, relatively speaking, for those who survived. It wasn't so good for the one third or more that perished in the Black Death. However, for those who survived, the demographic disaster made agricultural labor scarcer, which of course drove up the demand for it, which in turn gave surviving peasants opportunities for greater wages and opportunities than they would have had with the population that had died. Landlords of this period, too, typically commuted traditional feudal dues to rents, which gave them more liquid capital. They were paid in coin, rather than in kind, which was typical.

After about 1450, about the middle of the fifteenth century, the population began to increase once again. With a quickening of economic activity, the pressures between peasants and nobles began to mount. In central Europe, for example, the nobility tightened their control over the peasantry once again, while in England they appropriated previously common lands for their own use. They were beginning to raise sheep, to take advantage of the growing demand for wool, for the English textile market, used in the manufacturing of clothing.

In much of Western Europe, there was increasing tension between noble landlords and peasants in the decades prior to the Reformation, between the middle of the fifteenth century and the early sixteenth century. It came on the heels of three to four generations of relatively better times for the peasantry. In living memory, they knew that things had been better than they were presently. Their lands had not always been enclosed by the nobles so that they could raise sheep and become wealthy. It had not always been that they had had to pay a particular tax. They wanted to go back to the time when things had been better. They remembered back to sometime in that century, between the Black Death and the mid-fifteenth century.

We'll turn, now, from rural areas to towns and cities. Again, we're differentiating. We're talking about the way in which the society of ranks and hierarchy was organized. In towns and cities, we find a more diverse and variegated, but no less hierarchical, social order. To lay them out schematically, we'll start at the top of the main layers of stratification.

First of all, there were the wealthiest patricians and merchants. They were the members of the great elite political and trading family. They were characteristic of the towns in Western Europe in general. One rung down on the social ladder, we find various urban professionals. Their numbers have been growing in the West ever since the twelfth century. They included people like lawyers, civil servants, university professors, and to a certain extent, the clergy. The clergy's status was somewhat ambiguous, however. We'll discuss them at considerably greater length in the next two lectures.

Beneath the urban professionals stood the members of craft monopolies, the guilds. They were legally protected artisans specializing in certain crafts. They enjoyed jurisdictional protection for what they did, whether they were butchers, bakers, or candlestick makers; I should say "silversmith" or "blacksmith" if one was in the market for a candlestick. There wasn't a separate candlestick makers' guild, at least none that I know of.

Below the members of the guilds came domestic servants. They were very numerous, and typically lived in the homes of those they served. This was an extremely common occupation, for example, for young unmarried women; they would work as servants prior to marrying or entering convents. Also at this level, below that of urban professionals, there were wage-laborers, those who work, not as members of guilds, for a particular wage at a certain job. Many work in construction, others at trying to keep the streets as clean as they were in early modern Europe, which was not very clean, and so forth.

Finally, at the very bottom of the social hierarchy in towns and cities are the urban destitute. Homelessness as a problem has not just arisen in the last twenty or thirty years. In late medieval and early modern Europe, between 10 and 20 percent of the urban population are typically qualified as the indigent poor. They are the most vulnerable to disease and crime. They relied, in the end, on a combination of charity and their own wits for survival.

The towns and cities of late medieval and early modern Europe are characterized by extreme disparities of wealth. In early fifteenth-century Florence, for example, ten percent of the population owned 68 percent of the wealth. When Martin Luther was a monk in the German city of Erfurt, in 1511, seven percent of the population owned 66 percent of the wealth. The bottom 66 percent of the town owned only ten percent of the wealth.

The small size of these cities, as I mentioned a moment ago, were of a compact layout within stone city walls. This meant that wealthy patricians and educated civil servants crossed paths and rubbed elbows with artisans and indigent beggars. Only a small percentage of the overall populations lived in towns and cities. Remember, I mentioned that between 65 and 90 percent of the population lived and worked on the land in some direct capacity. Yet urban areas remained disproportionately important as centers of economic activity. There were greater opportunities there for education, especially university education. There was greater influence in terms of the circulation of ideas, including religious ideas. This will be very important in our course. In addition, social mobility was relatively higher in towns and cities than it was for those who lived in rural areas.

As in rural communities, however, widely shared cultural values, the deference of the lower toward the higher, and the paternalism of the higher toward the lower, comprised much of the cultural glue that held the society together. It was extremely important for providing social cohesion. Also important was the late medieval notion of the city as a kind of sacred collectivity, one that ideally sought the common good of all of its members, rather than allowing the self-interests of particular members or individuals to dominate it. This was again an ideal, and very often not a reality. These shared values and ideas of deference and paternalism were especially important in a society that lacked modern police forces and standing armies.

I've said something now about demographic realities, and about the social hierarchy. I'll turn now to political structures. I'll begin with local urban institutions, then look at local rural areas. Then I'll move on to consider the relationship between central and local political authorities, and say a little about the largest structures of governing political bodies. Finally, I'll make a note about the most important international rivalry in the early sixteenth century.

To begin with, we'll look at local political institutions in towns and cities. How were city political arrangements structured? Typically, a mayor or mayors oversaw some form of a city council. The Reformation began, and first took off, in the cities of the Holy Roman Empire in central Europe in the early 1520s. Here there were usually two town councils. The small council was usually dominated by wealthy patricians in de facto oligarchies. The great, or large, council was traditionally the preserve of representatives from the city's guild. The patricians had increasingly come to dominate the small council as well, however, by serving as guild representatives, in the German and Swiss towns after about the middle of the fifteenth century.

One can see, then, how the political structure of the city council generally mirrored the urban social hierarchy that I was laying out just a moment ago. One had to be a citizen in order to be a member of the councils. This meant that only male heads of households who, at a minimum, belonged to a guild could participate actively in civic government. Women were excluded, as they were excluded from essentially all forms of public political life in the era. Members of the clergy were exempt from both citizen status and from civic obligations, such as serving in the town militia, from fighting fires when one broke out, and from paying taxes. I'll say more about these special clerical exemptions in a subsequent lecture. An important point to be made is that town councils, then, are the arenas in which urban tensions come to the fore, and in which political decisions are made.

In rural areas, the peasants, who typically lived in small villages, farmed the surrounding land, and made up the large majority of the population in the later Middle Ages and in early modern Europe, had grown increasingly autonomous. They developed their own village councils and courts. However, they remained politically dominated by the nobles or monks whose land they worked, in the end. The nobles and monks retained important jurisdictional claims on them. In some areas, villages were less politically autonomous of the demands and pressures the local noblemen or monasteries made of them, around 1500, than they had been two or three centuries earlier.

This is in keeping with the gradual slide away from the "golden era," to exaggerate a bit, of medieval peasantry a century after the Black Death.

Now I'm going to say something about the central and local political authorities. There were kings, dukes, emperors, and counts, on the one hand, and the local communities on the other. Some towns were more independent of royal or imperial control than others were. All of them tended to fiercely guard whatever political independence and privileges they enjoyed. They wanted to make their own decisions. They didn't want to do someone else's bidding. Many cities in the Holy Roman Empire and in central Europe, for example, were free imperial cities. This was a technical legal status, which meant that they owed their allegiance directly to the emperor, not to the princes in the territories where the cities sat. Because the Holy Roman Empire was not there to see what was going on in Augsburg or Nuremberg on a day-to-day basis, for example, for all practical purposes these cities were self-governing entities.

On the other side of the coin, for their part, central authorities such as kings or emperors were constantly trying to extend their control at the expense of traditional, local urban privileges. This is the era when the bureaucracies of European states are expanding, as a way of extending central political authorities' reach.

The relationship between rulers and their localities, between central political authorities and what was going on on the ground in particular areas, was generally delicate and precarious. It depended much more on co-operation than on coercion. This was an age, again, without standing armies or professional police forces. Local resistance remained a pervasive and real possibility, if tensions strained this balance too much. We'll see a great many instances in early modern Christianity where this tension between central and local political authorities played an important role.

There was a move from this back-and-forth relationship between central and local authorities, then, to the large political organizations of the countries and territories of Europe, and a move out of the precarious balance between feudal lords and kings. From this emerged two basic patterns of political organization by the late fifteenth century. First of all, there was the increasingly centralized bureaucratic monarchy. It prevailed in Tudor England, in Valois France, and in Habsburg Spain. England, France, and Spain were the three great examples of the late-medieval centralizing bureaucratic monarchy. We shouldn't exaggerate. I mean, there wasn't very much centralized bureaucracy possible in a world without our sorts of modern communications present. Nonetheless, this was the trend, and this was the tendency. Through their advisory councils and their local officials, rulers sought to extend their sovereign control over their territories, to extract more money through taxes and loans, to fight their wars, and to enforce the laws that were made.

That was the first form of large-scale political organization. The second form was a kind of "conglomeration of territories" model. It prevailed on the Italian peninsula, and in the vast domain of central Europe known as the Holy Roman Empire. In Italy, by 1450, there were five major powers. There was no Italian state. The Italian state didn't exist in its modern form until the nineteenth century. There were five major powers by the mid-fifteenth century, in Italy. They were dominant cities who treated their surrounding hinterlands almost as if they were colonial possessions; Milan, Venice, Florence, the Papal States, under the direct political control of the Pope, and finally, the kingdom of Naples, which was under Spanish control in southern Italy.

In the Holy Roman Empire, there weren't just five. There was a dizzying variety of hundreds of different principalities, ecclesiastical lands, imperial cities, and territories. The Holy Roman Emperor was their elected overlord. Finally, a third example of this kind of conglomeration of territories was the Swiss Confederation. This was a sworn association of territories called "cantons." They had become independent of the Holy Roman Empire, for all practical purposes, in 1499. They were located in south-central Europe, essentially where modern Switzerland is.

Monarchies, as well as these territorial conglomerates, were significant for the story of Christianity in the sixteenth century. The importance of individual sovereigns in the monarchies meant that a king's decisions could, and did, affect matters of religion, and became the laws of the land. A king's decision, and the religion of the country, could officially change from one day to the next. The political dispersion and the heterogeneity of the Holy Roman Empire, for example, meant that the decisions of individual princes and of city councils would determine choices for or against the

Reformation, and they did. The individual Swiss cantons, too, would make independent choices about adopting or rejecting Protestantism.

Here, we're laying out the importance of the political orientation and framework for a subsequent understanding of how Christianity is imbedded and understood through them. We've got one more stop to make in our surveillance of the political institutions of the early sixteenth century. We've looked at cities, rural areas, the relationships between central and local authorities, and have talked just now about these monarchies and territorial conglomerates. Now I want to say just a couple of words about the most important European-wide political rivalry at the international level, in the early sixteenth century. That's the rivalry between the Habsburg Empire on the one hand, and Valois France, on the other. France was joined by its allies in southeastern Europe, the Ottoman Turks, which is perhaps surprising but true, and the Papacy.

By the time Charles V succeeded his grandfather Maximilian as the Holy Roman Emperor in 1519, he exercised control over Spain, over the Low Countries, Naples, and the eastern part of the Holy Roman Empire, Austria, Bohemia, and Moravia. It was an enormous amount of territory. He also had overlordship over the territories and cities in the rest of the Holy Roman Empire in central Europe. I mention this not for the sake of politics per se, but because of the antagonism between Charles V and the king of France, Francis I. This would matter greatly in the early Reformation, even though both remained Catholic. Charles V was preoccupied with simultaneously fighting the Muslims in southeastern Europe, and Francis I in France. He could not stop everything else he was doing, even though he was trying to deal with an expanding Spanish overseas empire. He couldn't drop everything to attend to the local problem in Germany.

By way of summary, it bears repeating that the basic social realities of hierarchy, as well as the many layers of political structure of Europe on the eve of the Reformation, from the humblest household, through local communities, to international political rivalries, are all extremely important to the development of Christianity in the period.

This lecture has looked at some of the fundamental demographic realities; the basic conditions of life, high infant mortality, a great deal of physical suffering, the possibility of epidemic disease, the ravages of war, and so forth. We also looked at the social hierarchy of early modern Europe. We looked at it in some detail, both in urban areas, and in rural areas. Finally, I've given a kind of overview of the political realities of the period in towns and rural areas. We've looked at the relationships between central and local authorities, contrasted the centralizing bureaucratic monarchy with the territorial conglomerate of the Holy Roman Empire, the Italian peninsula, and the Swiss Confederation. I mentioned, here at the end, this central international rivalry between the Habsburg Empire and Valois France.

Having discussed the demographics, social and political contours in this world, our next two lectures will discuss its oldest, most comprehensive, and most international institution, namely, the Catholic Church. We'll explore the worldview of late medieval Christianity.

Lecture Three

Late Medieval Christendom—
Beliefs, Practices, Institutions I

Scope:

To grasp the nature of the changes wrought during the sixteenth century, one must know something about the late medieval Christianity that preceded it. This understanding, in turn, requires a grasp of the complex interrelationships among basic Christian beliefs, institutions, and practices. Christian salvation history stretched from God's creation through his incarnation in Jesus Christ to the Church as the instrument of his salvation for humanity. Human life was seen as a transitory period before the afterlife and judgment by God. Necessary for eternal salvation was faith and the practice of faith. Central to medieval Christianity was the notion of divine providence; trust in God's abiding governance of the world; and sacramentality, the view of the spiritual manifest in and through the material, which included the Church's seven sacraments as part of a much broader sensibility.

Outline

I. Late medieval Christianity was an institutionalized worldview, a variegated amalgam of beliefs, institutions, and practices that cannot be separated.

   A. For example, baptism was a practice that presupposed certain beliefs, referred to specific biblical texts, and was institutionally administered by a priest in accordance with a prescribed ritual.

   B. Late medieval Christianity was not a rigid set of doctrines enforced by a monolithic Church, but a core set of beliefs and practices surrounded by a wide variety of elaborations that evolved over time, exhibited great local variation, and found diverse institutional expressions.

II. The basic story of Christian salvation history begins with God's creation and will eventually end with the apocalypse. Its authoritative source is the Bible, understood as God's revealed Word.

A. Adam and Eve's original sin of disobedience against God made all human beings subject to pain, suffering, and death.

B. In his mercy, God called a people to himself, the Israelites, and made a covenant with them, foretelling through their prophets a future messiah who would usher in a messianic age.

C. Jesus of Nazareth was this messiah, the incarnation of God who preached the "good news" (Gospel). Through his obedient death, humanity was redeemed and the possibility of salvation renewed.

D. After Jesus Christ's resurrection from the dead, he commissioned his followers to preach the Gospel to all nations and to baptize. From this early movement, emerged the Church, the instrument of God's salvation on earth, which derives its authority from Christ.

III. Human life was a transitory phase before judgment by God after death.

A. Depending on how one was judged by God, death was a transition to eternal salvation in heaven, eternal damnation in hell, or hope of eventual salvation in purgatory.

B. Right belief and right behavior were prerequisites for the possibility of eternal salvation; otherwise, one was not following Christ.

IV. Medieval Christianity taught that faith and the practice of the faith were essential for salvation.

A. Medieval theologians distinguished the act of faith from the content of faith and explicit faith from implicit faith.

    1. The act of faith (*fides qua*) refers to trust in God, in Christ as Lord and savior; the content of faith (*fides quae*) refers to the specific content of faith as preserved and elaborated by the Church.

    2. Explicit faith refers to the ability to articulate what one believes and why; implicit faith refers to obedience to, and participation in, Church life without explicit awareness of the content of faith.

B. Faith alone ("dead faith") was not enough for salvation. Only through a "living faith" expressed in concrete actions might one be saved by God's grace.

V. Medieval Christianity was pervaded by belief in divine providence and in sacramentality.

    A. Divine providence is the notion that God orders and governs all things in his creation, often despite appearances to the contrary.

    B. Sacramentality is the idea that transcendent spiritual reality manifests itself in and through created material reality. Its paradigm is God's incarnation in Christ.

Essential Reading:

R. N. Swanson, *Religion and Devotion in Europe, c. 1215–c. 1515*, ch. 2.

Supplementary Reading:

Eamon Duffy, *The Stripping of the Altars: Traditional Religion in England, c. 1400–c. 1580*, chs. 1–10.

Questions to Consider:

1. How would human life lived in the expectation of divine judgment likely differ from human life lived in the expectation that death is one's end?

2. How do the various aspects of medieval Christian belief reinforce one another?

Lecture Three—Transcript
Late Medieval Christendom— Beliefs, Practices, Institutions I

This is the third lecture of our course on the history of Christianity in the Reformation Era. It's entitled "An Institutionalized Worldview: Western Christendom in the Late Middle Ages, Part One."

In the last lecture, I sketched some of the basic demographic, social, and political features of Western Europe in the early sixteenth century. You'll recall that in our first lecture, I said that without some sense of what came before the religious developments and upheavals of the sixteenth century, we can't know what changed and how it changed; we don't have any basis for comparison. The purpose of this lecture and the following lecture, a two-part series, is to provide an overview of some of the most important beliefs, practices, and institutions of late medieval Christianity. These beliefs, practices, and institutions are entirely interwoven with one another, and they can't be separated from each other, except for the purposes of analysis and understanding, as I'm trying to do in these two lectures.

In this lecture, we'll concentrate on beliefs. In the following lecture, we'll concentrate on institutions and practices. These are not three separate, distinct spheres, but rather conjoined aspects of what we might call an "institutionalized worldview." They're rooted in a combination of scripture, in the Christian tradition, the Bible, in the Old and New Testaments, and tradition. We're really talking, then, about trying to reconstruct the basic framework of a religion as it was lived and experienced in the late Middle Ages.

Just to give an introductory example of what I mean by the penetration of beliefs, practices, and institutions, consider baptism in late medieval Christianity. As one of the Church's seven sacraments, it was part of the Church's practice. It also presupposed certain beliefs about original sin, for example, and its effects, how original sin came into the world, as well as Christian beliefs about Christian identity and destiny. Baptism was usually performed by a priest on an infant, in accordance with a prescribed ritual involving parents and godparents in a local church. Thus, it was administered through institutions.

Historically and scripturally, baptism derived from Christ's own baptism by John the Baptist, recorded in the Gospels, as well as from the commandment of the risen Christ from his disciples to teach all the nations, baptizing them in the name of the Father, and the Son, and the Holy Spirit.

Thus, we see just in this one example—and I could give you a hundred—it makes the point about the interwovenness of beliefs, practices, and institutions, scripture, and tradition in late medieval Christianity. It's important to keep this basic idea in mind throughout the next two lectures, because, as I said before, for the purposes of analysis, we'll be focusing on beliefs in this lecture and institutions and practices in the next.

It makes sense, as well, to think of late medieval Christianity not as a rigid set of doctrines enforced by a monolithic, homogenous Church, but rather as a core set of beliefs and practices around which an enormous variety of different elaborations, different particular local traditions and systems, had developed over time, often very long periods of time. By the time the Reformation begins, Christianity is nearly 1500 years old, after all. Three-quarters of the time between the time when Jesus lived and the present had already gone by at the time of the Reformation's inception. Outside of these core beliefs and practices—the Creed, sacraments, and structure of the Church—late medieval Christianity exhibited a great range of local variations, and found diverse institutional expressions. Remember the point I made in the beginning, in the very first lecture, about the local particularities and local character of life, as it was lived in the late Middle Ages and early modern Europe in general. It finds an expression here within Christianity itself.

The basic structure of this lecture, and points on which we'll be concentrating, are as follows. Firstly, I want to give an overview of the bare-bones picture of "Christian salvation history," as I call it. This is the basic view of the way the way that Christianity sees the course of time. Secondly, I want to give an overview of the Christian conceptualization of human life, then a bit about faith and the practice of it as it was understood in the late Middle Ages. Finally, I want to discuss two key ideas interwoven throughout late medieval Christianity; namely, these are "divine providence" and "sacramentality."

Let's start, then, with Christian salvation history. Late medieval Christianity had inherited a picture about the nature of the world and human history from the preceding centuries. This is known as "Christian salvation history." It incorporated many of the beliefs that are central to the religion. We cannot "get" late medieval Christianity on the eve of the Reformation without understanding at least the bare outlines of the picture. Consequently, it's a good place to start in our overview of the beliefs, practices, and institutions.

The basic picture runs something like this. The one, transcendent, omnipotent God, the true God, the creator of the Universe, created human beings as the crowning achievement of his creation. Genesis puts it thusly; man was created in God's image, and he set human beings in Paradise, in the Garden of Eden, but Adam and Eve, through disobedience to God, through pride and thinking that they knew better themselves than God what was good for them, rebelled against him, which is how sin entered the world, and human history.

All subsequent human beings, insofar simply as they partake of Adam's human nature, were subject to this original sin. This was the first sin that scarred and marked human nature. With original sin, pain, suffering, and death came into the world. Human beings were lost, separated from the God who had created them in love. Yet God, in his infinite mercy, called a people to himself, the Israelites. He made a covenant with them, establishing his holy law for them to follow. Through their prophets, they foretold of and prepared the way for a Messiah, a savior, who would lead the beleaguered nation to final triumph, the land of Israel. They would triumph over their enemies in a messianic age, an age of the Messiah.

According to Christians, this prophecy of the Old Testament prophets was fulfilled in the person of Jesus Christ, Jesus of Nazareth. He was believed to be not just a prophet or great ethical leader, but the literal incarnation of God himself. John's Gospel says that he was "the Word made flesh." This was a staggering idea. God himself reaches down, as it were, and gets his hands dirty in the muck of human existence. He takes on all the temptations, the weakness, and suffering of humanity. It was Jesus Christ's death by crucifixion, in perfect obedience to God's will, that undid Adam and Eve's disobedience and made eternal salvation possible once again, union between those separated human beings and God. God's love for humanity, then, extends to the point of himself becoming a human being, and suffering an excruciating, painful death.

Proceeding along—we're talking, again, about Christian salvation history, the basic picture of how things are—God raised the crucified Christ from the dead, a triumph over death itself, and Christ, before joining his father in heaven, commissioned his followers to "preach the good news," the Gospel, to all nations, to baptize them in the name of the Father, the Son, and the Holy Spirit. In medieval Christianity, the heir of this movement, of Christ's original followers, is understood to be the Church, described by Paul in the New Testament as the "mystical body of Christ" made up of all Christians; that is, all those who believe in Christ as their savior and are united to him by their shared common faith. The Church, the development of this original movement, derives its authority from Christ, who, again, is God incarnate, and the Church, then, is God's instrument on Earth for making salvation possible. The Church derives its authority from Christ; Christ is God.

Absolutely essential to this picture is the notion of divine revelation. God had revealed himself to human beings, and created them in his image—again, even to the point of becoming human himself. This is the exact opposite of the modern atheistic view that human beings imagine or create God or gods in their image. The initiative in the process is God's. The record of his revelation is preserved and promulgated, again, by the Church. Part of that record is the books of the Bible, the sacred scripture. This notion, as a kind of side-note here, is fundamental in the sixteenth century as well. What's at stake in Christianity, for those who subscribe to it, in the sixteenth century is "truth" with a capital "T." It is about the way that things really are, fidelity to God's teachings in the hope of eternal life, understood as salvation.

The final stage of Christian salvation history, in this basic overview, is that God's earthly instrument of salvation would persist until Christ came again, a prophecy that's foretold in the New Testament. The dead would be raised, reunited with their souls, and judged by Christ for eternity, some of them being sent to eternal salvation in heaven, and others to eternal damnation in hell. This would be the "apocalypse," the end of the world, and the Last Judgment, with a capital "L" and a capital "J."

That's the basic overview of Christian salvation history. It brings us to the basic conceptualization, the basic picture, of human life as seen within medieval Christianity. Human life, here, is viewed as a transitory phase between birth and death, a mere twinkle in time compared to eternal life with God in heaven, or eternal damnation without God and with Satan in hell. One might exist temporarily after death in an intermediate condition, purgatory, until one's sins had been purged sufficiently to enjoy eternal life with God.

Human life on earth, then, is lived as a transitory phase, in anticipation of judgment by God in the afterlife. "Right" Christian practice, "proper" Christian belief and practice—that is, orthodoxy, that is, following Christ truly and correctly rather than errantly—is necessary in order to have salvation. Otherwise, one is not, after all, following Christ, who said, "I am the way, the truth, and the light. No one comes to the father but by me." No one comes to the father but by me. That is a verse that's known very well to Christians, too.

Indeed, this notion of correct Christian doctrine and practice is absolutely fundamental to Protestants, Anabaptists, and Catholics in the sixteenth century. It cuts completely against the grain of the modern, subjectivist, liberal view, that individuals should be allowed to believe whatever they want to. From the perspective of late medieval and early modern Christians, such a view would have been supremely negligent. It would have meant literally risking the eternal fate of souls as a result of drifting away from right belief and right practice, away from Christ himself. The issue at this time is emphatically not about what human beings think and desire, but all about following what God has revealed. To put it even more dramatically, to say that matters of Christian teaching or "doctrine"—a term that comes from the Latin "doctrina," which means "teaching"—to say that they were matters of life and death is to understate the point. It would mean trivializing it. These are matters of eternal life and eternal salvation. To really try and grasp this, imagine for yourself how long you'll be dead, and how short your lifetime is in comparison to how long eternity is. That's the way to give yourself a kind of shiver, to get into the mentality of this period.

If human life is a snap of the fingers in the history of God's creation, to be followed by eternal judgment by God, nothing mattered more than knowing just what one had to do in order to be judged favorably by God, and so to inherit eternal life, rather than to suffer in hell. It makes perfect sense. If this is the way things are, then one ought to do the sorts of things that will lead to the good rather than the bad result. It's a perfectly rational approach. What were the requirements for salvation? How did one live such that s/he would be judged favorably rather than unfavorably by God? This can be summed up in one word; faith, and the practice of it. That's what we need to talk about next.

What did late medieval Christians mean by "faith?" I want to mention two distinctions made by theologians at the time, which will help us get a handle on this. This is our little crash course in late medieval scholastic theology. The first distinction involves two Latin phrases, "*fides qua,*" and "*fides quae.*" *Fides qua* is the act of faith itself, the trusting in God, in Christ as Lord and Savior. This is, as we might say, the "that" of faith, the act of having trust in God. *Fides quae* is the "what" of faith. It's the content of the faith, as preserved and elaborated by the Church, the specific articles that make up Christian faith. *Fides qua* is the "that" of faith, *fides quae*, the "what" of faith.

A second distinction concerns the relationship of the individual Christian to the content and practice of the faith. It's the distinction between explicit faith and implicit faith. Explicit faith refers to the self-conscious awareness of the content of the faith, implying the ability to articulate what it is that one believes, and why one believes it. Explicit faith, then, in this world, is the preserve of a very small percentage of learned clergy, especially theologians and preachers, together with an even smaller percentage of well-educated laity. Explicit faith tends to go along with formal education, the ability to understand and articulate what it is that you believe; this is explicit faith. Implicit faith, by contrast, refers to an obedience to, and participation in the life of, the Church, following its prescriptions without an explicit awareness or ability to articulate exactly what it is that one believes in, and why. "The priest tells me to do this, so I do it." That's implicit faith.

Most late medieval Christians, the vast majority of whom were illiterate with little formal education, were living as agricultural laborers, working on the land. Most late medieval Christians probably had only implicit faith. However, as understood at the time, this is sufficient for salvation, according to the teaching of the

Church. That is, to be a follower of Christ was not dependent upon being able to articulate specific points of Christian doctrine. That's the job of theologians. Your job as a Christian is to follow Christ. You can do that by living and participating in the life of the Church.

On the other hand, faith alone, understood as the knowledge of and mere assent to certain teachings, was not sufficient for salvation, at the time. This is known as "dead" faith, or "historical" faith. As medieval theologians said, "Even Satan himself knows perfectly all the content of Christian faith. He just doesn't do anything about it; he hates it." Mere knowledge itself—believing, but not doing anything with that belief—is not a saving faith, at the time. For faith to be sufficient for salvation, it had to be expressed in action. It had to be manifested externally in practices, in good works that were consistent with Christ's message of love, forgiveness, and mercy toward others. We'll discuss this further in the next lecture, when we talk about late medieval Christian practices. This is, again, that interwovenness. It's artificial to be pulling out the beliefs from the practices and institutions. I think the two lectures together will allow you to see how they fit together.

This idea that faith must get into action, and express itself externally, to be saving faith, is expressed in another Latin phrase, "*fides caritata formata.*" This means, "faith formed in love." This notion, that faith had to be expressed externally in order to be efficacious for salvation, is grounded in a host of scriptural passages. Jesus commands his followers, for example, to "Love one another as I have loved you." This is not mere assent to propositions. It's doing something. He asks them, "Why do you call me 'Lord, Lord,' and not do what I say?" Get into action. Belief cannot remain stagnant. In perhaps the starkest example, in the Book of James in the New Testament, James flatly states, "Faith without works is dead." This is the origin of the notion for "dead faith," as understood in medieval theology. We find in late medieval Christianity, then, a pervasive emphasis on the doing of good works of all kinds, performing acts of Christian charity as a part of living out one's faith. There's more emphasis on doing good works than on necessarily understanding the specifics of what the Church teaches, or why it teaches as it does.

In the terms that we've been discussing, I know I've thrown a few distinctions at you. One can be saved with active yet implicit faith, but one can't be saved with a "dead," perfectly knowledgeable faith that does not express itself externally. A "dead" yet explicit faith won't help you at all. At the same time, the Church condemned as heretical that one could earn or merit salvation as the result of one's own efforts done in faith. Faith and good works are both necessary for salvation, in other words, but they're never sufficient for it. One remains always reliant on God's good grace and his saving power, which he offers freely, and channels in through his instrument on earth, namely, the Church.

In looking at some fundamental Christian beliefs, I've sketched the core of Christian salvation history, I've said something about the conceptualization of human life, lived in anticipation of judgment by God, and I've discussed various aspects of faith and its relationship to salvation. Now I want to mention two further core beliefs that pervade late medieval Christianity, as a way of wrapping up our lecture. These are divine providence and sacramentality. "Providence" is the belief that God orders and governs all things, oftentimes despite contrary appearances. This is the idea, conviction, and trust that all things are in God's hands in the end, that God orders and disposes of things according to his will, no matter how much appearances might seem to imply the opposite. There is nothing, then, that happens, that is unknown to or stands apart from God. There is no "outside" to God's creation, removed from his providence.

As with all of these fundamental medieval Christian beliefs, there are biblical foundations for the idea. In Matthew's Gospel, for example, Jesus says to his followers that, "not a sparrow falls to the ground without the knowledge of my Father." He tells them that the hairs of their heads are all counted. This is to express the incredible intimacy of God with the world. The God who created the world does not just set it in motion, like the deistic Enlightenment God, the "watchmaker"—the Big Bang happens, and then God sits back and lets it take its course. No. God remains intimate with the world that he has created. This pervasive belief in divine providence, in the sense that I've described it here, would persist undiminished among virtually all Christians of the sixteenth century, including the overwhelming majority of those in the three traditions that are the main subject matter of the course. God knows, loves, looks out for, and disposes of all things for the good of his own.

Again, very importantly, this is not an empirical claim, based upon everything going according to one's wishes. "I had a bad day today; I broke my leg. My daughter died from a terrible disease. Therefore, divine providence isn't true." No. The view is, that you trust that all things are disposed according to God's will, even when they don't make any sense to you. That's divine providence; the trust that no matter what happens, God has his finger on the pulse of the world, even in the midst of the worst calamities, and there would be plenty of calamities for the respective groups that we'll be dealing with in this course.

Transcendent spiritual reality encompasses God, heaven, the saints in heaven, and those who've died before us. "Sacramentality" is the belief that transcendent spiritual reality manifests itself in and through created material reality, that all creation is in some sense a reflection of the creator, that God is present in and through the world. The correlation to this is that religion is not separated off from, or compartmentalized from, the rest of life. It's not something left for Sunday morning. It's a pervasive notion of the way the world is, and that God can manifest himself in and through the creation that he's made. The paradigm for sacramentality is God's incarnation in Christ to begin with—the transcendent God digging down and taking on human flesh, the purely spiritual becoming human, two natures in one person. In late medieval Christianity, far from this being a kind of one-time, bizarre aberration, with no connection to the rest of salvation history, it's the paradigm for it. Sacramentality expresses God's mysterious presence in and through the created world, his simultaneous transcendence and imminence.

God can be, then—and is—present in some places more than He is in others. It makes perfect sense, within this worldview, that God would manifest himself in some areas, but not in others. If there's a "why," that's for God to decide. We've no idea why. If he wanted a shrine to be located at Compostela in Spain, or in Einsiedeln, Switzerland, that's God's prerogative, not ours. Just below the surface of life, then, there hovers the constant presence of the holy, sacramentality. More than simply the seven sacraments of the Church—which belong to sacramentality to be sure, and we'll talk about those in the next lecture—sacramentality is a much broader category. Transcendent spiritual reality manifests itself in and through the material world.

To sum up this third lecture, then, we should recall that late medieval Christianity was an institutionalized worldview, with interwoven religious beliefs, practices, and institutions. We can't pull those three things apart, really. We can only analyze them serially, one at a time. I've concentrated here more on the beliefs. The next lecture, we'll look at the practices and institutions, and I'll refer back to things that we've talked about in this lecture.

Here, I've focused on Christian salvation history, the story of human beings and the rest of the world's creation, the fall in the Garden of Eden, redemption through Jesus, and judgment, eventually, by God—the second coming. I talked after that about the conceptualization of human life, a twinkle in time in God's eye, from birth to death, after which one would be judged by God, "thumbs up" or "thumbs down," with a middle thumb for purgatory. After that, I talked about faith, and the practice of the faith, producing some distinctions, *fides qua* and *fides quae*, implicit and explicit faith; a living faith that expresses itself externally, sufficient for salvation, as opposed to a "dead" faith, one that can know everything that there is to know about Christianity, but not do anything, and as a result, not be saved.

Next, I talked about two ideas, two convictions, really, about the nature of reality; providence and sacramentality. Providence is the idea that God governs all things. All things are in God's hands, even despite contrary appearances. Finally, I talked about sacramentality, the notion that the spiritual can and does manifest in and through material reality, just as God became incarnate in a human being. Again, we're talking here about convictions about the way the world is. Late medieval Christianity is an ontology: it's a view about what is, what has been, what is to come.

That concludes this third lecture, which, as I mentioned, is the first part of a two-part series. In the next lecture, we'll continue our discussion by examining some of the most important practices and institutions of late medieval Christendom.

Lecture Four

Late Medieval Christendom— Beliefs, Practices, Institutions II

Scope:

The fundamental institutions and practices of late medieval Christianity are inseparable from its beliefs. In its broadest terms, its basic institutional framework was partitioned in both space and time. Geographically, Christendom as a whole was overseen by the papacy, while bishops oversaw dioceses and secular priests and other lower clergy were responsible for laypeople in parishes. The members of religious orders, both male and female, coexisted with this geographical framework, and ecclesiastical institutions as a whole existed alongside secular authorities at every level of governance. The fundamental understanding of time was liturgical; Christian beliefs and worship structured the basic divisions of days, weeks, and the year as a whole.

The minimal practice of the faith expected (but not always enacted) of all baptized Christians included attendance at Mass, participation in the sacraments, and observance of basic ecclesiastical prescriptions. Common collective devotional practices included prayer, processions, pilgrimages, the making of endowments, and shared acts of Christian charity. At the committed end of voluntary devotion, practices included the extensive use of Books of Hours, the affective identification with Christ's Passion, and the pursuit of holiness—the exemplary practice of the faith—as one's highest priority.

Outline

I. Some ecclesiastical institutions were linked to the geographical organization of medieval Christendom, whereas others were not. Together, they provided a framework for the transmission of Christian faith.

   A. The Church was a hierarchical institution composed of all orthodox, baptized Christians, present and past, a community of the living and the dead.

1. The basic locus of authority in the Church lay with the clergy, who were distinguished from the laity by special vows and privileges.
2. Ecclesiastical institutions existed alongside secular institutions and frequently conflicted with them.

B. Some medieval institutions corresponded to Christendom's geographical organization.
   1. The pope, Christ's vicar, oversaw Christendom as a whole.
   2. Bishops, successors to Christ's apostles, were responsible for their dioceses.
   3. Parish priests (also known as "secular" clergy), deputies to the bishops, served the laity directly in their parishes.

C. Religious orders, both male and female, were overlaid on the geographically based institutions of Christendom and frequently coexisted uneasily with them.
   1. The male members of these orders were known as the regular clergy, because they followed a *regula* (rule).
   2. Contemplative religious orders (e.g., Benedictines, Cistercians, Carthusians, Brigittines) were devoted to cloistered lives of prayer and devotion.
   3. Mendicant religious orders (e.g., Franciscans, Dominicans, Augustinians, Carmelites) were dedicated to serving the laity through preaching, teaching, missionizing, and hearing confessions.

D. The most important lay religious institutions were confraternities, diversely constituted mutual aid organizations that were plentiful in both large and small towns.

II. In the Middle Ages, time was conceived and divided in liturgical terms based on Christian worship and beliefs. The basic idea was that no time stood apart from God.

A. In monasteries, the day was divided into the seven times of prayer that together comprised the "divine office."

B. The week was geared toward Sunday as a day dedicated to God and to rest.

C. The year was organized around Christ's life, from the preparation for his birth during Advent before Christmas, through the coming of the Holy Spirit at Pentecost, six weeks after Easter. Other major holy days were devoted to important events in the life of Mary.

    D. Every "ordinary" day was named in honor of one or more saints, Christ's special friends and Christians' intercessors with God.

III. Every Christian was expected to meet minimal requirements in practicing the faith.

    A. Every Christian was expected to be present each week at Mass, the priest's ritual reenactment of Christ's sacrifice on the cross.

        1. In this sacrament, God, through the priest's words of consecration over the bread and wine, makes present Christ's body and blood.

        2. This process was known as transubstantiation.

    B. Every Christian was expected to participate in the sacraments, the most important channels of God's grace, mediated through the priesthood.

        1. Building on inherited tradition, the Fourth Lateran Council (1215) established seven sacraments: baptism, penance, communion (Eucharist), confirmation, matrimony, extreme unction, and holy orders.

        2. The two most important and the only repeated sacraments were penance and communion.

    C. Every Christian was expected to observe basic religious and moral prescriptions and to avoid sins. Normally once a year, before receiving communion at Easter, Christians would confess their sins to a priest as part of the sacrament of penance.

IV. A wide range of collective religious practices was common in late medieval Christianity.

    A. Processions were ritualized local walks for various religious purposes; pilgrimages were journeys to specific sites distinguished in some way for their holiness.

    B. Large numbers of Christians, clergy and laity alike, invested money in practicing their faith, through the endowment of Masses or churches or through the purchase of indulgences or religious art.

C. Christians practiced their faith through the seven corporal acts of mercy and the seven works of spiritual comfort, which benefited both the practitioner and the recipient. Six of the seven corporal acts of mercy were drawn from the gospel of St. Matthew. These were:

    1. Feeding the hungry;

    2. Giving drink to the thirsty;

    3. Visiting the sick;

    4. Clothing the naked;

    5. Visiting the imprisoned;

    6. Accommodating the homeless.

    7. The seventh act was drawn from the apocryphal Book of Tobit regarding burial of the dead.

D. The seven acts of spiritual comfort were:

    1. Counsel;

    2. Correction;

    3. Comfort;

    4. Forgiveness;

    5. Endurance;

    6. Prayer;

    7. Instruction.

V. From the twelfth century on, more and more lay Christians adopted devotional practices that previously had been the preserve of the cloistered religious.

A. Books of Hours were prayer books that adapted monastic prayers for lay use. They were the most common type of printed book in Europe in the half century before the Reformation (1470–1520).

B. A wide range of practices centered on affective identification with Christ's passion.

C. Devout men and women made faith their highest priority, engaging in frequent prayer, ascetic routines, acts of Christian charity, and other practices.

Essential Reading:

R. N. Swanson, *Religion and Devotion in Europe, c. 1215–c. 1515*, chs. 3–5.

John van Engen, "The Church in the Fifteenth Century," in *Handbook of European History, 1400–1600*, ed. Thomas A. Brady, Jr., et al., vol. 1.

Supplementary Reading:

Eamon Duffy, *The Stripping of the Altars: Traditional Religion in England, c. 1400–c. 1580*, chs. 1–10.

Questions to Consider:

1. In what ways do the institutions and practices of late medieval Christianity imply basic Christian beliefs?

2. What sorts of tensions might have arisen between deeply devout Christians and those who sought to skirt even the minimal expectations of the faith?

Lecture Four—Transcript

Late Medieval Christendom—
Beliefs, Practices, Institutions II

Welcome to Lecture Four, entitled, "An Institutionalized Worldview; Western Christendom in the Late Middle Ages, Part II." In our last lecture, I laid out some of the basic beliefs of late medieval Christianity, which I said were intimately connected to its practices and institutions. In this lecture, we'll continue our exploration of this institutionalized worldview by looking at the institutional framework, and some of the most fundamental practices characteristic of late medieval Christendom. Again, our wider purpose here is to understand the matrix from which sixteenth-century Christianity emerged, to understand what the Protestant and the radical Reformations were reacting against, and the ways in which they differed from their late medieval forebears.

To pick up, then, from where we left off in the previous lecture, the preservation, the teaching, and the promulgation of Christian faith in terms of its content and of what Christians believed, required a stable means to ensure that Orthodoxy was preserved and maintained—that is, the correct following of Christ and the possibility of salvation. We've already had occasion to refer several times to this stable means, namely, the Church. The Church, in the late Middle Ages, included not only all living Christians, but the totality of all Christians who had ever lived, living now and dead. The idea of the Church, conceived as a community of the living and the dead, is crucial for understanding certain late medieval Christian practices; prayers and masses said for the dead, and supplications made to the saints.

The fundamental locus of authority within the Church lay with the clergy, with specially ordained ministers. It lay with priests, rather than with the laity. The clergy were set apart from the laity by special vows of celibacy and obedience, by a specific sacrament that they had received, namely, the Sacrament of Holy Orders. This was a vow I'll speak more about in a few moments. Theoretically, they were also set aside by commitment to holiness as a way of life, as well as by special privileges. The clergy were responsible for administering the sacraments, and for the doctrinal, moral, and spiritual supervision of the laymen and –women in their care. Finally, they were responsible for sustaining and staffing the increasingly complex and vast organization of the Latin Western Church.

It's important to note that the ecclesiastical institutions we'll be talking about in this lecture existed alongside the secular political authorities discussed in Lecture Two, the kingdoms, principalities, self-governing cities, and their relationships to one another. The Church had its own courts, its own jurisdictions. Throughout the Middle Ages, from a local level up through the most titanic struggles between popes and emperors, there was frequent friction between these two sorts of authorities, secular and ecclesiastical.

Some of the ecclesiastical institutions within Christendom centered on the clergy, and followed the geographic divisions of Christendom, whereas others did not. I want to consider each type in turn, beginning with those that track the geographical divisions of Christendom, and then talking about some institutions that were not geographically based. Starting, then, with the broadest geographic consideration of Western Christianity, namely, Christendom as a whole. We have it corresponding to the Pope, the Pope who presides over Christendom in its totality. He was normally resident in the city of Rome. He was its bishop, although for about 70 years in the fourteenth century, popes had been resident in Avignon, as we'll see in the next lecture.

The Pope's official title was, in the Latin phrase, "*vicarius Christi*," "the vicar of Christ," Christ's representative. It was his authority, derived from Saint Peter, which guided the Church, in the last instance. His authority was derived from Saint Peter, who was considered to be the first Pope, in the medieval Catholic perspective. He, in turn, had received his authority from Christ, according to the official interpretation of a key passage in Matthew's Gospel. I'm going to read that passage now, because it's critically important: "There," Jesus says, "You are Peter, and upon this rock I will build my church," (*ecclesia* is the Greek term) "and the gates of hell will not prevail against it. I will give you the keys to the kingdom of heaven. Whatever you bind on Earth shall be bound in heaven, whatever you loose on Earth shall be loosed in heaven." This is from Matthew's Gospel, the sixteenth chapter. Hence the reference to the "keys" here finds its visual representation in the papal insignia, the keys on the papal crest even to the present day.

Below the level of Christendom as a whole and the papacy, Christianity was divided into several hundred subdivisions known as "dioceses" and "archdioceses." They varied enormously in size, and were presided over in each case by a bishop or an archbishop, and the bishops were understood to be the successors to Christ's apostles, the first followers of Jesus, whom we talked about when we talked about Christian salvation history in our previous lecture. It's from their relationship to the apostles that the notion of the apostolic succession comes. The bishops and archbishops are understood as the successors to Christ's apostles. Each diocese was further subdivided into the local administrative units of Christendom, namely, parishes. In each parish, local parish priests were deputized by bishops to help them carry out their duties to preserve, transmit, and guide Christians in the practice of their faith.

Parish priests are also known by the term the "secular clergy." This means "secular" in the etymological sense, of being out in the world, the "*saeculum*," not in the sense of being distinct from religious priests. They're distinct from regular priests, who are not opposed to irregular priests. I'll talk more about regular priests in just a moment. These are secular priests in that they're out in the world, serving the laity, rather than being members of cloistered orders. Below the parish clergy, there are a host of other ministers in what are known as "lesser" orders, deacons and so forth, who won't play a very important part in our course.

Together, by about the year 1200, almost all of Western Europe had been organized into parishes, themselves organized into dioceses, within the totality of Christendom. The vast majority of Western Christianity had been so ordered by about the year 1000. By the time of the Reformation, the early sixteenth century, the institutional structure of medieval Christendom was centuries old. This was a very old institutional structure.

So much, then, for the basic institutions that framed Christendom in geographical terms. You'll recall that I mentioned that certain of the clergy were tied to geography, and certain other clerical institutions were not tied to geography. The most important ecclesiastical institutions were not geographically based. These were the religious orders, both male and female. The men among them are known as the "regular" clergy, a term I mentioned just a moment ago. Again, they were "regular" in the etymological sense of following a "*regula*," a "rule," in Latin, not because they were irregular. They were following specific orders laid down by the founders of their respective orders. The religious orders could be further subdivided into two main types; the contemplative orders on one hand, and the mendicant orders on the other. I'll say a little more about each one.

The contemplative orders were cloistered monks and nuns, living respectively in monasteries or convents, devoted, at least in principle, to the pursuit of Christian perfection through living lives of regular prayer and devotion. The contemplative orders, to mention a few of the most important, included the Benedictines, the Cistercians, the Carthusians, and the Brigittines. There were others as well, but I'm not going to go into an entire enumeration.

The mendicant orders, or the begging orders, from the Latin word "*mendico*," "to beg," were also known as "friars." They were dedicated to serving laity in the world, but not within the parish structure of the secular clergy. They missionized, they preached, they taught, and they heard confessions. The mendicant orders included, most importantly, the Franciscans, the Dominicans, the Augustinians, and the Carmelites. Thus, we have a distinction between contemplative orders and mendicant orders. They both fit within the rubric of the regular, as opposed to the secular—that is, the parish—clergy. The religious orders were extremely pervasive throughout Christendom, on the eve of the Reformation. A small town of 4000 or 5000 people might have six or eight different monasteries, of different religious orders, in it.

There was not always the most wonderful cooperation between the members of the various religious orders. Rather, they were oftentimes contentious among one another. There was also frequent friction between members of the regular clergy, parish priests, bishops, and members of the regular clergy, the religious orders. How would bishops oversee the relationship between the regular and the secular clergy within their dioceses? How would bishops and the abbots of great monasteries deal with conflicting claims over their jurisdictions and privileges? We really have two kinds of clergy that could, and often did, come into conflict with each other.

There were also ecclesiastical institutions that were run primarily by and for the laity, rather than by the clergy. The most important of these are "confraternities." Essentially, confraternities are lay mutual aid associations, run for the spiritual and social well-being of their members. They were organized in different ways. For example, sometimes they were organized according to the membership of a particular craft; all the printers or goldsmiths in a certain town belonged to a certain confraternity. They might also cut across different scholarly niches within the communities, or across different artesianal guilds, perhaps, in honor of a particular saint. There might have been a confraternity in honor of Saint Mark, or Saint Dorothy, whatever the case may have been.

The confraternity helped fellow members in need. They provided, for example, for the burial costs of fellow members. They carried out particular kinds of good works, very much in line with what we talked about in the previous lecture; it was about the importance of good works, and active faith for salvation. Confraternities existed in enormous numbers in the towns of Western Europe. A couple of examples; the northern German city of Hamburg, in the early sixteenth century, had a population of about 18,000. It had 99 confraternities. Many people belonged to more than one confraternity simultaneously. The town of which I'm aware had the greatest number of confraternities, in comparison to the population, goes to the Spanish town of Zamora. Zamora had some 8600 people, and over 100 confraternities, in the beginning of the sixteenth century. Confraternities were dense on the ground. They were very common associations. We can well see that an average urban Christian in the late Middle Ages, at the beginning of the sixteenth century, belonged to at least one confraternity.

Confraternities, we should be clear, were not set up in opposition to the clergy. Members of confraternities, for example, would have to contract out to have masses. They needed members of the clergy in cooperation with them for that. Neither should we imagine, however, that the late medieval laity were purely passive, and simply content to carry out clerical initiatives, without institutions for which they took the initiative and for which they sustained the tone.

We've seen the basic spatial divisions of Christendom. Now I want to turn to its principal divisions of time. I'll begin with the day, then move to the week and to the year. We're talking here, really, about the way that time was conceived within this worldview. This understanding was not nuclear or secular, but rather ecclesiastical. It was liturgical. That is, it was based on the Church's worship and its doctrines, again with a scriptural basis. In monasteries, for example, the day wasn't merely a neutral 24-hour period. It was punctuated by seven regular set times of prayer. Those were derived very specifically from one verse in the Psalms: "Seven times each day, I praise thee," talking about God.

The seven periods of prayer provided a daily rhythm of what was called the "divine office." In the divine office in monasteries, the entire cycle of 150 Psalms would be sung every two weeks. Depending on the monastery, the local laity often attended monastic prayers as well, while the secular clergy were expected to recite the divine office on their own.

Moving from days to weeks, throughout Christendom the week was organized around Sunday, as a day dedicated to God and to rest, as God himself had rested after creating the world. Saturdays came to be dedicated to Mary, Jesus' mother. Fridays were days of abstinence from meat, in remembrance of Good Friday, Jesus' sacrifice on the cross.

Moving from the week to the year, the entire year was organized fundamentally around Christ's life, death, resurrection, and the coming of the Holy Spirit after the resurrection. Following the lifecycle of Christ, first there were four weeks of preparation for his birth. This was Advent, the period just before Christmas. Then there was the feast of the celebration of his birth itself, Christmas. After that, there was preparation for his death, Lent, the period of six weeks prior to Easter. Then there was the celebration of his passion on Good Friday, then his resurrection on Easter, followed by the feasts of his ascension to heaven, the resurrection, and then of Pentecost, the coming of the Holy Spirit to the Church, six weeks after Easter, in accordance with Christ's promise.

In addition, other major feasts were tied to the life of Mary, Jesus' mother. Every single ordinary "in-between" day was named in honor of one or more saints, God's special friends. These were deceased Christians who were renowned for their holiness, and were now special intercessors for ordinary Christians with God. Remember that late medieval Christianity is a community of the dead and the living. These deceased Christians do not simply pass into non-existence. They're available for prayers for ordinary Christians. We have a thin remnant of this left in our Saint Patrick's Day, and Saint Valentine's Day. Imagine a society, though, in which every day is named for saints. Particular holy men and women are called to mind each day of the year. The basic idea in the liturgical ordering of time is related to the notion of divine providence that we discussed in the last lecture. It's namely that, just as nothing in the material world stands outside of God's spiritual influence, so no moment of time stands apart from God. Just as nothing in the material world is devoid of spiritual meaning, so no moment of time is separate from salvation history.

Institutions divided Christianity in time and space; the papacy and Christendom, bishops and dioceses, priests and parishes, religious orders, confraternities, and the liturgical ordering of days, weeks, and the entire year. Their structure provided a framework for the stable transmission and practice of Christian faith, ensuring that salvation remained possible. We can see, then, how these basic institutions interlocked and served basic Christian beliefs.

Let's turn, now, to Christian practices, which I'll group in three main categories. They are, firstly, the minimal practices expected of a Christian; secondly, some common Christian collective practices; and thirdly, some practices among the voluntarily devout. Remember throughout these practices that idea of sacramentality we talked about in the last lecture, as well as the idea that one's faith had to be expressed in action; it had to be a living faith, and had to be practiced in order to be efficacious.

A first minimal requirement expected of all Christians was attendance at the weekly celebration of the Mass each Sunday. The Mass was the central form of collective Christian worship in the late Middle Ages. It was a ritual reenactment of Christ's sacrifice on the cross. God, through the priest's word of consecration over the bread and the wine, makes Christ's body and blood present in the bread and wine. The bread was called the "host," that is, the sacrifice. In the categories of Aristotelian philosophy and theology, this process was known as "transubstantiation." It was based upon the biblical verse that came from the Gospels, in which Christ was saying to his disciples, "Take and eat; this is my body." The regular re-enactment of the Mass each week was based on Christ's commandment, "Do this in memory of me." Ordinarily, only the priest consumed the host and wine at Mass. Most of the laity received it only once a year at Easter.

This leads me to a second minimal requirement, expected of all Christians. In addition to weekly attendance at Mass, lay Christians were to participate in and to receive the sacraments. These were the most important specific channels of God's grace, as prescribed by the faith and mediated through the priesthood. We're talking about a condensation within the broader category of sacramentality. One of these was the reception of the consecrated host in communion, the Eucharist, as I just mentioned, at Mass.

In addition, building on inherited tradition, a very important Church council, held in the early thirteenth century, in 1215, had established seven sacraments in all. In addition to the Eucharist, communion, there was baptism. Baptism was administered to infants as the rite of initiation into the Church, and removed original sin. A third sacrament was penance, or confession. I'll say more about that in a moment. Fourth was matrimony, which was the Church's celebration of marriage. Fifth was confirmation, which was the second initiation rite. It confirmed baptism and was most commonly given in one's teen years. Sixth was extreme unction. It involved anointing a person on his or her deathbed with holy oil. Finally, the seventh sacrament was holy orders. It was the sacrament the clergy received, that set them apart from the laity. Only two sacraments were repeated, penance and communion. Again, God conferred his grace via the sacraments. They were the institutionalized expression of the notion of sacramentality, the idea that spirituality is present in and through the created world.

It was also expected that ordinary Christians would observe ecclesiastical regulations. These regulations told them, for example, to fast on certain days, to abstain from sexual relations on certain days, to attend Mass on special feast days in addition to those attended on Sundays, to strive to observe Christian moral prescriptions, which grew out of the Ten Commandments and the seven deadly Sins. The seven deadly Sins were pride, anger, lechery, envy, avarice, sloth, and gluttony.

Transgressions of the Church's prescriptions were sins, and they needed to be confessed to a priest in the sacrament of penance, or confession, each year. This was a prerequisite for receiving annual communion at Easter. The sacrament of penance involved discrete stages, the first of which was sorrow for one's sins, ideally, and for having offended God by not having done what he wanted. This was known as "contrition," the first stage of the sacrament of penance. The second stage was confession itself. This meant telling one's sins to a priest. The priest was functioning in this role as confessor, a priest to whom one told one's sins in the sacrament of penance. The third stage was absolution. It meant being absolved of one's sins by God, through the confessor. The last stage was satisfaction. It meant performing actions prescribed by one's confessor in order to make up for one's sins, for having offended God. "You have done things you shouldn't have; you ought to do these things in order to have your absolution be effective."

The sacrament was an annual ritual. It was done to restore ordinary Christians to a state of grace. Following that, of course, they would sin again, go to confession again a year later, and restoration would come once again. The cycle would repeat itself annually. Those were some of the most basic, ordinary expectations for lay Christians, regardless of anything else that they did.

Let's turn to a second category, and discuss a few common collective practices of medieval Christianity. Processions were among these. Members of a community followed a particular route through the streets of a town or village, or through a rural area, on particular saints' days. Processions were often accompanied by particular blessings of crops, animals, or particular places. Collective practices also included pilgrimages. These were related to processions, except that they were special journeys to particular holy places distinguished by past sacred events, or the presence of special sculptures, paintings, or relics—that is, the bodily remains of a holy man or woman. The most famous example of a pilgrimage from this period is Geoffrey Chaucer's *Canterbury Tales*. It tells a story of a group of pilgrims headed to St. Thomas à Beckett's shrine.

Other important shared Christian practices included financing the Church as a means of practicing the faith. It meant, for example, giving money for, or endowing, religious images, paintings, sculptures, or stained glass, to support or sustain an intensely visual religious culture. Remember, most people were illiterate and couldn't read. One had to make up for that with all sorts of images to nurture the faith. Another way was to endow priests to say masses to lessen the time a relative or oneself would spend in purgatory before passing to heaven, having had one's sins purged. One could also buy indulgences, to lessen the time in purgatory as well. Payment could be made in place of the satisfaction element of the sacrament of penance. Rather than do particular things to make up, a certain monetary value is attached instead, so that money was paid for that portion of the sacrament of penance.

Other widely shared types of Christian practice included the seven corporal acts of mercy. Six of them were drawn directly from Matthew's Gospel. They were feeding the hungry, giving drink to the thirsty, visiting the sick, clothing the naked, visiting the imprisoned, and accommodating the homeless. The seventh one was drawn from the Book of Tobit, namely, burying the dead. These were the seven corporal acts of mercy. Parallel to them are the seven spiritual acts of comfort; counsel, correction, comfort, forgiveness, endurance, prayer, and instruction. Such actions benefited not only the one who did them, for having done something good, but the fellow Christians who were on the receiving end as well. There was reciprocity to acts of Christian love, ideally done out of love for God and for one's neighbor, in imitation of Christ's example. Thus, there were material works, corporal works, and spiritual works, seven of each, and seven sacraments. These were part of that sacred numerology in the Middle Ages.

Having noted some of the minimal practices for all Christians, talked about a few common shared collective Christian practices, my final point for this lecture is to mention a few of the practices of the voluntarily devout. From the twelfth century onward, more and more lay Christians had been adopting devotional practices that had previously been the reserve of religious professionals, members of the contemplative orders. Remember that, within the regular clergy, there were the contemplative orders and the mendicant orders. These were the practices of cloistered monks and nuns.

This process was intertwined with the slow but steady rise of literacy, of education, and of urbanization in the late Middle Ages. For example, Books of Hours were prayer books that adapted monastic prayers from the cloister for use by the laity. They're best known today for those exquisite deluxe manuscript pages that I'm sure most of us are familiar with; at one time or another, those were beautiful illuminated manuscripts produced for the royalty and nobility who could afford them. Hundreds of cheap printed editions appeared in the decades between the advent of printing in the 1450s and the early Reformation in the 1520s. In fact, in the half century prior to 1520, there was no question that Books of Hours were by far the most common genre of any type of printed book in Europe.

In addition, practices among the voluntarily devout included the affective identification, the emotional identification, with Christ's passion, combining texts, images, and emotional imagination meant to deepen one's devotion to and love for Christ, thus becoming a better follower of him. This was not simply something that was done for the heck of it. There was a purpose behind it, to make oneself a better follower of the Lord. There was also an impulse among the devout to make faith and its practice the highest priority in their lives. This was not done just through a self-conscious, explicit faith, but through activities like frequent prayer, ascetic routines, frequent attendance at Mass, dedication to acts of Christian charity, and the scrupulous self-examination of one's conscience.

In sum, then, looking back over this lecture and Lecture Three, late medieval Christianity was an institutionalized worldview. This was a picture of the world believed to be revealed by God, with the most profound and ultimate implications for human origin, purpose, and destiny. This picture was preserved and taught by the Church, whose institutions were both stable and adaptable. It was practiced in widely varying ways, by men and women throughout the society, in the hopes of eternal salvation.

This presentation, though, as presented in this lecture and the preceding one, remains fairly static, a somewhat structural presentation of late medieval Christianity. How was it moving? What trends could be discerned within it in the decades leading up to the Reformation? This is the topic for our next lecture.

Lecture Five

Vigorous or Corrupt?
Christianity on the Eve of the Reformation

Scope:

The Church on the eve of the Reformation exhibits the seemingly contradictory features of widespread problems and pervasive vitality. Resentments, abuses, and vulnerabilities are apparent, including anticlericalism, structural problems derived in part from sheer institutional longevity, and the legacy of late medieval schism and conciliarism. At the same time, we see indisputable signs of vigor and renewal, including massive lay support of the Church, the proliferation of lay piety in a wide variety of forms, and widespread efforts at reform. The two broad aspects, perceived corruption and calls for reform, fit together logically. The Reformation emerged in a milieu not of religious decadence and indifference but of widespread concern and intense religiosity.

Outline

I. How we view the state of Christianity on the eve of the Protestant Reformation is important in shaping how we view the Protestant Reformation itself. We must be able to account both for the break from the Roman Church and for continued allegiance to it.

II. Difficulties afflicting the late medieval Church included anticlericalism, structural problems, and the legacy of schism and conciliarism.

    A. Anticlericalism is best understood as a general tone of resentment and complaints about the clergy. Its forms and prevalence varied greatly by region and specific locale.

        1. Some anticlericalism took the form of complaints about the existence of clerical privileges as such.

        2. These privileges included exemption from trial for civil offenses according to the secular law of cities and territories or kingdoms. Clergy could be tried only in ecclesiastical courts.

        3. Like the nobility, the clergy was exempt from paying most royal or civic taxes. The resentment that this

situation produced was coupled with resentment over the obligatory taxation that the laity owed to the local church in the form of the tithe. The ill will was exacerbated when economic conditions deteriorated, as, for example, during a crop failure.

4. Some resentment existed over clerical fees.
5. Some resentment was also felt over the fact that the clergy were exempt from certain civic duties, such as standing watch at night or fire fighting.
6. Other anticlericalism focused on the abuse of clerical authority in the form of greed, the holding of multiple church offices, the buying and selling of church offices, and the clergy's educational and moral shortcomings.

B. The late medieval Church faced several different types of structural problems.

1. Centuries of accumulated ecclesiastical institutions, theological traditions, and religious practices often caused friction. For example, a great Benedictine monastery might resent the encroachment of local parishes on its privileges to collect tithes.
2. In a society of low literacy, secular authorities called on the clergy, especially from the twelfth and thirteenth centuries on, to perform all kinds of tasks as administrators and lawyers. This increased the occasions for conflicts between ecclesiastical and secular employers and took the clergy away from their spiritual responsibilities.
3. Secular authorities at all levels exerted increasing control over aspects of the late medieval Church.

C. The "constitutional crisis" of the Western schism (1378–1415) raised questions about whether popes or church councils were the ultimate locus of authority in the Church.

III. Unmistakable signs of vitality make it impossible to characterize the late medieval Church as moribund or decadent.

A. The late medieval laity invested massively in religion by paying for churches and their upkeep, endowing Masses, and financing urban preachers.

B. Aided by the invention of printing, the fifteenth century saw an unprecedented proliferation of lay piety.

C. Impassioned, repeated calls for and movements of reform are themselves a sign of vitality, not decadence.

   1. Calls to improve the clergy's education and moral behavior were constant from the fourteenth century on.

   2. Many of the religious orders reformed themselves from within beginning in the late fourteenth century. This project is known as the Observantine movement.

   3. Individual Christians were urged to repent their sins and reform their lives by charismatic preachers, such as John Hus in Prague or Girolamo Savonarola in Florence.

IV. The perception of abuses and the calls for reform fit together, because people generally bother to complain only about things that matter to them. The devotional pitch of Western Europe was arguably higher on the eve of the Reformation than ever before.

Essential Reading:

Euan Cameron, *The European Reformation*, chs. 1–6.

John van Engen, "The Church in the Fifteenth Century," in *Handbook of European History, 1400–1600*, ed. Thomas A. Brady, Jr., et al., vol. 1.

Supplementary Reading:

Eamon Duffy, *The Stripping of the Altars: Traditional Religion in England, c. 1400–c. 1580*, chs. 1–10.

Bernd Moeller, "Religious Life in Germany on the Eve of the Reformation," in *Pre-Reformation Germany*, ed. and trans. Gerald Strauss.

Francis Oakley, *The Western Church in the Later Middle Ages*.

Questions to Consider:

1. What difference does it make for our perspective on the Protestant Reformation if we understand late medieval Christianity as vibrant rather than decadent?

2. Is it more difficult to reform a highly centralized, monolithic institution or a heterogeneous, labyrinthine one?

Lecture Five—Transcript
Vigorous or Corrupt?
Christianity on the Eve of the Reformation

This is Lecture Five, entitled "Corrupt or Vigorous? The Character of Christianity on the Eve of the Reformation." In the previous two lectures, we examined some of the fundamental beliefs, practices, and institutions in late medieval Christianity. This lecture will attempt to set this institutionalized worldview in motion. We'll look at some of the major trends in Western Christianity in the fifteenth and early sixteenth centuries, as well as continue to build up our background for understanding the emergence of the Reformation proper. How we view the state of the Church and the character of Christianity as it was practiced in the decades leading up to the Reformation is critically important, and will shape the way in which we view the Reformations themselves. Our view must be able to account sufficiently for what came after, or it wouldn't be a sufficient historical account.

Given the subsequent course of Christianity during the sixteenth century, we have to be able to account both for the break from the Roman Church, as well as continued allegiance to it. That being the case, the two positions that we should avoid, or at least regard with suspicion, are either that the degenerate state of the Church made the Reformation inevitable, or that things were so well-integrated that the Reformation became a kind of inexplicable anomaly.

First of all, we want to be suspicious of the view that's a traditional influential perspective; this saw the late medieval Church as so riddled with abuse and corruption, so remiss in meeting people's spiritual needs, that the Reformation was simply the logical outcome of an inevitable historical process. Such a view, however, makes it difficult, if not impossible, to understand why anyone would remain loyal to the Roman Church after Luther. If things were so bad, why did people stick with it? More recent scholarship has revised this picture of decadence and corruption, in some cases virtually reversing it altogether. It stresses the extent to which ordinary late medieval Christians seemed more or less fundamentally content with, indeed enthusiastic about, their religion. Here, though, the difficulty becomes understanding why the Reformation came at all, and especially why it enjoyed any popular appeal.

Our task, then, is somewhat tricky. We need to discern both the aspects of late medieval Christianity that make the Reformation intelligible, on the one hand, but also those that make the rejection of the Reformation intelligible. This is because both were subsequent outcomes. In this lecture, we'll look first at the minus side, the resentments, abuses, and vulnerabilities of the late medieval Church. Then we'll look at the plus side, the ways in which late medieval Christianity seemed to be functioning quite well.

Three major features of late medieval Christianity that presented difficulties to the Church, and are considered to be on the "minus" or "difficulties" side, included anticlericalism, structural problems, and the legacy of schism and conciliarism. The next part of the lecture will be devoted to talking about these three in turn.

Firstly, "anticlericalism" is essentially resentments of, complaints about, and actions directed against clerical privileges and/or abuses. Broadly speaking, we're speaking of complaints about the clergy, or hostility towards the clergy, by the laity. This is not a coherent program or organized movement, but rather a general tone of resentment against clerical privileges and abuses. It might erupt in specific instances, depending on local circumstances and whatnot. It was extraordinarily variable in its intensity. It seemed to have been much stronger, for example, in the face-to-face small cities of southwestern Germany and Switzerland than it was in England, or particularly in Spain, where there seems to have been very little anticlericalism in the late Middle Ages.

Some anticlericalism focused on complaints about clerical privileges as such, rather than about any specific abuses in particular. I'll talk about those in just a moment, but first, there were complaints about clerical privileges as such. This goes back to something I mentioned very briefly in a previous lecture—namely, some of those special clerical exemptions. This was when I was talking about the social hierarchy in late medieval towns; I noted that the clergy enjoyed a number of exemptions. Now is the time to explore those a little further.

The clergy, simply by virtue of being members of the clergy, enjoyed an exemption from being tried for civil offenses, according to the secular laws of cities, territories, or kingdoms. What does that mean, in concrete terms? If a priest was accused of theft, in the German town of Augsburg, or in Paris, he was not tried in a secular court for the crime. He was tried in an ecclesiastical court. Why? Because he was a member of the clergy. Another privilege was that, like the nobility, the clergy enjoyed an exemption from most royal or civic taxation. That was always bound to stir up resentment among those who weren't exempt from paying taxes. That's an analogy we can well understand in our own time. It was coupled with resentment over the obligatory taxation that all members of the laity owed to their local churches in the form of a "tithe," an annual ecclesiastical tax. This resentment was also exacerbated when economic conditions got tight. Remember when I talked about the possibility of crop failures? If members didn't have enough money to get enough food to eat, they certainly didn't have enough to give an extra six to eight percent, which was the ordinary amount of the tithe.

There was also resentment, sometimes, over the modest fees traditionally paid to the clergy for services such as presiding over wedding masses, hearing confessions, or blessing women in childbirth. Clergy were also exempt from certain civic duties, from having to stand civic watch over the city at night, for example, to make sure that no intruders tried to get in through the city wall. They also didn't have to help fight fires when they broke out in these towns with their wooden buildings.

A second problem was the abuse of clerical power as such. These resentments centered, above all, on clerical greed, as well the educational and moral failings of the clergy, or the fact that many of them kept concubines, for example, even though they were ostensibly supposed to have been celibate. The latter failings were criticized, but much less extensively than clerical greed. The greediness of the clergy was the most common complaint made on the eve of the Reformation. Complaints about clerical greed and avarice lay behind complaints about simony, for example, which was the buying and selling of Church offices. It lay behind complaints about clerical pluralism, meaning the holding of more than one Church office simultaneously, and drawing the endowed income from it on both. A particular bishop, for example, might be the bishop of four dioceses, and drawing the income from all four. If one was the bishop of four dioceses, he couldn't very well be overseeing all four with equal care.

The critique of clerical greed and avarice was particularly marked against the level of bishops and the papacy. The power wielded there was much greater, the ambitions higher, and the sums of money involved were also higher than they were with the ordinary parish clergy. The higher one went up the scale, the sharper and more intense the complaints about clerical greed were likely to be.

Anticlericalism was fueled, in part, by a perceived gap between the exalted status of the clergy as a privileged group, one that celebrated the Mass and distributed the sacraments on the one hand, and that seemed to use its status and privileges to further its own self-interests,on the other. Anticlericalism also took different forms depending on the specific context. For example, there was a kind of national edge to German anticlericalism against the papacy as a foreign Italian power. This wasn't the case in the anticlericalism of Italy. Similarly, because of the great variety within the clergy as a whole, as we saw in the previous lecture, the specific target of anticlericalism could vary, depending on the context. For example, we could distinguish antipapalism from antimonasticism, or antiepiscopism, meaning an attitude of resentment against bishops specifically. Thus, the target could vary depending on the specific category.

Criticism of clerical abuses and privileges in the early Reformation of the early sixteenth century, then, could tap into a deep and varied powerful stream of anticlericalism. That's the first major difficulty of the three major ones the Church was having on the eve of the Reformation. The second major problem was that the late medieval Church faced a number of structural difficulties, as I'll call them. I'm going to mention three. The first of these difficulties was its age, and what I'll call its "accretionist" character. I'll explain more about that in a moment. A second difficulty involved the wide range of functions that were performed by the clergy in addition to their spiritual duties. A third difficulty was the increasing degree of secular control over ecclesiastical matters in the fifteenth century. Let's look at each of those in a bit more detail.

First, in terms of its ecclesiastical institutions, its theological traditions, and religious practices, the Church represented centuries of accumulation and accretion in the decades leading up to the Reformation. This oftentimes caused friction. For example, institutionally a great Benedictine monastery might have resented the encroachment of local parishes upon its privilege to collect the tithe, or ecclesiastical tax, in a certain rural area. The Franciscans in a particular town might not have wanted the Augustinian monastery to move in, because it meant greater competition for them in terms of hearing confessions.

Another way in which the accretionist, age-heavy Church could cause difficulties was theologically. The emergence of nominalism in the fourteenth century did not displace another theological tradition, that of realism. Rather, the two coexisted. Many theologians drew from both, in eclectic and idiosyncratic ways. Finally, in terms of religious practice, the rise of devotions to one saint didn't usually displace existing devotions to another. It simply added to the total. Nor did endowing masses mean that one didn't read prayer-books, participate in processions, or go on pilgrimage, and so forth. Thus, depending on one's convictions or perspective, this could have been viewed as a situation of confusion and chaos. It is, in fact, almost the antithesis of the stereotype, that of the late medieval Church as a monolithic, single-minded, homogenous institution. If anything, it was the opposite. It had so much variety, and so many variations, so many competing and layered institutions and practices, that it is and was difficult to sort them all out.

The second difficulty in the structural domain, as I mentioned, was that over centuries, the clergy had come to perform a wide range of functions that reached beyond the Church itself. In addition to distributing the sacraments, providing spiritual guidance, and saving souls, secular authorities had called upon educated clergy in this low-literacy society to perform all kinds of tasks, especially since the twelfth and thirteenth centuries. Consequently, they also performed in such roles as administrators and lawyers. This provided occasions for conflict between ecclesiastical and secular employers, and also distracted priests from their explicitly spiritual responsibilities. If a priest was functioning as a clerical administrator, he couldn't see members of the laity who needed him for spiritual advisement.

The third difficulty in the structural domain was that secular control over the Church had grown in the fifteenth century. Behind this increased control lay unresolved tensions, over questions about authority in relationships between Church and state. For example, who had the right to appoint new bishops? Popes, as their ecclesiastical superiors; or kings and emperors, as the superiors in the territories over which they exercised ecclesiastical jurisdiction? Who had the right to appoint new priests to vacant benefices, laymen or clergy? Generally speaking, the fifteenth century saw a series of "negotiated settlements," we can call them, between the papacy and rulers across Europe. Kings and princes would nominate bishops for a vacant bishopric, and the papacy would approve and appoint their nominees. Occasionally, they came into conflict, but either side understood the other, so it went along pretty well for the most part.

In the towns of southwestern Germany and Switzerland, many cities took the initiative to endow preacherships. These were secular appointments of ecclesiastical positions. They raised the money, and they hired for the position. We shouldn't see this as a fundamental challenge to the Church, as such. It is an important shift, however, when compared to the stronger papal claims and practices of the thirteenth and early fourteenth centuries. It also exposes a kind of vulnerability. What happened, for example, if a secular ruler tested the limits of papal authority by challenging it altogether? What happened on the local level if secular magistrates repudiated or thwarted the Church's claims to fill its own positions? The Church had made its own bed, in a way, through its legacy of schism and conciliarism. This is our third major area of difficulty within the late medieval Church.

In the fourteenth and early fifteenth centuries, internal power struggles at the highest levels of the Church raised questions about the locus of its authority. Where was authority situated within the Church hierarchy? Those questions stimulated an urge for wider participation in, and input in, the decision-making of the Church. A story comes, now, with quite a few facts, dates and names, so you're prepared. In 1377, at the end of the fourteenth century, Pope Gregory XI was persuaded to return the papacy from Avignon, where it had been for nearly 70 years, to Rome. Gregory XI died the following year, and the new Pope elected, Urban VI, soon proved objectionable to the majority of the cardinals who had elected him. The cardinals declared the election invalid, and elected a different Pope, Clement VII. This ushered in, not a changeover to the new Pope, but competing groups of cardinals, and almost 40 years of rival popes and rival allegiances that split Western Christendom. This provoked what was really a constitutional crisis; how should one resolve disputed claimants to a monarchy? The answer was, by means of a council. When the two monarchs didn't agree, everyone else who mattered around them was brought together to resolve the difficulty.

This was why the Council of Piazza was called in 1409. It was convened to try and create an end to the schism.

In fact, however, it made the situation worse. It succeeds, not succeeds but actually fails, by adding a third Pope to the mix of the two. Now it was really a problem. Those involved had to go from three popes to one again. Thus, the Council of Constance was convened in 1414. It was attended by many cardinals, bishops, and theologians—above all, to end the schism. It didn't fail again and add a fourth pope. It did succeed, and elected Pope Martin V in 1417. Along the way, the council asserted authority of "councils over popes" in 1415. The relationship between conciliar authority, the authority of a council, and papal authority, authority of popes, remained very active through the 1430s, the Council of Basel, yet another council. However, from the pontificate of Nicolas V in the middle of the fifteenth century, the issue had essentially been decided in favor of the papacy. The Renaissance papacy was located back in Rome, and re-established papal supremacy over councils; that would hold sway into the sixteenth century.

Why do I mention all of this, especially when there is no direct connection between the great schism of competing popes within Christendom and/or conciliarism on the one hand, and the Reformation on the other? Luther emerges as a figure decades after the Renaissance papacy has been ree-stablished in Rome under Nicholas V. However, conciliarism, and the legacy of schism, raised issues and questions that remained "in the air" until well into the sixteenth century. To what extent is authority in the Church a matter of consultation and collective decision-making at whatever level? How, exactly, is authority in the Church exercised and preserved? Where in the Church's hierarchical structure is it anchored? Where does it reside?

In sum, then, the late medieval Church faced anticlerical resentments of clerical abuses and privileges It did so within a complex, multi-layered, ancient ecclesiastical structure, and in a society fraught with friction. In addition, there were ideas current regarding the nature of ultimate authority within the Church.

What about the other side of the picture? A considerable amount of recent research has altered the picture of the late medieval Church as a decadent, corrupt institution, filled with a discontented laity yearning for something better. There is some evidence for this altered view. The first, and probably most important, cluster of evidence comes from lay support for clerical activities. This makes any simplistic opposition between the laity and the clergy, for example, highly problematic. There was, for example, massive lay financial investment in the late medieval Church. If we use the principle that people don't pay for things unless they like what they're paying for, particularly when they don't have to pay for them, then I think we're on solid ground here.

For example, an extraordinary amount of money is given for the building, renovation, and decoration of churches in the late Middle Ages. Something like two-thirds of the more than 10,000 parish churches in England are either built or substantially renovated in the century and a half prior to the Reformation. With unprecedented enthusiasm, people paid for statues of saints, endowed stained-glass windows, and paid for all the accoutrements and materials needed for the ordinary upkeep of the churches and the celebration of the masses. There were altar cloths, candles, priests' vestments, ordinary masonry repairs, and the like needed. Countless individual bequests were left to parish churches, and to monasteries.

Another example of lay investment in the Church was the purchase of masses for family members, or in honor of the saints. As an example of this, the number of endowed masses was rising continually in upper Austria between 1450 and 1480, and reached a peak in 1517. This is the red-letter date, traditionally, denoting the beginning of the Reformation. In England, the laity often controlled, or even owned, side altars in churches. They left detailed instructions about the types of masses they wanted said, how many, on what days, how the altar should have been decorated, on down to the most minute details. These are not, I submit, the actions of people who thought that the Church's teaching on purgatory, for example, was a problem or imposition, but rather of those who embraced it, and wanted to avail themselves of it all the more.

Another example of late medieval lay investment was the lay and civic support of preaching. Individuals left bequests for the support of, and urban city magistrates contracted for, the mendicant orders to preach, especially so on Sundays, saints' days, and during the two great liturgical preaching seasons of Advent, prior to Christmas, and Lent, before Easter. These included both local and so-called "star" preachers of the late Middle Ages. Perhaps the most famous example of a "local" preacher was in the city of Strasbourg, which had a detailed annual contract with their great city preacher, Johann Geiler von Kaysersberg; they renewed this every year with him between 1478 and the year of his death, 1510. There was no tenure for him; he had to earn the contract every year. The "star" preachers preached during the liturgical seasons. Famous ones included Giovanni Capistrano in Italy, and Olivier Meijer in France. I could go on and on. These preachers taught Christian doctrine, urged amendment of life, and preached in the vernacular, so that ordinary people could understand them. They often preached to large crowds in public squares.

Far from suggesting hostility, I would suggest that all of this investment implies approval, and embracing of the teachings and practices at the heart of late medieval Catholicism. Indeed, it has made some scholars go so far as to suggest that much of late medieval piety was actually driven by lay demand, and was far from being imposed by the clergy. The clergy was giving the people what they wanted: More masses, more saint sculptures, more endowed preaching, and so forth. It's a rather different view of the late Middle Ages than the traditional one, that's more in line with what I sketched earlier in the lecture.

This brings us to the next point to be made. The fifteenth century saw an unprecedented proliferation of lay piety and devotion, in a bewildering variety of forms. It was a kind of breaking down of the monastic walls, as we can conceive it. It accelerated a process that had begun in the twelfth and thirteenth centuries. The invention of printing in the 1450s played an important part in this expansion of lay piety. By 1500, printed devotional treatises, collections of saints' lives, prayer sheets, Books of Hours, are all available in relatively cheap editions, and in large quantities throughout Western Europe, in the vernaculars.

Nor was the vernacular Bible itself neglected. It's not widely known, but at least 22 complete editions were published in German by 1522 of the complete Bible, plus 131 vernacular editions in German of the Sunday Gospel and Epistle readings.

There were also printed editions of the Bible or parts of the Bible in French, Italian, English, Spanish, and Czech. All of this printing had an important impact, especially in higher-literacy urban areas. In addition, people who were literate could read aloud to those who weren't. Thus, there was a wider dispersal of the texts beyond those who could simply read them, We're used to reading silently by ourselves, reading wasn't like that all the time in this world. We shouldn't neglect to mention that many of these sources had a strong visual component. This made them accessible in certain ways to the semi-literate and illiterate.

As these religious texts were widely dispersed and penetrated to the level of more humble Christians, so too did practices that had been restricted in previous centuries. Indulgences, for example, had originally been granted only for extraordinary actions, like going on a crusade, or heroic charitable actions. They became attached, though, to more and more religious acts. They became less and less exceptional in the later Middle Ages. For example, instead of making a pilgrimage all the way to the Holy Land to see Jerusalem, it's domesticated, regularized, and brought inside churches, in the Stations of the Cross. In Catholic churches today, you can still see the fourteen stages that trace Christ's pattern, his walking on the way to his crucifixion and through it.

At the devout end of the spectrum, the activity I'm talking about here found expression in a mixed lay and clerical movement that began in the Netherlands in the 1380s, after which it spread into Germany and to Northern France; namely, the "*devotio moderna*," the "modern devotion." These were groups of voluntary, devout men and women, living in separate communities but together, called respectively the "Brothers" or the "Sisters of the Common Life." They come together to cultivate the life of the soul, but don't take formal clerical vows. The most important work to emerge from this circle was the very well known *Imitation of Christ*, by Thomas à Kempis. Talk about a best-seller. Over 70 Latin editions, over 50 vernacular editions before 1500 were produced, in addition to 800 surviving manuscript copies in seven languages. This does not look, I would submit, like a society seeking to change its religious orientation. Rather, it looks like one entering more deeply and enthusiastically into devotional sensibilities available to it. There were increasing numbers of the laity appropriating what previously had been the preserve of monastic piety.

Finally, the vitality of the late medieval Church could itself be seen in the acknowledgement of its shortcomings, abuses, and problems. The widespread calls for reform, in other words, were themselves a sign of vitality, not a resignation about decadence. An example of this were the calls for improvement in the moral behavior and education of the parish clergy, out of a concern that they perform their jobs of caring for souls better. These calls for reform were heard consistently from the fourteenth century on. Another example was the internal reform of the monastic orders, the Observantine movement; that is, the internal reform of the orders was self-imposed, in order to rid the Dominicans, Franciscans, Augustinians, and so forth, of their perceived abuses and shortcomings, usually when measured against their original foundations. This began in the fourteenth century and continued throughout the fifteenth.

Individual Christians were exhorted to repent their sinfulness and reform their lives, often in the shadow of apocalyptic expectations. This was a pervasive characteristic of the late Middle Ages. There was a sense of the imminent end of the world. The most famous preacher who fits in here is probably Savonarola of Florence. It's also in this context that we should place the impassioned calls for reform that fit the preaching of John Hus, the great Czech preacher of Prague. In the early years of the fifteenth century, he harangued huge crowds about abuses, penance, and moral reform. Hus disputed the capacity of priests in mortal sin to perform sacramental functions and exercise their privileges. He was tried as a heretic at the Council of Constance. He was condemned and executed in 1415. His death created a massive reaction in Bohemia, which led to the creation of an independent Hussite church, that rejected papal authority. In some respects, it prefigured the Reformation of the sixteenth century.

Viewed in terms of religious participation, devotional sensibilities, and concern with reform, it's impossible, I think, to say that late medieval Christianity was decadent or lacking in commitment. That leaves us with a problem that we have to resolve here very quickly. Can we put these two paradoxical faces of late medieval Christianity together, that of the abuses and the problems, as well as that of the vigor and the vitality?

I submit that there's a logical relationship between the perceptions of abuses and the calls for reform, religious commitment, and religious criticism. Generally, people only bother to complain about things that matter to them. To this extent, the Reformation emerges not out of a milieu of neglect, decadence, or indifference, but out of widespread concern and religious integrity. The devotional pitch of

Western Europe was arguably higher on the eve of the Reformation than it had ever been. Not only were religious sensibilities strong, but the limited success of previous reformative efforts to effect sweeping change was causing frustration. It was exacerbated by the frightening sense that time was running short. The end of the world was near. Time was running out, running faster.

Fundamentally, calls for reform remained conservative, in the sense that they sought to correct what the late medieval Church was, not to radically remake it. The entire age, indeed, was conservative in this sense, both in the Church and in society at large.

That's a view, then, of the corruptions and problems with the late medieval Church, as well as with its signs of vitality and vigor. In the next lecture, we'll look at a powerful movement that shared in this drive toward reform with a self-conscious appeal to the purity of the past in the learned circles of Europe, namely Renaissance and Christian humanism.

Lecture Six
Christian Humanism—Erudition, Education, Reform

Scope:

One of the most important strands of reform in the early decades of the sixteenth century was Christian humanism, especially important in northern Europe. It emerged out of the broader movement of Renaissance humanism, an attempt to recover the classical Greek and Latin rhetorical and literary tradition and apply it to contemporary morals and politics. The humanists' general admonition to "return to the sources" meant a return to the text of the Bible in the original Hebrew and Greek, plus a return to the writings of the Greek and Latin Church Fathers, to reform Christianity through philological erudition and moral education. Christian humanism offered a notion for Christian renewal that differed from and antedated those of the Protestant Reformation and Counter-Reformation Catholicism, both of which appropriated certain of its emphases in their own ways.

Outline

I. Renaissance humanism was an intellectual movement devoted to the recovery and advocacy of the humanistic disciplines as embodied in their ancient Greek and Latin expressions.

    A. Renaissance humanists sought to learn and teach authentic Greek and Latin based on original, ancient works of rhetoric, literature, oratory, history, poetry, and moral philosophy.

    B. They sought above all to cultivate many of the values and ideals of the ancient world and to integrate them into their own times.

    C. On the whole, Renaissance humanism was not a program that sought knowledge for its own sake but rather knowledge that produced virtue, enabling man to engage in useful moral and political activity.

    D. The humanists were concerned about the degenerate state of Latin as taught at that time and about scholasticism as an overly intellectualized and rationalistic method that failed to effect moral change.

II. For Christianity, going "back to the sources" meant above all returning to the Bible (in the original Hebrew and Greek), and to the writings of the Greek and Latin Church Fathers, with a practical aim.

    A. Christian humanists saw "sacred philology" as key to establishing the best texts and editions of scripture and the Church Fathers.

    B. Consistent with the humanists' general practical aim, sacred philology sought not to attack the Church or Christianity per se, but to provide solid foundations for genuine reform. This project had both critical and constructive aspects.

        1. The Bible and Fathers provided criteria for criticizing practices deemed superstitious or harmful, for deploring the ignorance of many Christians, and for criticizing sub-par clergy.

        2. Christian humanists envisioned a purified Christianity based on norms derived from scripture and the Fathers, combined with a relatively optimistic view of human nature that was partly the product of their immersion in other classical sources.

III. The most important Christian humanist was Erasmus (1466–1536) whose "philosophy of Christ" sought the gradual moral improvement of Christendom through scholarly erudition and education.

    A. By the 1510s, Erasmus's education, travels, and writings led to his wide acknowledgment as the "prince of the humanists."

    B. Erasmus viewed the central problems plaguing Christendom as ignorance and immorality, to be addressed through the scholarship and education of the "philosophy of Christ," the inculcation of Christian virtue based on the Bible and the Church Fathers.

        1. As a straightforward, moralizing reformer, Erasmus wrote his *Handbook of the Christian Soldier* (1503), which confidently urged individual Christians to moral self-mastery of their passions and temptations in a neo-Platonic view of the human being.

        2. As a satirist and critic with a moral purpose, Erasmus wrote his *Praise of Folly* (1511), which included some of the most common devotional practices on the eve of the Reformation.

3. As a philologist and translator, Erasmus published a Greek edition of the New Testament with his own Latin translation (1516).

Essential Reading:

Richard Rex, "Humanism," in *The Reformation World*, ed. Andrew Pettegree.

Ronald G. Witt, "The Humanist Movement," in *Handbook of European History, 1400–1600*, ed. Thomas A. Brady, Jr., et al., vol. 2.

Supplementary Reading:

James McConica, *Erasmus.*

Charles Nauert, *Humanism and the Culture of Renaissance Europe*, ch. 4.

Hilmar Pabel, ed., *Erasmus' Vision of the Church.*

Questions to Consider:

1. What sorts of potential threats did the program of Christian humanism represent to late medieval Christianity?

2. What values and assumptions are presupposed in the humanists' disdain for "the Middle Ages"? In what ways has this legacy persisted to the present, at least in the popular imagination?

Lecture Six—Transcript
Christian Humanism—Erudition, Education, Reform

In the previous lecture, we concluded by pointing out the relationship between perceived problems in the Church and calls for reform. Today, we will pursue one strand within these calls for reform, an intellectual movement crucial for understanding the emergence of the Reformation, namely, Renaissance humanism. Then we'll move on to consider its application in Christian humanism. Finally, we'll look at the greatest exemplar of Christian humanism, the "prince of humanists," as he was called, Desiderius Erasmus.

Renaissance humanism should not be confused with later notions of humanism that carry different connotations—for example, today's secular humanism. Nor was it a particular philosophy or a particular school, or any sort of straightforward precursor to modern rationalism or the Enlightenment. Rather, Renaissance humanism was an elite intellectual movement that began in Italy in the first half of the fourteenth century, and had spread by the late fifteenth century throughout learned circles in Western Europe. It was dedicated, above all, to the recovery and the advocacy of the *studia humanitatis*, the humanistic studies: Literature, poetry, oratory, history, and moral philosophy, all of which had rhetoric at their center. It was dedicated to the recovery of all of these, in their ancient Latin and Greek expression. The humanists sought, above all, to recover and to imitate the classical Latin style, rather than to use the medieval Latin that they had been brought up with. Perhaps above all, they sought to cultivate many of the values and beliefs, the ideals, of the ancient world and to integrate them into the social, political, and moral life of their own times.

The fact of using ancient texts per se wasn't new. Think of the widespread use of Aristotle, for example, in the medieval philosophy and theology in the beginning of the thirteenth century. The humanists took a new attitude toward ancient texts, however. Theirs was a philological and an historical approach to understanding texts as integral wholes, integral works of their own time and place, to be reassembled and understood from the "where" they'd come from. They wanted to think, speak, and live as their ancient predecessors had done. Hence, the rallying cry of the humanists was another of those Latin phrases you'll take away with you from this course: "*Ad fontes*;" "back to the sources." Back to the sources, rather than simply accepting customary interpretations, or receive translations of particular authors.

This program, "back to the sources," supposes an excellent knowledge of the original languages in which the works were written, so that you can understand them as texts that came from a particular time and place. Hence, Leonardo Bruni, as an example, was a humanist who served as chancellor for the city of Florence the first half of the fifteenth century. He raved about the way in which his city had restored classical Latin and rescued Greek from oblivion, "enabling one to encounter ancient authors," as he put it, "face to face." The humanists felt, then, like they were living in a new age, that a new era was dawning after a period of neglect—the wisdom of the ancient world. In fact, it was Renaissance humanists who coined the term "Middle Ages." They understood what its connotations were, as a period of negative backwardness and decline between the summit of ancient times, and the rebirth of modern times.

What was their object of criticism? They were concerned, above all, with attacking the degenerate state of the Latin language that was taught in the schools and universities. They were also upset with the scholastic method in philosophy and theology; they thought of it as an overly intellectualized, rationalistic approach, one that failed to effect moral change. Thus, there was the importance of rhetoric for the humanists, who sought fundamentally to persuade and to move the reader or listener, rather than of philosophy; philosophy's goal, above all, is to rationally demonstrate. They wanted to persuade or to move, rather than to demonstrate, per se. Generally speaking, Renaissance humanism was not a movement of knowledge for its own sake, but ideally, knowledge that produced virtue as understood in classical terms, a certain nexus of values, including the dignity of man, and confidence in his faculties, as well as a sense of responsibility to engage in socio-political life, to serve the larger collectivity, to pursue fame, honor, and glory for one's self, one's family, and one's city or kingdom.

Knowledge of the ancients, of ancient Latin and Greek texts, was useful, because of its moral and civic implications. This, we should note, entails a reassessment of certain values central to medieval Christianity. We can see that if we juxtapose Leonardo Bruni's encouragement of learning for the sake of fame, glory and wealth, with Frances of Assisi's emphasis on voluntary poverty as the heart and ideal of Christian holiness. By the early fifteenth century, humanists were functioning not only as schoolteachers, and bit by bit as university professors, but also as civil servants in cities and courts in Italy. They carried out diplomatic correspondence in their polished Latin, served as ambassadors and secretaries for political regimes, including, as one Italian principate among others, the papacy. The popes employed humanists to carry on correspondence and take care of administrative aspects of the Church at its central highest level.

As an educational program, humanism became the paradigm for the governing elites of Western Europe, beginning in Italy, and spreading north and west to other countries. A humanist training became trendy. It became a way to distinguish oneself by education and culture.

Let's move, now, to consider the significance of the humanists' rallying cry, "*ad fontes*," or "back to the sources," specifically for Christianity. Especially in Northern Europe, beginning around the middle of the fifteenth century, humanists started to apply the humanist program to the reform of Christendom. In this context, the rallying cry, "back to the sources," means a return to scripture and to the writings of the Church Fathers, influential Latin and Greek theologians who lived between the second and the sixth centuries after Christ. The humanists deliberately bypassed later medieval theology and philosophy, accusing these ways of thinking, teaching, and writing of having strayed from the sources, and of having produced empty intellectual systems, we would say. These systems failed in the essential task of Christian theology, as the humanists saw it, of producing devout, self-conscious Christians.

For Christian humanists, the crucial tool for understanding the Bible was not scholastic theology, but rather classic philology, the scientific and critical knowledge of languages. This meant understanding the Bible, not through the traditional Latin Vulgate translation produced by Jerome in the late fourth century, but rather, on the basis of understanding the Greek language of the New Testament and the Hebrew of the Old Testament, comparing and collating, ferreting out as many manuscripts as possible, and trying to produce the most accurate texts possible of both. We might call this project, this application of philological techniques, this program of reforming Christendom, "sacred philology." The Christian humanists' reform program also meant the production of printed scholarly editions of the Church Fathers' writings. The humanists thought that writers like Augustine and Jerome were closer to early Christianity, and had more appreciation for classical literature before classical Latin and Greek had been eclipsed in the West. This made them, they reasoned, more profound theologians than more recent medieval scholastic theologians like Thomas Aquinas, Bonaventure, or Duns Scotus.

Consistent with the practical aim of humanism in general that I mentioned a moment ago, which was to produce virtue, the point of all of this philological work was ultimately pragmatic. It sought not to attack the Church or Christianity, but to provide the basis for a genuine reform built upon solid foundations. The humanists wanted to recover, present, and disseminate a legacy that they thought had been obscured over the course of the medieval centuries. The distortions had to be fixed before this could be undertaken. Therefore, the Christian humanists' return to the sources had both a critical and positive aspect to it. Let's take each of these in turn.

On the critical side, the Bible and the Church Fathers provided criteria for criticizing practices that the humanists judged to be superstitious, silly, or even harmful. For example, these included the veneration of saint's relics, or the use of images as devotional aids, processions, and pilgrimage, whenever their use was divorced from some moral value. Humanists also deplored the abysmal ignorance of many so-called "Christians." They thought that these "Christians" knew nothing of God's word, Christ's message, or the practice of Christian love toward their neighbor. We should note that this amounted to a kind of attack on the distinction between explicit and implicit faith. The humanists essentially said here that 99 percent of the time, implicit faith was nothing but a cover or euphemism for ignorance and superstition.

It was also a criticism of the clergy, to the extent that clerical self-indulgence and greed had paved the way for anticlericalism, and had sullied the dignity of the priesthood. For example, the humanist priest, John Colet, railed against clerical vices in a sermon given to a large congregation of clergy assembled in London in 1512. This was a few years before we'll meet Martin Luther. Colet rails in particular against clerical avarice and greed, which as I mentioned was the most common complaint within anticlericalism as a whole in the late Middle Ages. We might call an address like this of John Colet's a "clerical anticlericalism," to use a rather paradoxical phrase. He himself was a priest, and he was criticizing the shortcomings of the clergy. It was done in a humanist key; that is, directed toward the clergy's reform. This led to a second, pragmatic part of the humanists' return to the sources. On the positive side, humanists sought to derive norms for the practice of a purified Christianity from the Church Fathers. They based this on a relatively optimistic view of human nature, that was partly the product of their study and admiration of the non-Christian classical sources in the ancient Greek and Latin worlds. In their enthusiasm for these ancient texts, humanists encountered powerful examples of men like Socrates and Plato, Cicero and Seneca. They admired these men for their moral virtue, even though they had not been Christians. This prompted the humanists to reflect on the relationship between moral virtue and Christianity.

At a very bare minimum, the humanists' esteem for pagan moral virtue in the non-Christian ancient world, in its own right, led humanists to hold an optimistic view of human nature. This view stressed, for example, man's being created in God's image, and the dignity of human beings, rather than the completely devastating effects of original sin. They argued that one could live a truly informed Christian life in the midst of the world's temptations, through moral education, proper instruction in Christian virtue, through the exercise of that virtue in self-control, and charitable concern for others. The humanists' positive program extracted from the Bible and from the writings of the Church Fathers. It filtered them through their understanding and admiration for non-Christian values. They read the Bible through the values of classical antiquity.

Just to look ahead, now, for a moment, to our next lecture, Martin Luther's call for a return to scripture didn't occur in a vacuum or come out of nowhere. Rather, it had been part and parcel of the humanist call for reform for decades prior to the Reformation. As we shall see, however, this similarity marks even more fundamental differences that would become apparent in the early years of the Reformation. I'll say more about that in subsequent lectures. The exemplar of this approach to Christian reform in the first two decades of the sixteenth century was Desiderius Erasmus, or Erasmus of Rotterdam. He was the Northern Christian humanist par excellence. I want to give a little bit of biographical background before proceeding to discuss his vision of reform.

Erasmus was born around 1466; some scholars think it was 1469. Oftentimes it's extremely difficult to be exact with the birth-dates of people born in this era. We don't have the baptismal or birth records from which scholars can determine people's ages. We have to be content with knowing that Erasmus was born in the late 1460s. In his later childhood and adolescent years, he spent several years at the famous school run by the Brothers of the Common Life, an organization I mentioned in a previous lecture. This particular school was located in the Dutch town of Deventer. One alumni from the same school was none other than Thomas à Kempis, author of the *Imitation of Christ*, an extraordinarily popular late medieval devotional work that I mentioned in the previous lecture. From an early age, Erasmus is exposed to the "Modern Devotion," the "*devotia moderna*," as he was learning Latin and becoming acquainted with humanism. In 1487, Erasmus entered an Augustinian monastery, because he thought it would provide opportunities for study. He took solemn vows, and was ordained a priest in 1492. Not everything that happened in 1492 had to do with the New World.

His later criticisms of monasticism were shaped by an unsatisfying experience at the monastery. In 1492, he obtained a position as a secretary to the Bishop of Cambray. The bishop permitted Erasmus to go to Paris three years later in 1495; it was the center of theological study of Western Christendom. Erasmus, though, was deeply turned off by scholastic method and objectives. His aversion to scholastic and academic theology in general would be a recurrent theme in his later writings.

Invited by one of his students, Erasmus went to England in 1499. This was a decisive trip for him. During the trip, he met John Colet, the same humanistic priest who would address the London clergy with his "clerical anticlericalism" in 1512. John Colet was lecturing on Paul's letters from the New Testament at Oxford, using the new humanist techniques. Erasmus was smitten. He was inspired from that point to devote himself to applying the humanistic scholarship to scripture, in order to revitalize theology in Christian life. During his stay in England, he also met other humanists, including Thomas More, whom he would be friends with for the rest of his life.

After 1500, Erasmus returned to the continent. He spent future years leading a traveling scholar's existence, working on editions of the writings of Church Father Jerome, as well as on the text of the New Testament, improving his Greek all along. The first editions of his *Adages* were published in 1500, and of his *Enchiridion* in 1503. These helped to establish his reputation. After the early first years of the sixteenth century, Erasmus was famous in the learned circles of Europe. Between 1506 and 1509, he spent time in Italy, including a visit in 1509 to the papal court of Julius II. It utterly disgusted him as conspicuous extravagance, along with the fact that there was a man as Pope who also led military campaigns, mounted as a warrior on a white horse.

All of this was fresh in his mind when he returned to England between 1509 and 1511, and among other things wrote the work for which he is probably most famous, *In Praise of Folly*. It was written in 1509 and published in 1511, and dedicated to Thomas More. This was not because he thought More was a person filled with folly himself, but because they were close friends, and he knew that More would appreciate it. Between 1514 and 1521, Erasmus' main base of operations and place of residence was Holland, with forays over to England. He spent time living in the town of one of my alma maters, Louvain. He spent time at the university there. He worked hard on his scholarly edition of the New Testament during these years; it appeared in 1516.

When Luther first became a public figure in 1517, Erasmus had been Europe's leading intellectual for a decade. He was known, as I mentioned at the outset of the lecture, as the "prince of the humanists." For a bit of biographical background, what is Erasmus' program? He saw the essential problem plaguing Christendom as one of ignorance and immorality. It was to be addressed by a partnership of scholarship and education in what he called the *Philosophia Christi*, the "philosophy of Christ," teaching Christian virtue based upon the Bible and on the Church Fathers. Erasmus envisioned humanistic scholars making texts available to be used by humanistic teachers, who would gradually indoctrinate and raise the moral behavior and levels of genuine piety among Christians throughout society, via education. Whether he wrote as a satirist, a moral reformer, or a Biblical scholar, this was Erasmus' basic vision.

Relatively speaking, it was a patient reform vision. By that, I mean that it was not one driven by apocalyptic urgency, the sense of the imminent end of the world. Erasmus had a longer-term view of things. It was also a highly intellectual vision, with the Christian scholar, really, as the hero of the story, the one on whom the texts and education were ultimately based. The genuine practice of Christianity, then, depended crucially on scholarship.

I want to mention three different works now, which show Erasmus at work in three different modes. Namely, I want to show him as a moralizing reformer, a satirist, and finally, as a biblical scholar, to close out this lecture.

First of all, there was Erasmus, the straightforward, moralizing reformer, in his *Handbook of the Christian Soldier*, his *Enchiridion,* as it's called. It was written in 1501 and published in 1503. Throughout the work, Erasmus used the metaphor of Christian life as a warfare against sin and temptation. This was a very traditional metaphor, and found, for example, in Paul's letter to the Ephesians. Erasmus sets it, though, in a heavily Platonic view of man, as a rational soul struggling to transcend the baser nature of his body, and doing so by turning to Christ as the exemplar of all virtue. Here's a quotation to give you a flavor of what I mean: "This is the only way to virtue," Erasmus says. "First, that you know yourself." Socratic principle, there.

> Second, that you act, not according to the passions, but the dictates of reason. Seize with a stout heart upon the principle of the perfect life, and press forward in your purpose. Never has the human spirit failed to accomplish something it ardently demanded of itself. A large part of the Christian life is to wish wholeheartedly to become a Christian. What will seem unattainable at the outset will become more accessible as you approach it, easy when you use it, and at last, delightful, when you get accustomed to it.

There's a real sense, here, of the confidence in human capacities for self-mastery; of Christianity as a gradual process, the incremental growth in the practice of virtue and the love of neighbor. The entire work, Erasmus' entire *Enchiridion*, contains almost no mention of the sacraments or of the Mass. In his second mode, Erasmus was a satirist, the critic of superstition and ignorance, of misdirected piety and self-importance masquerading as religiosity. This we see in his *Praise of Folly*. This was a complex work, dealing with multiple senses and complex manifestations of folly in human affairs. Here he was, ridiculing the disputatious methods and questions of academic scholastic theologians. What was the exact moment of divine generation? Was it a possible proposition that God the Father could hate his son? Could God have taken the form of a woman, a devil, a donkey, a gourd, or a flintstone? If so, how could the gourd have preached sermons, performed miracles, or been nailed to the cross?

There are any amount of quibbles, even more refined than these, about concepts, formalities, and quiddities, which no one could possibly perceive unless he could see through blackest darkness, things which don't exist. We're close, here, to stereotypes about medieval theologians debating about how many angels could dance on the head of a pin. I'm going to answer the question, which, of course, is that it's a category mistake. Angels, because they're spiritual beings, don't have any extended bodies; you can't compare something that's not extended in space to something that is, however small, such as the head of a pin.

Erasmus was attacking certain religious practices that were thriving, as we've seen in previous lectures, in late medieval Christianity. He was lampooning the hypocrisy of monks and clergy. Again, the wider purpose was not an attack on devotion, theology, or monasticism as such, but rather on their corruption, or their perversion. It was a satire on abuses as part of a call to renewal, serving his wider program.

A third and final example was Erasmus' scholarly edition of the New Testament. It was published in 1516. What's interesting about this edition is that it was published in Greek, but with his own parallel text Latin translation of the Greek set side by side. The Latin translation was much more threatening, because it diverged from the Latin of Jerome's Vulgate, the Church's official text in all of its worship and liturgical prayers. Some of those differences had doctrinal implications. I'll give one example. In the Gospel of Matthew, Chapter 3, Verse 2, John the Baptist is preaching. Erasmus translated the Greek term as "Be turned to me," rather than the traditional, "Do penance." That is, "Be turned to me," even "Come back to your senses," not "Engage in the sacrament of penance," or "Go confess your sins to a priest." This transformed an exhortation about the sacrament of confession into an imperative to reorient one's person toward Christ.

The question could be raised, then, that many of the Church's practices had been based upon inadequate or even misleading scriptural translations, for centuries. This is potentially an extremely subversive idea. Erasmus' translation provoked both immediate hostile criticism, as well as fulsome praise. It became a real touchstone. This edition of the New Testament, which illustrates Erasmus' desire to put the Bible into the hands of all Christians through vernacular translations, was part of his vision for the reform of Christendom. I'd like to read a passage from its preface as we near the end of our lecture. Erasmus said:

> I disagree very much with those who are unwilling the Holy scripture, translated into vulgar tongue, be read by the uneducated, as if Christ taught such intricate doctrines that they could scarcely be understood by very few theologians, or as if the strength of the Christian religion existed in men's ignorance of it.

> I would that even the lowliest women read the Gospels and the Pauline Epistles, and I would that they were translated into all languages, so that they could be read and understood not only by Scots and Irish, but also by Turks and Saracens. Would that, as a result, the farmer sing some of them at the plow, the weaver hum some parts of them to the movement of his shuttle, the traveler lighten the weariness of the journey, with stories of this kind.

Very soon, Erasmus got his wish. The results of putting the vernacular scriptures into the hands of the full swath of the population certainly made him rethink twice about what he desired so earnestly, in 1516. To conclude our lecture, on the eve of the Reformation Christian humanism comprised a powerful and patient international reform movement, for the renewal of perceived problems within Christendom. It married erudition with education, classical values with Christian ones, and sought to raise the levels of Christians' moral behavior. The humanists weren't the only ones advocating a return to Scripture, however. Another was one who came from one of the very monastic orders Erasmus had ridiculed. His name was Martin Luther. We'll meet him in the next lecture.

Lecture Seven
Martin Luther's Road to Reformation

Scope:

Martin Luther is one of the most remarkable and influential figures in all of European history. In 1517, he was an obscure Augustinian monk and university professor; by the spring of 1521, he had defied both Pope Leo X and Emperor Charles V on behalf of his understanding of Christian faith and life. After his early life and university education, he joined the Observant Augustinians in 1505. In October 1517, he objected to abuses regarding indulgences in his *Ninety-five Theses*, which appealed to Christian humanists. At the Leipzig Disputation of June 1519, he asserted that scripture alone, not popes or councils, possesses ultimate authority for Christians. In the latter half of 1520, he published three important treatises after the pope threatened him with excommunication: *Address to the Christian Nobility of the German Nation, Babylonian Captivity of the Church,* and *The Freedom of a Christian.* After his excommunication, Luther refused to recant his views at the Diet of Worms (April 1521) and was condemned as a heretical outlaw by Charles V. Four factors crucial to Luther's success from 1517–1521 included the protection of his territorial prince, Frederick of Saxony; anti-Roman sentiment in Germany; support from humanists, including Erasmus; and the widespread, rapid diffusion of his writings via print.

Outline

I. After his early life and university education, Luther joined the Observant Augustinians in Erfurt, the strictest monastic order accessible to him, in 1505.

   A. Luther was born in Eisleben in central Germany in 1483. He attended school in Mansfeld and Eisenach before studying in the arts faculty at the University of Erfurt.

   1. At Erfurt, Luther was trained philosophically as a nominalist, an influence that would remain with him.

   2. Though he developed a love of Latin literature in Erfurt and had a high regard for the fruits of humanist learning, Luther was not deeply influenced by humanism.

B. After a traumatic experience in 1505 (he was thrown to the ground by a bolt of lightening), Luther made the decision to enter the Observant Augustinian order as a monk. This religious order was the strictest, and the monastery would be the matrix for his Reformation.

    1. Luther's "revolt" against the Church came from a consummate "insider," one who had sought for years the path of Christian perfection through the rigors of monastic life.

    2. As a monk, Luther was deeply stricken with anxiety about his own sinfulness and inability to live up to God's commandments.

II. In late 1517, Luther's *Ninety-five Theses* first brought him to public attention.

    A. Luther objected to the campaign of papal indulgences being promoted by the Dominican Johann Tetzel under the authority of the Archbishop of Mainz. At this stage, he was concerned that the laity was getting a distorted understanding of good works.

    B. Luther sent his objections to the Archbishop of Mainz and posted them on the door of the castle church in Wittenberg on October 31. He gained his first public notoriety when humanists immediately translated the objections into German and had them printed in multiple editions.

III. At the Leipzig Disputation in June 1519, Luther stated that scripture alone, not popes or councils, is the locus of ultimate authority for Christians.

    A. Luther's skilled Catholic opponent in the disputation, Johannes Eck, pushed Luther to claim that neither popes nor councils can interpret scripture infallibly. This unsettled those humanist supporters who had seen him as an anti-papal conciliarist in his views on ecclesiastical authority.

    B. The Latin phrase describing Luther's view that the Bible alone is authoritative for Christian faith and life is "*sola scriptura.*"

IV. In response to the threat of excommunication, Luther wrote three important treatises in late 1520. He was excommunicated, then condemned by Emperor Charles V after the Diet of Worms in April 1521.

A. After the theologians of Louvain and Cologne condemned propositions from his works, Luther was threatened with excommunication in June 1520 by Pope Leo X in the papal bull *Exsurge domine.*

B. Between August and November 1520, Luther wrote three treatises that addressed different audiences and issues and were widely read in Germany, Switzerland, and the Low Countries.

1. In August 1520, Luther published the *Address to the Christian Nobility of the German Nation*, urging the nobility to reform the Church in Germany, because the papacy had made reform impossible through its tyrannical monopoly of power.

2. In October 1520, Luther published *The Babylonian Captivity of the Church*, a manifesto for the reform of the Church's worship, with considerable attention devoted to the sacraments. This work was written in Latin and intended for an educated audience.

3. In November 1520, Luther published *The Freedom of a Christian*, his early programmatic statement of his theology of justification, which reconfigured the relationship between faith and works in the Christian process of salvation: Humans are saved by faith alone. Faith is a free gift from God.

C. After his excommunication in January 1521 by Pope Leo X, Luther refused in April to recant his views before Charles V at the Diet of Worms, whence he was secretly taken into protective custody and translated the New Testament into German. In May 1521, the Edict of Worms condemned him as a heretical outlaw.

V. At least four major factors contributed to Luther's success between 1517 and 1521.

A. Frederick of Saxony, Luther's powerful territorial prince, protected him politically.

B. German anti-Roman sentiment benefited Luther.

C. Humanists esteemed Luther for his emphasis on scripture and hostility to scholastic theology.

D. Luther's many early writings were widely and rapidly diffused through print.

Essential Reading:

Martin Brecht, "Luther's Reformation," in *Handbook of European History, 1400–1600,* ed. Thomas A. Brady, Jr., et al., vol. 2.

Euan Cameron, *The European Reformation*, ch. 7.

Carl Truman, "Luther and the Reformation in Germany," in *The Reformation World*, ed. Andrew Pettegree.

Supplementary Reading:

Roland Bainton, *Here I Stand: A Life of Martin Luther.*

Heiko A. Oberman, *Luther: Man between God and the Devil.*

Questions to Consider:

1. How did the course of events intersect with the development and expression of Luther's own views between 1517 and 1521?

2. How would Luther's experience as a monk have helped him in the trajectory of events that led to his excommunication and imperial condemnation in 1521?

Lecture Seven—Transcript
Martin Luther's Road to Reformation

We've set the stage, now, for the early Reformation itself. I've talked about the basic conditions of social and political life, we've looked at the institutionalized worldview of late medieval Christianity, we've explored the character of the late medieval Church on the eve of the Reformation, and finally, in our last lecture, looked at the reform movement of Christian humanism.

This is the first of two lectures devoted to one of the most remarkable and influential figures in European history, namely, Martin Luther. He was a religious and passionate man, a penetrating and relentless thinker, and a tireless writer and propagandist. He was also the initiator of a movement that would eventually become known as the Protestant Reformation. This lecture will primarily be devoted to a narrative of Luther's early career as a reformer, between 1517 and 1521, trying to understand how an obscure monk and university professor on the edge of Christendom became known throughout Western Europe, and eventually dared to challenge the authority of both the pope and the Holy Roman Emperor. The next lecture will explore the character and implications of Luther's theology.

In this lecture, we'll talk about five major topics. First, we'll talk about Luther's life up to 1517; after that, the indulgences controversy and the famous *Ninety-Five Theses* of the year 1517. We'll move on to the critical watershed of the Leipzig Disputation; then the three famous treatises of 1520 and the Edict of Worms; and, finally, conclude with talking about four factors that were crucial to Luther's success.

Luther's life, then. He was born in 1483, in Eisleben, a small town of about 4000 people in central Germany. He was born to Hans and Margaret Luther. He was a copper miner from a peasant background, and she was from a fairly prosperous burgher family. They were not wealthy, but neither were they destitute. Luther himself would often refer to having been of peasant stock. This was a bit of a stretch of the truth. His father was descended from peasantry, but in fact was a fairly well-to-do miner.

Luther moved when he was young to Mansfeld, a town even smaller than Eisleben; that's where he first attended school. He said it wasn't a good experience. He got a much better educational experience in the town of Eisenach, where he moved afterward and went to Latin school. This prepared him to enter the University of Erfurt. He attended between 1498 and 1501. It was one of the leading universities in the Holy Roman Empire, and a distinguished one, to be sure. While at Erfurt, Luther studied in the arts faculty, not in the fine arts, but what we would call the liberal arts, the standard medieval undergraduate university curriculum, apparently with an eye toward eventually following law. Law, medicine, and theology were the three "professional" faculties in the medieval curriculum.

He was trained philosophically in Erfurt as a nominalist; that is the late medieval epistemological view that took a critical attitude toward authorities, that insisted that all philosophical speculation be tested on the basis of experience and reason, that all theology be based on the authority of the Bible as interpreted by the Church, and drawing a fundamental distinction between God's word, on the one hand, and human reason on the other. Nominalism was an important influence that remained with Luther throughout his career.

At Erfurt, Luther developed a love of classical Latin literature. Plautus and Virgil were among his favorite authors. He was not touched by humanism in a deep, fundamental way, however. Throughout his career, he would have a high regard for the fruits of humanistic learning. He was very excited, for example, about the publication of Erasmus' New Testament, the one we talked about in our last lecture. For Luther, however, it was always a means to an end. Luther was not a religious thinker who was interested in knowledge for its own sake, scholarship per se. It is misleading to characterize him as a humanist. The matrix for his Reformation, his formation and the emergence of his theology, was really the monastery. In order to understand the emergence of his Reformation theology, we need to understand something about his experience in the monastery. How did he get there? It's an interesting story in its own right.

Just after beginning the study of law, in July of 1502, Luther was caught in a ferocious thunderstorm. He was thrown to the ground by a bolt of lightening, and absolutely terrified. He called on Saint Anne to protect him. He vowed to become a monk if she did. The storm passed, and Luther didn't perish. Two weeks later, to the great disappointment of his father, who wanted him to pursue the law,

Luther instead enters the monastery. It wasn't just any monastery, but the Observant Augustinians in Erfurt, the strictest monastic rule available. He was ordained a priest in 1507.

An aside right here, and an important point to be made, is that Luther's eventual revolt was eminently a revolt by an insider. It was not a critique of the Church from the outside, but the inside, by someone who had lived an exacting, ascetic version of Christianity for years. Observant Augustinians were not the self-indulgent, lax monks of popular caricature, or of Erasmian satire. Rather, they were part of that monastic reform movement of the late Middle Ages, the Observantine movement we saw in an earlier lecture. Luther was pursuing a rigorous way of life. He was seeking Christian perfection through self-denial, prayer, and service, doing battle against the temptations of the devil. His later rejection of the idea that monasticism was somehow inherently a holier or better way of life than callings in the world, was based upon this sincere and serious experience with it, not on a rejection of it simply in its corrupt or self-serving manifestations. This was an important formative experience. Luther had been a monk for over a decade by the time he became a public figure.

Part of the service that Luther engaged in while in the monastery was the hearing of confessions. He was acting in his role of confessor with the sacrament of penance, as we've talked about before. He heard the confessions of local lay parishioners who were coming to him. In addition, he himself was an extraordinarily self-conscious, scrutinizing sort of person. He was very aware of, and concerned with, his own spiritual progress, in addition to being intimately familiar with lay perceptions and experience of the sacrament of penance, and preparations for it.

Luther, then, had a wide-ranging familiarity with human sinfulness, above all, his own sinfulness, and a nagging, persistent sense that carrying out penances, however rigorous or severe, would never be enough to assuage the punishing wrath of an angry God, or of Christ, who would come again to judge the living and the dead, as the Creed put it, as we talked about when discussing Christian salvation history. Moreover, Jesus had told his followers in the very Sermon on the Mount "to be perfect as your heavenly Father is perfect." He had pushed the Ten Commandments to the level of intentions. "Everyone who looks at a woman with lust in his heart, is already guilty of adultery." Luther asks himself, "If that's the standard to which we're being held, what possible chance do we have? How can we possibly meet that standard?" What would happen if the contrite sinner didn't feel the liberation that the sacrament of penance was supposed to provide? That was Luther's situation. We'll leave him there for the moment.

In 1511, he moved from Erfurt to the new University of Wittenberg. In the same year, he visited Rome for several weeks on Augustinian business. He was shocked by the public blasphemies and the irreverence. We'll recall from the last lecture that Erasmus, too, went to Rome and had a very negative experience. In 1512, Luther received his doctorate, and he began lecturing on scripture two times a week, as a professor of biblical theology at the University of Wittenberg. Luther was a man who was extremely intimate with scripture, both from his experience in the monastery as well as from his own teaching and study. This was not simply scholarly knowledge. We're talking here about experiential knowledge, knowledge based both on academic learning and its interwovenness with the monastic life of prayer. He was highly respected within the Augustinian order, and became the second-ranking Augustinian within the Observant Augustinian order in 1515. He oversaw ten Augustinian monasteries and the Augustinians at two universities.

In retrospect, looking back and knowing what came afterward, elements of Luther's theology are visible in his biblical lectures on different books of the Old and New Testaments, from about 1513 on. In 1517, even, no-one could have foreseen the remarkable events of the next four years, however.

Let's move on now to the indulgences controversy. Indulgences, as you'll recall, are an amount of money paid for papally-commissioned graces, including a remission of sins, which replace the satisfaction portion of the sacrament of penance. This only works for someone who is properly contrite and confessed. They are not a substitute for the sacrament of confession in toto, nor a substitute for the necessity of confessing one's sins; it's not a matter of buying one's way into heaven, even though it's sometimes portrayed that way in Reformation polemic.

In the summer of 1517, then, the Dominican Johann Tetzel was aggressively promoting an indulgence campaign, under the authority of the local archbishop, Albrecht of Mainz. They were trying to help raise money, to build, of all things, St. Peter's Cathedral in Rome. Tetzel had a real sense of urgency. He was telling people to seize the opportunity, to be more concerned with the salvation of their souls than for material possessions.

Right at that time, Luther was in contact with laity who were coming to him, and to other Augustinians in the monastery as well, for confession. Based on what he was hearing from people, he was concerned that souls were being misled by the indulgence campaign, because good works were being undercut by money. He draws up 95 technical theological propositions in Latin, for academic debate at Wittenberg. This was the origin of his famous *Ninety-Five Theses*. He posted them on the door of the castle church at Wittenberg on October 31, according to custom. He sends a copy, along with a letter, to Archbishop Albrecht of Mainz, asking him to change his practice.

At this stage, in 1517, during the indulgences controversy, Luther was concerned that good works are being undermined. This is not the way he's often presented, as opposing good works in the name of faith right from the outset. I'll give an example by reading four of the 95 theses. These are Theses 41–44. Luther says:

> Papal indulgences must be preached with caution, lest people erroneously think that they are preferable to other good works of love.
>
> Number 42: Christians are to be taught that the pope does not intend that the buying of indulgences should in any way be compared to works of mercy.
>
> 43: Christians are to be taught that he who gives to the poor or tends to the needy does a better deed than he who buys indulgences."

Because, this is 44:

> Love grows by works of love. Man thereby becomes better. Man does not, however, become better by means of indulgences, but is merely freed from penalties.

"If a pope can truly free souls from purgatory," Luther asked, "why not free them all, for no charge whatsoever?" The reckless promotion of indulgences, he was concerned, exposed the papacy to criticism and ridicule from the laity.

Luther first emerged into the public eye in late 1517, as a university professor and monk. He protested against indulgences on the basis of scripture. His publicity at this point came, above all, from circles of humanists. Humanists saw in his theses common points with many of their own concerns, such as the importance of scripture, and the renewal of religious life. The theses were translated into German without Luther's consent, and published in multiple editions. The humanists were the ones who saw to this, above all. In months, the obscure monk was known throughout Germany and Switzerland, all the way from Amsterdam in the north, to Berne in Switzerland in the south. Humanists were essential, then, to making the 95 theses more than just narrow matters for academic debate. They gave Luther his first real public exposure.

At this stage, Luther was concerned with the misunderstanding of a Church practice by the laity. He didn't want to attack the Church, but access it from within, to call it to do its job rightly, to not mislead the faithful, or undermine their understanding of Christian life. In October of 1518, to jump ahead to the next stage in our story—to the Diet of Augsburg, an important meeting of lay and ecclesiastical political leaders in Germany—the general of the Dominican order, Cardinal Cajetan, was sent as a papal representative, to meet Luther and to secure his recantation of the recently expressed views on indulgences. Discussions took place, largely behind closed doors.

Luther refused to recant his views, unless he could be shown the reason for it on the basis of scripture, rather than canon law, the Church's law. He was increasingly pushed to question whether papal authority was sufficiently infallible to interpret scripture. He was tipped off that Cajetan had been told to bring him back to Rome bodily, and fled from Augsburg at night. There was an emergence, here, at the Diet of Augsburg, of a divide. The divide was between the authority of tradition, on the one hand, embodied in the Pope, and of scripture, on the other. This view had been associated with medieval heresy, with John Wycliffe, with John Hus. It was still largely a private debate at this point, however, in late 1518. That changes dramatically with the Leipzig Disputation.

In June of 1519, Luther publicly debated the young and very capable Johannes Eck, in Leipzig. With his disputational skill, Eck backed Luther into a corner, and pushed him to say things that he didn't necessarily want to say. He forced Luther to push his own lines of thought to their logical extremes. In fact, Luther later acknowledged and thanked Eck for helping him fully see the implications of his views. Eck got Luther to admit that neither councils nor the pope had the sanction to interpret scripture infallibly. This came as a shock to those of Luther's humanist supporters who thought that he was an anti-papal conciliarist. He was not saying that councils, rather than popes, were authoritative. He was saying that the Bible has an independent authority, as God's word, that is contingent on neither popes nor councils. The public emergence was what was visible here, the public emergence of Luther's Reformation, exegetical view. This was his approach to the interpretation of scripture. His view was that scripture alone was authoritative for Christian faith in life.

After the Leipzig Disputation, events moved rapidly. Luther was gaining a wider reputation, and his position became sharper. After the condemnation of propositions from his works by the theology faculties of Cologne and Louvain, Pope Leo X issued the bull, "*Exsurge domine*," in June of 1520. "*Exsurge domine*" gave Luther 60 days to recant his condemned views, or face a final excommunication. Luther responded to the bull defiantly and energetically. He produced three important treatises in the second half of 1520, in which he addressed different issues and audiences. These were widely published and distributed in Germany, Switzerland, and the Low Countries. I'll talk briefly about these three treatises.

In August of 1520, he produced the *Address to the Christian Nobility of the German Nation*. It was written in German, and was an impassioned appeal to the German nobility to reform the Church in Germany themselves, since the papacy had insulated itself from the possibility of change through a tyrannical monopoly of power. It had erected three walls around itself, and had made change impossible, Luther said. First of all, it had subjected temporal power to spiritual power. Second of all, it had subjected councils to popes, and had said that only papally convened councils could be valid; thus, they had closed off the conciliar path, an independent route to reform. Third of all, it had closed off scripture as a basis for reform, since it claimed the sole authoritative interpretation of the Bible.

The work contained extraordinarily sharp attacks on the papal court. Luther referred to it as a "crawling mass of reptiles," for example. He attacked the abuses, avarice, and corruption of Rome and high-ranking prelates, with numerous detailed reform proposals of his own. In short, Luther was flatly accusing the papacy of trying to stifle secular authorities, councils, and scripture in its arrogant greed for power. Over against this, he issued a flattering appeal to the nobility, to go over the heads of ecclesiastical authority, as a kind of emergency program to salvage the Church. It was a move of desperation, to rescue society, if it was to remain a Christian society. This was a decisive gesture towards the nobility, in the long-standing medieval tension between secular and ecclesiastical authority, to go back again to a theme from a previous lecture.

The second of the three important treatises of late 1520 appeared in October. It was *The Babylonian Captivity of the Church*, which was a deliberate echo of the Babylonian captivity of the fourteenth century, when the papacy was in Avignon. This work was written in Latin. It was intended for a different, more educated audience. Its concern was really the reform of the Church's worship, with a great deal of attention given to the sacraments. The key here was that, on the basis of Luther's own understanding of scripture, he said that the number of sacraments should be reduced from seven to three. Only baptism, communion, and, in certain somewhat ambiguous respects, penance should be retained. Again, here we see the explicit use of scripture over against tradition in a sharply critical, antagonistic way.

The third treatise of 1520 was Luther's *Freedom of a Christian*. It was written in Latin and German. It had separate editions in each language. It was Luther's early, programmatic statement of his theology of justification; that is, there was a profound reconfiguration of the relationship between faith and works in the Christian process of salvation. According to Luther, human beings are saved by faith alone. Salvation is an absolutely free, unmerited gift received from God, to which human beings contribute literally nothing. At the same time, however, people are no less obligated to do good works toward their neighbors; rather, they should do so out of Christian love. In other words, one should no longer be concerned with whether one's good works are good enough for God. All anxiety and uncertainty about salvation is transcended. It's God's gift of grace from the outset. Thus, one can concentrate completely on loving and serving one's neighbor, as a result. I'll talk much more about this in the next lecture, when we focus on Luther's theology explicitly.

These three treatises together—*Address to the Christian Nobility*, *The Babylonian Captivity of the Church,* and *Freedom of a Christian*—together comprised a hard-hitting, sharp-edged attack on Rome, the papacy, and on many of the late medieval Church's practices and ideals. They made it absolutely clear that Luther was not going to back down from the papal intimidation and the threat of excommunication.

In January 1521, long after the 60 days that he'd been given to recant his views were over, Luther was excommunicated by Pope Leo X. In April 1521, at the Diet of Worms, with the newly elected emperor, young Charles V, a staunch defender of Catholic orthodoxy, present, Luther was given one last chance to avoid a secular condemnation, meaning a condemnation by the emperor, as well as the excommunication by the Pope. Luther refused to recant, unless it could be shown on the basis of scripture that his arguments were wrong. Repeated open and "behind doors" discussions failed to make him give any ground on this position. He was condemned a month later as a heretic, by the emperor.

On April 26, Luther was abducted by men working for Luther's prince, Frederick of Saxony. They took him into protective custody, so that he couldn't be taken away by the papacy. This is what happened to John Hus, who was promised passage to the Council of Constance, and then was double-crossed. Luther was taken into protective custody in Frederick's castle at the Wartburg, overlooking the town of Eisenach, where Luther had attended Latin school all those years before. Rumors flew about that he'd been seized and secretly murdered. However, he remained in hiding for almost a year. Doing what? He continued his writing, and translated the New Testament into German himself. This was the origin of Luther's famous translation of the New Testament. He didn't have the Old Testament for several more years, a much longer body of texts. Thus, Luther was in protective hiding. He had scuttled away from the Diet of Worms in 1521, and while in protective custody, translated the New Testament into German.

The refusal of those self-governing, free imperial cities of southwestern Germany to enforce the Edict of Worms and to suppress Luther's teachings—those sympathetic to him— inaugurated a new phase of the Reformation, one that we'll take up beginning in Lecture Ten. I want to close the lecture today by mentioning four factors that were crucial to Luther's success in those early years between 1517, when he first emerged as a public figure through the indulgences controversy and the *Ninety-Five Theses*, and his condemnation after the papal bull, "*Exsurge domine*," and at the Diet of Worms.

The first factor, probably unquestionably the most important of all, was the political protection of his prince, Frederick of Saxony. He was a powerful German territorial prince. This protection was absolutely crucial to Luther at this time. Why? Without it, if Frederick had been hostile to Luther, he could easily have handed Luther over. Luther would have been tried, condemned as a heretic, and almost certainly executed. This was the first crucial factor, political protection from his prince, Frederick of Saxony.

The second factor crucial to Luther's success was the popularity and the notoriety that he enjoyed because he was German. This is because there was already this existing German hostility toward Rome and the papacy, to some degree; they were seen as being greedy foreign powers, sucking Germany dry of its wealth. "Why do we have to give all of this stuff to these Italians, and those papists, south in Italy?" The third important factor I've mentioned was that Luther enjoyed esteem in humanist circles, right from the start, because of his emphasis on scripture, and on scholastic theology. "Those things sound just like Erasmus." In fact, in the early years, there was a widespread perception that Luther and Erasmus were part of one and the same reforming movement. We'll see shortly that that wasn't the case.

Finally, the fourth crucial factor was the rapid and widespread diffusion of Luther's writings through printing. At a time when print runs for a given work averaged between 1000 and 1200 copies, Luther's *Address to the Christian Nobility* sold out 4000 copies, and required a second edition in only a few days. It was an extraordinarily popular work. Further editions followed in Leipzig, Basel, Strasbourg, and other cities. Just as an example, another work by Luther, his *Sermon on the Meditation on Christ's Passion*, which is another late medieval theme that we've talked about, went through 24 editions between 1519 and 1524. I could go on and on with statistics that support the popularity of his work. Luther was the most published author of the early sixteenth century in Germany.

Step by step, not all at once, or with a clear idea or program for reform in mind, starting with his own life as a monk, his own immersion in scripture, anxiety about his own sinfulness in the monastery, and through his experience as a confessor, Luther eventually gained public notoriety by challenging abuses regarding indulgences, not by trying to eliminate the practice from the start. His interactions with theological opponents, most importantly Johannes Eck, pushed him further, and led to his repudiation of papal and conciliar infallibility. Finally, he took the logical institutional step, and defied both Pope Leo X and Emperor Charles V, in 1520 and 1521.

That's an overview of Luther as a public figure, of the emergence of his fame, as it were, between 1517 and 1521. I've left out a good deal of the substance. What was the big deal, after all? So what? A monk and university professor has different views on the way Christians are saved. What did Luther's theology say, and how did it threaten traditional medieval Christianity? We'll take up this subject in our next lecture.

Lecture Eight
The Theology of Martin Luther

Scope:

Three core ideas of Luther's theology include his "Reformation discovery" of justification by faith alone, his insistence on scripture as the sole normative authority for Christian doctrine and life, and his idea of the "priesthood of all believers." Common popular misconceptions about his theology and intentions include the idea that he championed a subjective "right" of individuals to interpret the Bible as they pleased, that he was primarily motivated by the desire to correct abuses and corruptions in the Church, and that he sought to establish his own church. Luther's theology was deeply subversive of numerous late medieval Christian beliefs, practices, and institutions. The gulf between Erasmus's and Luther's views of Christianity and reform came to a head in 1524–1525 in their debate over the place of free will in Christian life.

Outline

I. Luther's forceful expression and apocalyptic expectations are constant features of his theology.

   A. Luther's gritty, and sometimes vulgar language is more than merely an expression of his personality. It is an attempt to move people.

   B. Like many of his contemporaries, Luther thought he was living in the Last Days, which lent urgency to his theology.

   C. Luther was not a systematic, academic theologian, but rather primarily a preacher, biblical interpreter, and pastor who expressed his theology in a wide variety of genres: sermons, treatises written for specific occasions, biblical commentaries, letters, hymns, and in conversation.

II. At the heart of Luther's theology are the notions of justification by faith alone, the Bible as the sole and final authority for Christian doctrine and life, and the "priesthood of all believers." His theology emerged gradually between about 1513 and 1519.

   A. Luther's "Reformation discovery" was a new idea about, and experience of, the way in which Christians are saved: not by contributing in any way to their own salvation but by faith alone in Jesus Christ as savior.

    1. Before his breakthrough, spiritually anxious and convinced that absolute sinfulness was the universal human condition, Luther thought that a just God could not but condemn everyone to damnation.

    2. By seizing on Paul's dictum that "The just will live by faith," Luther understood that salvation is something passively received. Only by trusting in Christ's redemptive sacrifice are sinners justified in God's sight.

B. According to Luther, scripture alone possesses an authority independent of, and higher than, the authority of both popes and church councils, neither of which is infallible in interpreting scripture.

C. Luther's "priesthood of all believers" is directed against the idea that the clergy is intrinsically holier or closer to God than the laity.

    1. All legitimate callings in the world are equally good and holy insofar as they are pursued out of obedience to God.

    2. The primary purpose of the clergy is not to mediate grace through the sacraments but simply to proclaim God's word and to teach.

D. Luther distinguished sharply between the domains of faith and secular authority. His social and political views remained profoundly conservative.

III. Three popular misconceptions of Luther's theology and purpose include the idea that he supported a subjective "right" of individuals to interpret the Bible as they desired, that he sought primarily to correct abuses in the Church, and that he sought to establish his own church.

A. Far from offering an "alternative" Christianity or proclaiming the right of each individual to understand the Bible as he or she wished, Luther thought he had properly understood the one and only Christianity that existed, rescuing it from medieval distortions.

B. According to Luther, abuses and corruptions in the Church were symptoms of deeper, doctrinal errors. Even at its best, medieval Catholicism was inherently perverted insofar as it taught that human beings contribute to their own salvation.

C. Luther did not seek to establish his own church but rather to call the one and only Catholic Church back to what he regarded as true doctrine, worship, and practice.

IV. The implications of Luther's theology and his principle of *sola scriptura* were subversive of numerous late medieval Christian beliefs, practices, and institutions.

A. Luther rejected many important traditional Catholic beliefs.

1. With his principle of *sola scriptura*, Luther rejected the medieval view that scripture must be understood in the tradition of the Roman Church and its authority.

2. According to Luther, good works are important as an expression of Christian love, not as attempts to please God. Liberated by faith, Christians are free to love others.

3. Luther rejected the notion that the Mass was a reenactment of Christ's sacrifice, as well as the Catholic doctrine of transubstantiation.

B. Luther condemned many late medieval Catholic practices as illegitimate or harmful.

1. He repudiated four of the sacraments as being unbiblical, retaining only baptism, communion, and confession (all of which he reinterpreted).

2. He rejected any and all practices inconsistent with justification by faith alone, including prayers to saints, the purchase of indulgences, participation in pilgrimages, and bodily asceticism.

C. Luther's theology ran deeply counter to many traditional Catholic institutions.

1. Luther's reconception of the clergy robbed monasticism of its rationale and subverted clerical vows of celibacy.

2. Because he claimed that they fostered harmful particularisms and factions, Luther rejected confraternities.

V. Erasmus and Luther disagreed fundamentally on the nature of Christian faith, Christian life, and reform. Their differences came to a head in 1524–1525 in their debate over the role played by free will in Christian salvation.

A. Luther thought Erasmus grossly misconceived Christian life as a process of gradual moral reform based on education, as opposed to the liberating power of faith radically to transform the depraved sinner. Luther's view of human nature was much less optimistic than that of Erasmus.

B. In 1524, Erasmus wrote *On the Freedom of the Will*, which argued against Luther that human beings must play some role in responding freely to God's commandments. Luther responded in 1525 with *On the Bondage of the Will*, which ridiculed Erasmus and argued that salvation was entirely God's initiative.

Essential Reading:

Euan Cameron, *The European Reformation*, chs. 8–11.

Bernard M. G. Reardon, *Religious Thought in the Reformation*, 2nd ed., chs. 3–4.

Supplementary Reading:

Desiderius Erasmus and Martin Luther, *Discourse on Free Will.*

Martin Luther, *Martin Luther's Basic Theological Writings.*

Heiko A. Oberman, *Luther: Man between God and the Devil.*

Questions to Consider:

1. How might Luther's impact have been different if he had presented his theology in a milder, less combative manner?

2. What might have been especially appealing in Luther's message to ordinary lay Christians in Germany in the early sixteenth century?

Lecture Eight—Transcript
The Theology of Martin Luther

In the previous lecture, we traced the story of Martin Luther's early reforming career, from his emergence as a public figure in 1517, to his defiance of Pope Leo X and Emperor Charles V in 1520 and 1521. We ended the lecture by asking what all the fuss was about. What was it in Luther's message and manner that caused such a reaction? Hence, this is the subject matter for this lecture, entitled, "The Character, Content, and Implications of Luther's Theology."

I'll proceed in five main parts. First, I'll talk a little bit about the character and temperament of Luther and his theology. Second, I'll talk about three key ideas in that theology; "*sola fide*," "*sola scriptura*," and "the priesthood of all believers." Next, I'll mention three popular misconceptions of Luther's theology, and what it was all about. I'll talk a little about the subversiveness of his theology, vis-a-vis late medieval Catholicism, and finally, I'll talk about the famous conflict between Erasmus and Luther, and salvation.

The character and the temperament of Luther's theology. Many of Luther's contemporaries, including Erasmus, complained that he lacked "*modestia*," modesty, in his manner and in his writings. Luther was indeed an extremely passionate writer. He almost always expressed himself forcefully, in earthy, gutsy, sometimes obscene language, to get his point across. This was part of his personality, but more fundamentally, it was a part of his concern to move people, to appeal to their hearts as well as to their heads. Luther would say that the most sophisticated, nuanced theology was useless, unless it had an impact on ordinary men and women, unless it reached them and moved them, regardless of their social or educational backgrounds. This was a point that he shared in certain respects with the humanists, this desire to move people, persuade them, and to affect them. Luther, though, had a much better sense of appealing in the vernacular to ordinary folk, rather than in the detailed, educationally-based reforms of the humanists per se.

Luther's urgency and intensity throughout his theological writings were undergirded by a pronounced apocalyptic sense, apocalypticism being an expectation of the imminent end of the world, the idea that time is running out; running faster, as we mentioned in an earlier lecture. We should contrast this to Erasmus' vision. Remember, it was a patient, long-term reforming vision, one based on education that would gradually seep into society and have its effects. Luther's growing conviction between 1517 and 1521 about the extent to which the papacy had corrupted the Church exacerbated his sense that the Antichrist foretold in the book of Revelation had been unleashed, that Christ's second coming was just around the corner. His apocalypticism colors, and makes even more forceful and strident, the things that he says.

We should also note that Luther was not primarily an academic, systematic theologian, who wrote detailed theological treatises in the manner of medieval scholastic theologians. He wasn't a professor of theology at Wittenberg, but of sacred scripture, biblical interpretation. Luther is above all, and should be seen as, a preacher, a biblical interpreter, who expressed his theology in a wide variety of genres—in sermons and treatises written for a specific occasion and certain circumstances, biblical commentaries written to correspondents, hymns, and in casual conversations that were written down after the fact. One of the things that makes the scholarly interpretation of Luther so demanding and difficult is that he wrote so much. Writings in the modern critical edition fill 100 large volumes. If you're going to be a Luther scholar, you need to study and focus on Luther. It's hard to get a lot beyond it. It's one of the reasons Luther is not my sole focus. If he were, I couldn't be giving this course, so be glad for that.

Let's turn now to three crucial convictions at the heart of Luther's theology, namely, justification by faith alone, or "*sole fide*," the Bible as the sole authority for Christian doctrine and life, or "*sola scriptura*," and finally, the "priesthood of all believers." Most scholars would say that these ideas emerged gradually between 1513, when Luther was still an Augustinian monk, well before the indulgences controversy, and 1519, where, with the Leipzig Disputation, we could say that we've had the first full early manifestation of his theology.

What was the central truth of Christianity for Luther? It was an answer to his years of experience in the monastery, with his spiritual anxiety and inability to find consolation within the practice of penance, as satisfaction for sins. Luther's emphasis was a subtle one. It was a concern with human sin, in the singular. It wasn't a concern with individual transgressions against God's will or the Church's prescriptions, or shortcomings that contravened moral guidelines, but rather a pervasive, deeply-rooted sense of utter human inadequacy in God's sight, which nothing that human beings could offer could make up for. That anxiety, that ineradicable sense of human sinfulness, was only intensified by the way that he was immersed in scripture, the way he dwelt on particularly crucial passages from Paul's letter to the Romans.

Here's the first passage from Paul's Letter to the Romans that gave Luther particular difficulty: "The Gospel is the power of God for salvation to everyone who has faith, for in it, the justice of God is revealed through faith, for faith. As it is written, the just will live by faith." Luther's problem was this; how could one be saved by God's justice, when it's understood as God's judgment against sinful human beings? The only thing available for human beings who've failed to live up to the standards as set by Christ in the Sermon on the Mount is surely damnation. Nobody can meet that standard. No human being ever has, or ever will.

Luther's breakthrough came in the way that he understood that passage, and ones like it, in the Letter to the Romans. His understanding was, namely, that this justice or righteousness of God is not something active that human beings "do." It is something passive, something that human beings receive, not something that they earn, or contribute to, in any way. It's something that we receive or accept, in Luther's image, as empty-handed beggars. In short, the impossibility of fulfilling God's commandments was precisely intended to drive sinners to trust in Christ, and so to find salvation. He saw that God's law is there, not as something to be fulfilled, but to show people that they can't fulfill it. It forces sinners to turn to the Gospel, to acknowledge their need for a savior.

Thus, the catch phrase for Luther was "justification by faith alone," "*sola fide*," "by faith alone." We are made acceptable to God by trusting in Christ's redemptive sacrifice for our sins, offered as a free gift by God. This is what Luther understood by "grace." It's not by doing anything ourselves, but rather recognizing that we can't contribute to our own salvation. That's the beginning of the path to real faith. The greatest obstacle in this, of course, is the natural, egoistic assumption that we have to do something to get on God's good side. "If we can't measure up, then God won't accept us." Luther said that that was exactly the problem.

For Luther, this was not an abstract doctrine. It was an experience of liberation after years of anxiety. God's grace does not come in little parcels doled out bit by bit in the sacraments; it comes all at once. Salvation is no longer in doubt, no longer in question. It's guaranteed, because it's based on God's promise that whoever has faith in Christ will be saved.

As Luther's conviction about, and experience of, "justification by faith alone" emerged, he also came to believe that the Church councils, especially popes, had arrogated control of God's word and scripture to themselves, as we saw in a previous lecture. "Justification by faith alone" was there, in the Bible, but had been choked off, obscured, and mangled by centuries of self-serving ecclesiastical control. By the 1519 Leipzig Disputation with Eck, as we saw in the previous lecture, Luther had rejected that either popes or councils had a guarantee of interpreting the Bible infallibly. Thus, we arrive at Luther's second key principle, "scripture alone," or "*sola scriptura*," in Latin. As God's word, the Bible is the sole normative authority for Christian faith and life. Its authority is independent of both popes and Church councils, and neither a pope nor a Church council can make any rule that contravenes God's word in scripture. That's justification by faith alone, and scripture alone.

A third central claim of Luther's theology was his notion of the "priesthood of all believers." This principle is directed against the idea that the clergy are intrinsically holier, or closer to God, than the laity by virtue of their vows or their way of life. Over against this, Luther maintained that all legitimate callings of the world are equally good and holy, insofar as they're pursued out of obedience to God. A priest, monk, or nun is not better or holier than a butcher or baker, than a housewife or a hangman. If all Christians are, in some fundamental sense, priests, then, what becomes of the clergy's role? Remember that grace comes, now, all at once, through justification by faith alone. For Luther, their primary purpose was not to mediate God's grace through the sacraments, but to simply proclaim God's word, and to teach, to offer spiritual counsel and guidance to the men and women in their care.

Before we move on to consider several common misconceptions about Luther and his theology, it should be noted that his radical reinterpretation of the way in which Christians are saved by God, and of the independent authority of scripture over against tradition, did not have significant social or political implications. It was radical in terms of its understanding of justification. It was not radical in political or social terms.

Based especially, again, on Paul's Letter to the Romans, in this case the thirteenth chapter, Luther held to a very traditional view. I'm going to quote one verse, because it's crucial. Paul's Letter to the Romans, Chapter 13, Verse 1: "Let every person be subject to the governing authorities, for there is no authority except from God, and the authorities that have been instituted by God." The most straightforward reading of that verse regards established governments as inherently legitimate, regardless of their actions. That was Luther's view. There was no imperative in Luther, then, to integrate the domains of faith and politics. Luther saw this, indeed, as a huge part of the problem throughout the Middle Ages. Each had poisoned the other. He thought these were two "separate kingdoms," as he called them, that should remain distinct. As a result, Luther's social and political views remained deeply conservative and traditional. I mention this in part at this stage, because we're going to see reformers down the road for whom this was decidedly not the case.

All right, then. More than many major figures in European history, Luther has been subject to numerous misinterpretations and misreadings, oftentimes because subsequent historical developments are read into him. I want to mention three such common misconceptions here. The first one is that he advocated the subjective right of individuals to interpret the Bible as they wished. The second one is that he sought primarily to correct abuses in the Church. The third one is that he sought to establish his own church.

First of all, then, Luther was not concerned with proclaiming his view, understood as a subjective right to read the Bible however one liked. His persistence and refusal to change his views when pressured to do so came, rather, from his conviction that "the" truth of Christianity is at stake. He was convinced that he had disclosed "the" essence of Christianity, which had become increasingly obscured. He was not proclaiming an alternative Christianity; "that's theirs, this is mine." No, he was claiming that he had authentic insight into the one and only one that there is. Remember back to Lecture Three, when we had discussed that God had revealed himself. A corollary of that is that there cannot be competing Christian truths. God doesn't contradict himself.

The idea of Christian pluralism, in other words, is inherently self-contradictory. Luther believed that he was rescuing the one authentic Christianity from its medieval distortion. As a result, he heaped scorn on other reformers who rejected Rome, but disagreed with him. We'll see the first example of that at the end of today's lecture, and other examples in subsequent lectures. Luther is not proclaiming his own subjective interpretation of scripture.

Now to a second popular misconception; Luther did not reject papal authority and the Roman Church primarily because of its pervasive abuses and corruptions, greedy clergy, ignorant laity, power-hungry papacy, superstitious practices, and the like. As we've seen, humanists like John Colet and Erasmus also criticized such abuses. For Luther, though, these abuses were merely symptoms of a much more fundamental and problematic doctrinal error. Even at its best, Luther was saying, medieval Christianity, medieval Catholicism, was inherently perverted, insofar as it had taught that human beings contribute to their own salvation, and insofar as it had missed the boat on the core notion of justification by faith alone. All of the other corruptions flowed from that fundamental error, and had corrupted the totality of Christian life and practice. Remember that Luther had been an extremely scrupulous and conscientious Augustinian monk, not a lazy and indifferent one. He knew what it was to try and live the ideal of medieval Christianity. His was not a fundamental concern with abuses per se; he thought that those were merely symptomatic of deep doctrinal errors, above all, an infringement upon justification by faith alone.

Thus, there was no advocacy of individuals' rights to interpret scripture as they wish, and no mere concern with correcting abuses. The third popular misconception to correct is that Luther sought to establish his own church. He did not. Just as there couldn't be contradictory readings of God's truth in the Bible, just as there couldn't be contradictory doctrines in Christian truth, so could there not be more than one Christian Church. Luther did not seek to establish his own Protestant church. Rather, he sought to call the one and only Catholic Church back to what he considered to be true doctrine worship and practice. When Pope Leo X rejected, rather than accepted, his criticisms, Luther then drew the conclusion that the Church had been taken over by the Antichrist, and that Christ's second coming could not be far away.

We see, then, how Luther shared many of the same fundamental assumptions as traditional medieval Christianity; that God's truth was one, had been revealed, was a true picture of the world, and was necessary for salvation. He also thought that there was one Christian Church. Neither Luther, nor the Reformation era, marks a self-conscious move toward a subjective or relativist view of religious belief. I can hardly emphasize this point enough. Rather, it is the proliferation of competing claims to the one objective, absolutist Christian truth. This is a fundamental point. We'll see it made in many ways over the course of these lectures. Since I trust that you've been following those lectures with care, I'm sure that you can see how subversive Luther's basic theological claims were for much of late medieval Christianity. Nevertheless, let's run through a few of the challenges that his theology represented, beginning with late medieval beliefs, then passing to practices and institutions, mirroring the structures of Lectures Three and Four.

As for beliefs, Luther's view of "*sola scriptura*" juxtaposed the Bible to the Church's tradition, in a way that was virtually unheard of except among a few other medieval heretics, or those who'd been condemned as heretics. It had not been pressed to its logical conclusion to the extent that Luther pressed it: That scripture might be seen as an independent—as a basis for rejecting the authority of the ecclesiastical tradition—was unknown. Luther rejected, then, the implicit medieval view that scripture had to be interpreted within the Church and its authority, that it could not be used against tradition.

So too, Luther's doctrine of justification by faith alone dramatically reconfigures the relationship between faith and good works, as we saw. Luther didn't champion faith rather than good works, but rather reconceived their relationship to salvation. Because Christians no longer have to worry about their salvation, or about piling up enough meritorious actions to outweigh their sins, they are free to concentrate entirely on serving others in love. Hence, Luther called himself the "doctor of good works;" "no theologian has taught a doctrine of good works as well as I have." Freed by faith, Christians are bound to others in love. This undermined, though, the implicit medieval Catholic understanding of active faith. Remember, that involved contributing to one's salvation by cooperating with God's grace, by doing all of those good works. According to Luther, we contribute nothing to our salvation in that sense, and it is blasphemous to suggest otherwise. It's all in God's hands.

A final example of Luther's threat to Catholic beliefs was his rejection of the teaching that the Mass was a reenactment of Christ's sacrifice; he said that it could only have been once and for all. He repudiated the Catholic teaching of transubstantiation, although not because he rejected the real presence of Christ in consecrated bread and wine. Rather, he objected to the claim that the nature of this presence could be sanctified, in Aristotelian categories of essence and accident, appearances and substances, and so forth. The way in which God effected the miracle of becoming present in the bread and wine, in other words, could not be known to us. That it was the case, we should not and could not doubt. Indeed, since God gives his gift of salvation freely to all who receive it in faith, the very legitimacy of a priesthood that emphasizes the sacrifice-offering character, meaning a sacerdotal priesthood with an emphasis on the sacrifice in the Mass, is overturned as a notion. As noted earlier, the function of the clergy in the priesthood of all believers is simply to proclaim and to teach God's word.

Turning from traditional beliefs now to traditional practices, Luther rejected an enormous swath of them as being misleading or even dangerous. On the basis of his principle of "scripture alone," for example, he denied that there was a scriptural basis for the sacraments of matrimony, confirmation, extreme unction, and holy orders, although his Catholic adversaries did not, as we'll see. He retained baptism, communion, and penance, although the latter was somewhat ambiguous, as I mentioned in the last lecture. He also reinterpreted these according to his own theology, even the ones that he retained. Additionally, Luther rejected a whole host of practices, those that gave the impression that human beings could contribute to their salvation. Among these were things like prayers to the saints. "Wasn't Christ's sacrifice good enough?" he asked. It was completely efficacious for salvation. You don't need additional intercessors. He rejected indulgences, of course, and pilgrimages. Again, these are superfluous. You don't have to do these things in order to receive the gift of faith.

Finally, to examine a few central institutions, we've already seen that Luther rejected the authority of a papacy as the successor to Saint

Peter. Indeed, his reconception of the clergy robs monasticism of the whole idea that some people live inherently holier lives than others; it robs monasticism of the rationale for its existence. Clerical celibacy is not inherently holier or better than marriage; hence, clergy should be free to marry like anyone else. Luther himself did. He married a former nun, Katherine von Bora, in 1525. Luther also rejected confraternities, those extremely common lay mutual-aid organizations, because he thought that they fostered factions and particularisms. Christians should simply belong to, and be content to participate in, the life of the parish in which they find themselves. Confraternities are superfluous and distracting. This list could be extended; I could go on and on. It doesn't take much to see, though, that Luther's core teaching, the liberating experience of justification by faith alone, had implications that tore deeply at the fabric of late medieval Christianity. Since those beliefs, institutions, and practices were interwoven so tightly, tearing could only affect the whole, a point I tried to make in Lectures Three and Four.

To conclude this lecture, I'm going to say a few things about Luther's theology in comparison to Erasmus' vision for the reform of Christendom. I've already mentioned in the previous lecture that from late 1517, into 1518–19, many humanists and others thought that Luther and Erasmus were part of a single movement to reform the Church. Both urged theology that touched the heart and moved Christians to genuine piety, and both ridiculed scholastic theology and corruption in the Church. These similarities, however, can't disguise the profound differences between the two, on the nature of Christian faith, Christian life, and Christian reform. For Luther, Erasmus' view of Christian life as a gradual process of moral improvement based on education was a kind of cruel joke. It was worlds away from Luther's conviction that utterly depraved sinners could do nothing to help themselves in God's sight. They could not possibly fulfill his commandments.

Remember Erasmus? "Seldom, if ever, has a human being ever failed to achieve something it desired of itself." For Luther, that was pathetic. You cannot fulfill the commandment that says, "If you look at another woman with lust in your heart, you've committed a sin." Luther thought, "Who is this Erasmus? That's pathetic." Luther's view of human nature was much less optimistic than Erasmus'. Erasmus was strongly influenced by ancient classical notions of virtue; Luther thought Erasmus was just deluding himself. Erasmus thought Luther had run off the rails, in his zeal and passion. These differences became clearer in the early 1520s. They came to a head in the famous debate between Erasmus and Luther over the nature of free will in relationship to salvation.

In 1524, against his own inclinations and nature, Erasmus published *On the Freedom of the Will,* after considerable prompting and goading from others. I say "very much against his own inclinations" because Erasmus was not inclined to jump into the cut and thrust of theological controversy. He wanted to gradually reshape good Christians, not to get people arguing with one another. *On the Freedom of the Will* argued against Luther in a very moderate, carefully-crafted fashion, that human beings must, after all, play some role in responding freely to God's commandments. Why on Earth would God command things that were literally impossible to fulfill? This was Erasmus' core position.

Luther came back the following year with *On the Bondage of the Will.* It had exactly the opposite title, and exactly the opposite message. It was a fierce attack on Erasmus, and argued that any degree of human contribution to the process of salvation effectively robbed God of his omnipotence, and grossly underestimated human sinfulness besides. It took salvation out of God's hands, and effectively made it dependent on human beings. Luther said, in the end, "If we contribute to our own salvation, then we are effectively saving ourselves. What's the point of God, then?" That's the core of Luther's comeback to Erasmus. Luther and Erasmus would remain far apart on this issue, as on so many others. There would be no one-to-one correspondence between Christian humanism and the Reformation. Moreover, as we shall see, there would be no unanimity within the Reformation movement itself.

In this lecture, we've looked at some of the key ideas, some of the most important aspects, and the temperament of Luther's theology. We've considered some common misconceptions about that theology, and we've looked at the subversiveness of it vis-à-vis late medieval beliefs, practices, and institutions. Here, I've summarized, in a very brief form, the debate between Luther and Erasmus on free will. In the next lecture, I'll look at the other most important reformer of the early Protestant Reformation, namely, Huldrych Zwingli and the early Reformation in Zurich and Switzerland.

Lecture Nine

Huldrych Zwingli—
The Early Reformation in Switzerland

Scope:

Deeply influenced by Christian humanism and Swiss urban values, Huldrych Zwingli was the leader of the early Reformation in the Swiss city of Zurich during the 1520s. Hired as a preacher in 1519, Zwingli was instrumental in the elimination of Catholicism and implementation of a Reformed Protestant regime in Zurich between 1522 and 1525. Unlike Luther, Zwingli conceived civic government and the church as two aspects of one and the same Christian community and thought that scripture should be the foundation for its every aspect. The intersection of religious disagreements between Catholic and Protestant with the political independence of the Swiss cantons provoked tension and finally war, in which Zwingli himself was killed in 1531. Zwingli's longstanding dispute with Luther over the Lord's Supper, dramatically epitomized in the Marburg Colloquy of 1529, was the beginning of a divisive doctrinal difference between Lutheranism and Reformed Protestantism.

Outline

I.   After his early education, a strong influence of Christian humanism, and more than a decade as a priest elsewhere, Zwingli was hired as a priest in Zurich.

   A. Zwingli was born in 1484 in the small Swiss canton of St. Gall, part of the Swiss Confederation. His early education took place in the Swiss cities of Basel and Bern, then at the universities of Vienna and Basel.

      1. Zwingli was intimately familiar with the life and institutions of the towns in which he lived, which would be crucial to his reforming career in Zurich.

      2. Zwingli's outlook was shaped by the politically independent Swiss Confederation and its individual cantons.

   B. Much more so than Luther, Zwingli was deeply influenced by the emphasis on scripture and reform in Christian humanism.

1. After an initial acquaintance with humanism as a student, Zwingli immersed himself in Greek, scripture, and the Church Fathers after becoming a priest in 1506.
2. Zwingli met Erasmus in Basel in the mid-1510s and was close to him for several years.

C. Zwingli held several positions as a priest before coming to Zurich at the beginning of 1519, where he preached directly from scripture in a humanist vein.
1. From 1506–1516, Zwingli was a priest in Glarus, then went to the pilgrimage town of Einsiedeln from 1516–1518. Like Luther, he was intimately acquainted with Catholic belief and practice.
2. In 1519, Zwingli began preaching regularly in Zurich, garnering support and provoking resistance.
3. In 1521, Zwingli became a member of the Zurich city council.

II. Between 1522 and 1525, the Zurich city council and Zwingli's leadership combined to eliminate Catholicism and to introduce Protestant worship and institutions in the city.

A. In 1522, Zwingli preached against traditional Catholic practices, defended the actions of those who had eaten meat during Lent, and appealed to the Bishop of Constance in favor of clerical marriage.

B. In January 1523, at the First Zurich Disputation, the Zurich city council decided in Zwingli's favor that all disputed religious issues were to be decided on the basis of scripture.
1. Zwingli was content to have the city council, whose members he had influenced, make decisions and policies regarding religion.
2. The city council's decision implicitly repudiated Catholic claims of authority in religious matters.

C. In October 1523, at the Second Zurich Disputation, the Zurich city council concurred with Zwingli that the Mass should be abolished and images removed from churches in due course.
1. Zwingli deferred to the magistrates as to the timing of the changes.

2. Those critical of Zwingli's capitulation included future Anabaptists (see Lecture Twelve), who were not content to let the city council determine the pace of reform.

D. In 1525, the Zurich city council mandated infant baptism, established an evangelical communion service, created a marriage tribunal, and institutionalized biblical study (the "prophecy"), for the study of Greek, Hebrew, and Latin.

E. Throughout his reforming efforts, Zwingli wanted every aspect of life in Zurich to be guided by biblical teaching.
  1. According to Zwingli, civic government and the church were but two aspects of the same Christian community.
  2. The close cooperation of civil and ecclesiastical institutions striving to create a godly polity would be characteristic of the Reformed Protestant tradition (later exemplified in Calvinism).

III. In the later 1520s, some Swiss cities and cantons accepted Zwingli's reforms, but others remained Catholic, resulting in opposition and war.

A. The political autonomy of the Swiss cantons enabled them to accept or reject Zwingli's changes. The most important to accept them were Bern (1528) and Basel (1529), which together with Zurich, headed a Protestant alliance.

B. As early as 1524, five rural Swiss cantons rejected Zwingli's changes and defended the traditional faith, banding together in a Catholic alliance.

C. An economic blockade of the Catholic cantons by the Protestant cantons led to war in 1531. Zwingli himself was killed at the battle of Kappel on November 11, 1531.

D. Switzerland's early division into Protestant and Catholic states prefigured on a small scale the religious divisions of Europe in general in the Reformation era.

IV. Zwingli's theological differences with Luther, especially over the Lord's Supper, were highly influential in the subsequent history of Protestantism.

A. At the Marburg Colloquy in 1529, Luther and Zwingli sharply disagreed and refused to compromise their respective views of the Lord's Supper.

1. Zwingli taught that Christ's presence in the Eucharist was only spiritual, whereas Luther affirmed the real presence of Christ in the Eucharist.
2. The failure of Luther and Zwingli to agree on this doctrine prevented the formation of a political alliance between Zwinglian and Lutheran cities and territories.

B. The disagreement between Luther and Zwingli is the fountainhead of the distinction in Protestantism of the Lutheran and Reformed Protestant traditions.

Essential Reading:

Bruce Gordon, "Switzerland," in *The Early Reformation in Europe*, ed. Andrew Pettegree.

Bernard M. G. Reardon, *Religious Thought in the Reformation*, 2nd ed., ch. 5.

Mark Taplin, "Switzerland," in *The Reformation World*, ed. Andrew Pettegree.

Supplementary Reading:

G. R. Potter, *Zwingli.*

W. P. Stephens, *Zwingli: An Introduction to His Thought.*

Questions to Consider:

1. How does the urban and communal emphasis of Zwingli's thought differ from the thrust of Luther's thought?

2. In what ways did Switzerland's political configuration affect the course of the Reformation and resistance to it?

Lecture Nine—Transcript

Huldrych Zwingli—
The Early Reformation in Switzerland

In the last two lectures, we examined the early career and the theology of the most important early Protestant reformer, namely, Martin Luther, including the monastic matrix within which his religious experience and his thought took shape. We also looked at the course that his path from the Augustinian monastery to the Diet of Worms in 1521 assumed. In this lecture, we'll look at the other most influential early Protestant reformer of the 1520s, namely, Huldrych Zwingli, a native of the Swiss Confederation rather than a territory in central Germany. His theology was forged in a late medieval city, rather than in a monastery.

An important point to keep in mind here, particularly since we just finished two lectures on Luther, is that from its earliest years, the Reformation was not a unified movement, even among the magisterial Protestant reformers. The differences between Luther and Zwingli, in particular, are the origin, in retrospect, of the differences between the Lutheran and the reformed Protestant traditions. This will become much clearer, but I just want to set that up at this point.

This lecture has four main parts. First of all, I'll give an overview of Zwingli's life and education, up to his appointment as a preacher in the city of Zurich. Secondly, we'll look at the major changes with the introduction of the Reformation in Zurich between 1520 and 1525. Thirdly, we'll look at the wider setting of the Swiss Confederation, and the conflict between the "cantons," or territories, that adopted the Reformation and those that rejected it. Finally, we'll discuss the Marburg Colloquy, and Zwingli's dispute with Luther over the nature of the Eucharist.

In this lecture, note especially both the religious and the military conflicts between Protestant and Catholic cantons, as well as the theological disagreement between Luther and Zwingli. Both types of conflict, political and military, as well as theological, would be small-scale indicators of larger and more extreme, more destructive disagreements in Europe during the entire Reformation era. Switzerland in the 1520s, in other words, is a sort of prelude to, and a microcosm of, the Reformation in Europe as a whole.

Zwingli was born the son of a farmer in the mountainous small Swiss canton of St. Gall. It's part of the Swiss Confederation, the sworn association of small territories in south central Europe that was essentially the same as modern-day Switzerland, in terms of the territory that it covered. By 1499, the Swiss Confederation had essentially gained de facto independence from the control of the Holy Roman Emperor. Each of the cantons that made up the Confederation was itself independent of the others, and fiercely guarded its autonomy.

It's important to bear this political setting in mind, because Zwingli was intimately familiar with the life and institutions of the towns and regions in which he lived. It's crucial for understanding his reforming career in the city of Zurich, a town of about five or six thousand people. Again, these are those small communities in which the early Reformation unfolded. Certain aspects of his theology, for example, the relationship between ecclesiastical and political authority, were influenced by the nature of the communities in which he lived. Here, we should note a contrast with Luther. The most important matrix for his Reformation was not the city and its institutions, but rather, the monastery, his own anxiety, and his attempt to overcome it. Similarly, Zwingli's outlook was shaped by his sensitivity to the political independence of each of the cantons of the Swiss Confederation. They were a sworn association for purposes of military defense, for common concern in that regard. In all of the decision- making, however, they guarded their autonomy.

Part of the context for Zwingli's reforms was his Swiss patriotism, his concern for the Swiss Confederation, as a whole. For example, throughout his reforming career, Zwingli opposed the dissipation of Swiss strength, as he saw it, through the use of the famous Swiss mercenary soldiers in foreign military involvements. He didn't want the Swiss losing their strength because they were having their soldiers go off to die in foreign wars.

A bit about Zwingli's education. After his earliest education by his uncle, who was a priest, Zwingli learned Latin, first in the Swiss city of Basel, not far from where he grew up. Then he went on to study Latin literature, in the Swiss city of Berne. At the age of 14, in 1498, he went off to study at the University of Vienna, where he gained his first acquaintance with humanistic learning, as well as with traditional scholasticism. From Vienna, he went on in 1502 to the

University of Basel, in other words coming back to where his education had begun, earning his bachelor's degree in 1504, and his master's in 1506.

In that same year, 1506, Zwingli was ordained a priest, at the age of 22. He went to Glarus, where he served as a priest for a decade. This proved to be a pivotal period in his life. Besides the clerical duties as a preacher and pastor, he immersed himself in the study of Greek and the Greek and Latin classics. He corresponded during the decade with other important humanist scholars. There was a major impact on Zwingli of Erasmus. Zwingli called Erasmus "the greatest of all scholars." His meeting with him personally in Basel, in 1515 or early 1516, converted Zwingli to the program of Christian humanism.

He turned his humanist training, that intensive study of Greek, and the Greek and Latin classics, to the intensive study of scripture and the Church Fathers. There was nothing more indicative of this than the fact that as soon as Erasmus' edition of the New Testament was published, Zwingli bought a copy immediately. Indeed, Zwingli would remain personally close and in touch with Erasmus for several years, until the early 1520s. The differences between the two broke their friendship.

Much more so than Luther, Zwingli was deeply influenced with the thrust and the program of Christian humanism. It remained with him as an important influence throughout his later reforming career. Zwingli, indeed, we could say, was the prototypical case of how Erasmus' emphasis on scripture, reform, and the elimination of abuses in the Church could, and frequently did, lead especially younger humanist scholars to embrace some form of the Protestant Reformation. Another example would be Luther's right-hand man in Wittenberg, Philip Melanchthon.

In 1516, after being in Glarus for ten years, Zwingli went to the Swiss pilgrimage town of Einsiedeln, from 1516 until 1518. This was the site of a major Marian shrine, a shrine devoted to the Virgin Mary. This was again part of that late medieval Catholic sensibility that we've talked about in previous lectures. He continued, there, to carry out his clerical duties, and he gained a reputation for being an excellent preacher. He also, during these years, lived with a woman as his concubine, as quite a few late medieval priests did.

We shouldn't forget that, like Luther, Zwingli was intimately acquainted with Catholic belief and practice, through first-hand experience of having been a priest, and having carried out clerical duties. His eventual rejection of Roman authority, then, like Luther's, was that of an insider, someone who'd been a priest for more than a decade. In 1518, two years after going to the pilgrimage town of Einsiedeln, Zwingli's renown as a preacher brought him to the attention of a chapter of the Grossmuenster Church, the main church in the city of Zurich. Once Zwingli convinced the chapter that he had left off his concubine, the chapter hired him, in order to be the official church preacher.

He began preaching at the church in Zurich in January of 1519. He proceeded, though, from the outset in a very unconventional manner. Rather than following the liturgical prescriptions, and doing a sermon on each of the prescribed readings for the day, Zwingli said, "No, I'm going to do it differently. I'm going to start with the Gospel of Matthew, and I'm going to do a sermon on this bit, and this bit, and the next bit, working my way through different books of the New Testament." In other words, he proceeded with sermons in the way a humanist scholar might. This stirred up controversy. Nothing like this had ever been seen in the city before. It was the first of many controversies of which Zwingli would be at the center.

He was a powerful and persuasive preacher. Zwingli gained a significant following, and he grew popular in the first few years in Zurich. He moved from Erasmus' strong emphasis on scripture, to the view that all preaching and worship must be based exclusively on the Bible. This was a subtle but important difference, from an emphasis, to saying that the focus should be exclusively on the Bible. This mandate, that all preaching be based on scripture, is a mandate that is laid down by the city council of Zurich in 1520.

This is a crucial point. Zwingli's reforms in the 1520s, beginning here and going through the essential completion of them in 1525, are the story of a kind of symbiotic co-operation and negotiation between a preacher, theologian, and reformer on one hand, and the political authorities of the city on the other, the members of the city council that we talked about in Lecture Two. Zwingli himself got a seat on the city council, beginning in 1521. He was in daily common contact.

In 1522, Zwingli had carried his preaching through to the point of denouncing numerous traditional Catholic practices. In the same year, he also defended the actions of Zurich citizens who had eaten meat during Lent, the season of the liturgical year prior to Easter, when Catholics were supposed to fast. He also wrote to the Bishop of Constance in the same year, petitioning for clerical marriage, that priests be allowed to marry. This was after he himself had secretly married a widow. We see his concubinage past coming back in a different form here. He married a widow in Zurich, in secret, because of course, at this point, priests were still prohibited from marrying.

Tensions over religious belief, practice, and authority within the city were growing. This led the city council to call a public theological disputation in the city, in January of 1523. This was known as the First Zurich Disputation, a rather flashy title there. The central issue in the First Zurich Disputation was this: What was the basis for religious authority - was it scripture alone or, as understood by the Roman Church, was it the authority of the Roman Church itself, a question that was definitive for Christian faith in life. Far from being an abstruse, uninteresting event, over 600 people attended the First Zurich Disputation, and on Zwingli's insistence, the proceedings were not in Latin but in German, so that everyone could understand what was being said.

Zwingli came well-prepared. He came with a list of 67 specific articles that summarized the substance of what he'd been preaching in the city. The city council, in the end, decided in Zwingli's favor, against the representatives for the Bishop of Constance, who also attended. The council decided that Zwingli's preaching was scriptural, and that all disputed religious issues were to be decided on the basis of scripture. Note that this is the city council making this decision. This amounted to political authorities making decisions not only about religious policy, but indirectly about religious content as well. In effect, they claimed that Catholic claims to religious authority in the city are no longer going to be acknowledged. This was a political decision about religious content. We see here, then, a continuation of the intertwined relationship between Zwingli on the one hand, and the city council on the other, between a religious leader, and political authorities, which would carry through all the religious changes of the 1520's, as I mentioned.

If it was granted that the scripture should be the sole basis for Christian life, what was next? How should the reform have proceeded? What form should it have taken? How rapidly should it have taken place? These were the questions immediately raised after the conclusion of the First Zurich Disputation, and they came to a head after it. It led, surprisingly—yes, you guessed it—to the Second Zurich Disputation, It was held in October of 1523, nine months after the first.

In this instance, the Zurich city council concurred with Zwingli that the Mass should be abolished, and images removed from churches. Remember that we talked about all of that stained glass, all of those sculptures and paintings, that were so much a part of late medieval Christianity. They concurred with Zwingli, in other words, that these things should be removed, but in due course. Zwingli deferred to the magistrates as to the timing of the changes, sensitive as he was to the political hand that fed him. Magistrates were concerned, for their part, about preserving order, as they always were. They didn't want religious agitation, or movement for change, to get out of hand.

Zwingli's critics at the time of the Second Zurich Disputation included only traditional Catholics, who didn't want to see the Mass abolished, or the images that they might have endowed removed from the churches. There were also other critics, though, those who thought that the timing of the changes should not be left up to the local authorities. They were disgusted by Zwingli's capitulation to the council, of his letting a political body determine the pace of the reform. They wanted the reform to go forward, regardless of when the magistrates saw fit to remove the images. With the truth of God clear, why wait to enact it? Among the critics, at this point, of the Second Zurich Disputation are future Anabaptists. They were part of the radical Reformation, whom we'll discuss in Lecture Twelve.

In Zurich, though, the changes kept coming in the next few years. In 1525, for example, in response to disputes between Zwingli and what, by that time, are emerged Anabaptists regarding the nature of baptism and Christian life—as a result of those conflicts, infant baptism was mandated as a law by the city council. I'll say more about this in Lecture Twelve when we talk about the Anabaptists.

It was also in 1525 that the Mass was officially abolished, and an evangelical communion service was established in its place. It was worship understood in terms that were deliberately opposed to those of the traditional Mass. Other changes that occurred in 1525 included the establishment of a marriage tribunal, created under the control of a city government, rather than under the control of the Church. Again, this was in keeping with Zwingli's downgrading of marriage from a sacrament to no longer a sacrament. It went from being under church control to being under political authorities' control.

Finally, there was an institutional change in 1525. There was the creation of an institution known as "Die Prophezei," "the prophecy." It's kind of a strange name. It works better in German than in English. This was an institution established for the study of Greek, Hebrew, and Latin.

Despite a great deal of substantial agreement, and while on many points Zwingli and Luther saw eye-to-eye, nonetheless the "feel" of their respective thought, the theologies, was quite different. Zwingli, for example, was much more influenced by humanism, by neo-Platonic philosophy, than Luther was. Remember that Erasmian influence on Zwingli. Another important difference, perhaps the most fundamental except for the Eucharist, which we'll talk about momentarily, was the difference between the respective views on the relationship between the domains of faith and religion on the one hand, the Gospel, and the domain of secular authority on the other, the law. In contrast to Luther's sharp distinction between the two domains—remember that he called them the two kingdoms, to be kept separate and from poisoning one another—Zwingli wants every aspect of urban life to be guided by biblical teaching. In his view, the civic government and the Church are not fundamentally different domains, pertaining to the "outer" and the "inner" man, as Luther said. No, rather, Zwingli saw them as essentially two different aspects of one and the same Christian community.

It was here that Zwingli's urban background showed itself. Already in the fifteenth century, the leaders of those Swiss and southwest German cities viewed themselves as localized examples of Christendom as a whole. Both ecclesiastical and political aspects ideally cooperated for the sake of the common good. Similarly, Zwingli contended that all of the government's laws conformed to God's laws. He thought that the secular political order should be brought into line with scriptural mandates. This close cooperation between civic and ecclesiastical institutions, striving to create together a godly polity, would be characteristic of the Reformed

Protestant tradition as distinct from the Lutheran tradition. We'll see this again, that is, this sort of cooperation perspective, when we look at Calvin and Geneva in Lecture Seventeen.

We've started with Zwingli himself; we've expanded to the Reformation in Zurich, the fundamental changes of which were in place by 1525. Now we need to expand our circle, our context, further, and look at the wider setting of the early evangelical movement, and the early Reformation, in the context of the Swiss Confederation. The key point here is that while some of the Swiss cantons accepted Zwingli's reforms in the later 1520s, others deliberately rejected them and remained Catholic. This gave rise to opposition, and to war between alliances of cantons on each side.

Remember the political autonomy of each of the Swiss cantons in the Swiss Confederation. This enabled, provided the institutional framework for, each of them to decide either for or against Zwingli's reforms, once it became known, especially from the mid-1520s, what was going on over in Zurich. We'll see something similar to this, in terms of the political autonomy and decision-making, when we discuss the growth of the early Reformation in the towns and territories of the Holy Roman Empire.

The most important (because they were the most politically influential), Swiss cities with their cantons to accept the Zwinglian changes; were Berne, in 1528, and Basel, 1529. You'll also recall the two cities where Zwingli himself had in part been educated. Together with Zurich, these three stood at the head of the Swiss Protestant alliance. They were Berne, Basel, and Zurich. On the other hand, as early as 1524, even before Zurich's reforms had been enacted, five rural Swiss cantons decided that they'd seen enough. They rejected Zwingli's changes. They vowed to uphold and defend the traditional faith. They banded together and formed a Catholic alliance. Indeed, they sought to expel Zurich from the Swiss Confederation altogether, to have it eliminated because it hadn't remained true to traditional ways.

By the late 1520s, there are opposed Zwinglian and Catholic blocks of cantons. There were those who embraced the Reformation, and wanted the superstitious traditionalists to join them, and those who'd rejected the Reformation and wanted the destructive innovators to come back to their senses, or exclude them from the Swiss Confederation. The tensions between the two came to a head. The first time it happened, in 1529, that ended in a deadlocked treaty between the two sides. In 1531, an economic blockade of the Catholic cantons by the Protestant cantons leads to a Catholic attack on the canton of Zurich, however. This happened at the Battle of Kappel on November 11, 1531. When Zwingli himself was riding into battle to spur on the Protestant troops, he himself was killed.

As I mentioned at the outset of the lecture, the important thing to keep in mind here is the way in which Switzerland's early division into hostile Protestant and Catholic alliances prefigured on a small scale the religious divisions in Europe in general, in the Reformation era. It didn't take long for the religious differences of the Reformation to lead to armed conflict. We'll see a great deal more of this sort of thing before our course is over.

Passing to our last major subject for the day, for this lecture, we've seen Zwingli's disagreements with Catholics, we've mentioned his disagreements with those whose calls for reform were more radical than his own, at the Second Zurich Disputation, who did not want to wait for the timing that the magistrates established. Today's lecture concludes with a look at his most famous and influential disagreement with a fellow Protestant reformer, namely, Luther. That disagreement would prove to be the origin of the distinction between the Lutheran and the reformed Protestant traditions within magisterial Protestantism.

The dispute between Luther and Zwingli over the Lord's Supper, over the Eucharist, had been brewing for several years, at the time that they wrote major works against one another, in 1527 and 1528. The Lutheran prince Philip of Hesse desperately wanted the two sides to resolve their differences, so that a political alliance of Zwinglian and Lutheran towns and territories might be formed against Emperor Charles V. He'd condemned Luther, of course, in the Edict of Worms. Philip of Hesse calls for both Zwingli and Luther to head groups of theologians from both sides to meet at the Marburg Colloquy. This was a theological meeting in Germany, held in October of 1529.

After three days of discussion, Luther and Zwingli reached agreements on 14 of 15 disputed issues. Neither would compromise or alter their respective views on the nature of the Lord's Supper, however, regarding the way Jesus is present to Christians in the bread and wine. Luther remained close to the traditional Catholic position, although, as I mentioned in my previous lecture, he rejected the traditional Aristotelian categories in which the Catholic doctrine of transubstantiation was expressed. Although he denied that the Mass was a sacrifice offered to God, he maintained that the Eucharist, communion, Christ's body, was really present in the bread and wine, according to a straightforward reading of Christ's words in the Gospel, "This is my body." The fact that this couldn't be comprehended by human beings was neither here nor there for Luther. God had chosen to, and did in fact, share himself with Christians in this way, just as God had really become incarnate in a human being. That was incomprehensible as well.

Zwingli, by contrast, rejected the traditional doctrine. He was influenced by a neo-Platonic metaphysical view, in which spirit and matter are sharply opposed to one another; again, he was influenced by Erasmus. Christ's human and divine natures were more sharply distinguished from each other than they were for Luther. He's also influenced by humanist exegesis, biblical interpretation, that took Christ's words, "This is my body," to mean, "This signifies my body," not literally "is my body." Christ's presence in the bread of communion, then, was purely spiritual, not bodily. The purpose of the Eucharist was to proclaim oneself a follower of Christ, and to recall and memorialize his death, not literally to receive him again. Zwingli said that Christ was seated at the right hand of God the father; how on earth could he be present in the bread as well? His was a very different notion of the sacraments in general than we find in Luther, and certainly than we find in late medieval Christianity.

The dispute between Luther and Zwingli was bitter, especially on Luther's part. He refused to shake Zwingli's hand, or to acknowledge him as a brother in the faith, in Marburg. Indeed, he even said after the fact that he didn't consider Zwingli to be a Christian. After Zwingli's death, Luther said, "Ha! That's God's judgment against one who erred so egregiously in the matter of the Eucharist." Remember the last lecture? I talked about Luther's temperament, and his rejection of views other than his own. Why? He had understood the one Christian truth.

The failure of Luther and Zwingli to agree on this doctrine at the Marburg Colloquy prevented the formation of a political alliance between the Zwinglian and Lutheran cities and territories. If ever evidence or proof were needed that politics was influenced by theology in the sixteenth century, this was the ultimate example. Both sides had every reason to want a broader Protestant alliance, against the threats of Charles V. What happened? Two men couldn't agree on the proper interpretation of the Lord's Supper. As a result, no political military alliance was formed. I've mentioned several times, and you'll hear it from me again in these lectures, that religion is not separate from the rest of life in the sixteenth century.

We're talking here, then, too, about not only disagreements between Protestants and Catholics, of course. This is a disagreement within Protestantism itself. That is, within magisterial Protestantism itself, there are reformers who accept political support for their positions. As I mentioned, this distinction, this stand-off, of Lutherans mainly, is the fountainhead for the formation of distinct Lutheran and Reformed Protestant tradition.

In sum, then, we've traced Zwingli's career both before and during his Zurich years, we've seen the conflict between the Protestant and Catholic cantons in Switzerland, and noted the importance of Zwingli's and Luther's disagreement over the Lord's Supper. Having looked at the two most important leaders in the early Reformation in our last three lectures, Luther and now Zwingli, we now need to turn to the spread of the movement itself in the cities and towns of Germany. This is the subject for our next lecture.

Lecture Ten
Profile of a Protest Movement—
The Early Reformation in Germany

Scope:

In the early 1520s, the evangelical movement became a major social and political force in the towns and cities of southwest Germany. Outstripping the control of such individual reformers as Luther or Zwingli, this was an impatient, zealous urban protest movement directed against many traditional Catholic practices, with more critical than constructive components. It was transmitted and spread through a profusion of printed pamphlets, through satirical and instructional woodcut images, through preaching, and by informal word-of-mouth communication, as well as by forms of hybrid media. Socially and politically, the movement exhibited considerable local variety from town to town. It is still possible, however, to form a general picture of the process by which Reformation changes were introduced in urban settings, from humanists' initial enthusiasm for Luther, through popular agitation by "middling sorts" in the towns, to action by civic magistrates charged with preserving peace and order.

Outline

I. In the early1520s, the early evangelical movement spread throughout dozens of towns in central Europe, especially in southwest Germany.

   A. Drawing on apocalypticism and anticlericalism, the early Reformation was an impatient, even militant, protest movement with a strongly bipolar, "for or against," character.

   B. Most leaders of the movement were members of the clergy, often former mendicant friars, fed up with the Church's inertia regarding reform.

   C. Already from the early 1520s, the movement's leaders were unified neither in their beliefs nor prescriptions, but at this stage, their similarities were more important than their differences.

D. The movement's critical aspects included the voicing of anticlerical views, attacks on ecclesiastical practices and regulations, hostile actions against clergy, and iconoclasm.

E. The movement's constructive aspects were less important than its critical aspects. The former centered on calls to preach "the freedom of the Gospel" and "the pure word of God" to the "common man."

II. The early Reformation movement spread by a variety of means that mutually reinforced one another, including printed pamphlets, woodcut images, preaching, and word-of-mouth communication.

A. The early years of the Reformation in Germany saw Western history's first massive propaganda campaign in print.

    1. More than 3,100 pamphlets appeared from 1517–1522, with over 1,000 more in 1524 alone, most of them in German, covering a wide range of interrelated religious, social, and political issues.

    2. The pamphlets' direct appeal to the laity in religious matters was a sharp break with tradition.

    3. The nature of printing itself, combined with the political configuration of the territories and cities in the Holy Roman Empire, made effective censorship almost impossible.

    4. Although the majority of the population was illiterate, pamphlets were often read aloud to those who could not read for themselves.

B. A wide range of satirical and instructional woodcuts helped spread evangelical themes to an audience that was deeply familiar with religious imagery. To mix metaphors, these might be viewed as the "sound bites of the Reformation."

    1. The woodcut of "Christ and the Sheepfold" draws on John 10 to contrast traditional Catholics who seek to circumvent Christ and a humble peasant whom the Lord beckons to enter.

    2. The woodcut entitled "The Distinction between True and False Religion" is an elaborate, mirror-image contrast between evangelical truth and "the idolatrous teaching of the Antichrist."

      3. Satirical woodcuts could be extremely coarse, as in one depicting an early Catholic opponent of Luther, "Johann Cochlaeus, the holy apostle, prophet, murderer, and virgin, born from a papist bowel movement."

C. In a largely pre-literate society, the importance of both formal and informal means of oral/aural communication in spreading Reformation ideas can hardly be underestimated.

      1. Preaching by clergy sympathetic to the Reformation was crucial to the spread of the movement.

      2. Informal, word-of-mouth communication was central to the way in which news and ideas spread in early modern Europe.

D. Hybrid forms of communication also helped the spread of the early evangelical movement.

III. Only by attracting sufficient social and political support did the early evangelical movement become institutionally efficacious.

A. A typological distinction between a grassroots "Reformation from below" and a political "Reformation from above" does not do justice to the incremental and dialectical way in which German and Swiss towns typically accepted the Reformation.

B. Individuals' support for the Reformation cannot be deduced from social standing or political views, but the Reformation clearly appealed to many citizens from the "middling ranks" of the towns.

C. Generally speaking, towns received and implemented the Reformation as part of a four-stage process.

      1. First, circles of humanists in touch with one another often expressed enthusiasm for Luther as early as late 1517.

      2. Second, evangelical preachers began proclaiming "the Gospel" in the towns as they denounced Catholic practices, while pamphlets in favor of the new ideas circulated, neither of which were suppressed by civic magistrates.

      3. Third, significant numbers of the urban "middling sorts" agitated for changes in preaching and worship, threatening and sometimes causing serious social and political unrest in the city.

4. Finally, civic magistrates, faced with losing order, began the process of instituting changes that were being called for, in a dialectical process of negotiation with popular pressure.

Essential Reading:

Thomas A. Brady, Jr., "In Search of the Godly City: The Domestication of Religion in the German Urban Reformation," in *The German People and the Reformation*, ed. R. Po-chia Hsia.

Berndt Hamm, "The Urban Reformation in the Holy Roman Empire," in *Handbook of European History, 1400–1600*, ed. Thomas A. Brady, Jr., et al., vol. 2.

Supplementary Reading:

Thomas A. Brady, Jr., *Turning Swiss: Cities and Empire, 1450–1550.*

Euan Cameron, *The European Reformation*, ch. 15.

Bernd Moeller, *Imperial Cities and the Reformation*.

Robert W. Scribner, *For the Sake of Simple Folk: Popular Propaganda for the German Reformation*.

Questions to Consider:

1. How was the early Reformation able to spread so rapidly in the towns of Germany and Switzerland?

2. Besides matters of doctrinal conviction, what else would civic authorities have had to take into account in their stance toward the early Reformation?

Lecture Ten—Transcript

Profile of a Protest Movement—
The Early Reformation in Germany

In the last three lectures, we looked at the two most influential reformers of the early Reformation, namely, Martin Luther and Huldrych Zwingli. If significant numbers of people hadn't listened to them, and the other reformers, however, and they hadn't had some appeal, their ideas would have remained nothing more than footnotes in the history of theology.

That's not what happened. The early evangelical movement of the Reformation very quickly grew into a major phenomenon in the early 1520s, above all in the towns of southwest Germany and Switzerland. Today's lecture looks at three major aspects of this movement. First of all, simply, what was it? Secondly, how was it spread? Thirdly, who supported it, and how did their support sit with urban authorities?

The imperial "line in the sand," that had been drawn by Emperor Charles V at the Edict of Worms in May of 1521, made outlaws of those who supported Luther and his cause; these people were literally "outside the law." Yet, in the early 1520s, the early Reformation grew tremendously, affecting dozens of towns in Germany as well as Switzerland. The rapid, unexpected growth of the movement made plausible the view that God himself was indeed behind it, and that the apocalypse was just around the corner.

The early evangelical movement was basically an impatient, zealous, even militant urban protest movement, in the early years of the Reformation, in the early 1520s. It was directed against many traditional Catholic practices and institutions, with a hard edge fueled by apocalypticism, and the conviction that centuries of Christians had been misled by the very institutions that claimed to embody supreme religious authority. While claiming to show them the way to heaven, it had been endangering their chances for salvation. The early evangelical movement had a strong bipolar, "for or against" character. It was reinforced by many passages in the Bible, including the New Testament. Good versus evil, darkness and light, God and the devil. One was either for the Gospel, the word of God, over against the old ways, or one was against it. There's something in this, I think, of that 1960s slogan: "If you're not part of the solution, you're part of the problem."

The leaders of the early evangelical movement were mostly conscientious clergy, who were fed up with abuses and problems in the Church, frustrated by institutional inertia and failure to effect significant change. Many of them were former mendicants, especially Franciscans and members of Luther's own order, the Augustinians. On the whole, they tended to be better educated than the average clergy. Oftentimes, they had university degrees, and had been exposed to humanism. They, though, took humanist criticism further, against practices not simply regarded as superstitious or misguided, but now seen as diabolical, evil, sinful in themselves. As I've mentioned already in previous lectures, this wasn't a unitary party, simply repeating Luther's views. We saw that already in the case of Zwingli.

You'll recall that we left Luther translating the New Testament into German, while in protective custody at Wartburg Castle. As soon as he returned in the spring of 1522, he too faced challenges about the exact nature and implementation of the changes to be made. We'll see additional divergent groups in the next two lectures, as we begin to examine the early radical Reformation. I want to reiterate this point again, because it is so fundamental.

At this stage, though, in the early 1520s, reformers' similarities were more important than their differences. It was only when they began the positive project of defining Protestant doctrines and building Protestant institutions, which happens, for the most part, in the later 1520s, that their differences would emerge more sharply, and would come to define different groups within Protestantism. We saw this yesterday in the previous lecture, when I talked about the distinction of Luther and Zwingli over the Eucharist. They were trying to define positively what the content and proper understanding of the Eucharist was, and there they began to run into difficulties.

In the early 1520s, the similarities among the various groups who were acting against traditional practices and beliefs were more important than those differences. There were both critical and constructive aspects to this early evangelical movement. As I just mentioned, the critical were more important than the constructive, but we'll take both in their turn. The critical aspects were critical ideas and critical action. Perhaps the most fundamental critical idea was a prominent anticlericalism, something we saw already in talking about challenges and discontentment within the late medieval Church. Appeals were made directly during the evangelical movement to the laity, against the clergy; they were accused of being exploitative, and rapacious. Laity were warned about clerical fraud and deceit. For example, one early evangelical preacher, a former Francisca n named Johann Eberlin von Gunzburg, wrote a pamphlet entitled, "I Wonder Why There Is No Money in the Land." It was published in 1524. He sarcastically juxtaposed clerical wealth and extravagance to the deprivation of ordinary folk, asserting that clerical greed had led to lay impoverishment.

Because virtually every group had or could bring some grievance against the clergy, anti-clericalism was a common strand that helped bind together groups as diverse as peasants, artisans, nobles, civic magistrates, and former frustrated clergy, in the early years of the Reformation. It was an important ideological glue that helped hold the early protest movement together.

We also had, in the early evangelical movement, a critique of practices and regulations of the Church on the basis of scripture; criticized for being unjustified human inventions, burdening people with rules and regulations that had nothing to do with genuine Christian practice, and served only to enrich the Church. For example, a layman, the city secretary of Nuremberg, in Germany, Lazarus Spengler, published a pamphlet in 1522 called "The Main Doctrines by Which Christendom Has Been Deceived." There wasn't a lot of subtlety there. From the belief that one could contribute to one's own salvation, idea that one could contribute through good works, Spengler said, had come the deceit of pilgrimages, indulgences, endowing monasteries and Masses, decorating churches, fasting, etc. We see Luther's idea that it wasn't the abuses per se, but the underlying doctrine that was responsible for all the difficulty. There was a direct attack here, then, on many of the integral practices of late medieval Christianity, as we also saw when we discussed the implications of Luther's theology.

Frequently, many of the criticisms in the early evangelical movement went beyond the level of ideas to the level of action. Clergy were heckled and harassed, for example, in public, disrupting Mass, processions, or sermons not according to the Gospel. In Saint Ulrich's Church in Augsburg, a man exposed himself as a sign of contempt at the Catholic Mass being celebrated. I'm sure that didn't go over too well with those who remained loyal to the old ways. In some cities, especially those influenced by a Zwinglian view of religious images, there were the first manifestations of vandalism against sacred objects. This is "iconoclasm," the destruction of statues, images, and churches, shrines, stained glass, both from a sense of having been duped: "We were pouring our money into this for all of these generations and it was a waste," and from a belief that the use of such images as part of worship was idolatrous, was a direct violation of the Second Commandment. "You shall not make for yourself an idol." This was understood, very straightforwardly, to apply to a whole host of manifestations of the material culture of late medieval Catholicism.

Iconoclasm could, and often did, take the form of a kind of ritualized, deliberate mocking of Catholic practices. For example, mock trials of statues were conducted, in which a religious wooden statue would be made to answer for itself. They would say, "Saint John, what do you have to say for yourself?" Saint John would reply, of course, or was reluctant to reply, and they would shout, "Off with his head!" They would take an ax, and chop the head of the statue off. They would also do things like urinate or defecate into a baptismal font, using letters of papal indulgence as toilet paper. There was not a lot of subtlety here. There was an extraordinary amount of anger being expressed. So much for the critical ideas and actions in the early evangelical movement.

What about the constructive components? As I mentioned, these were less important than the negative, critical aspects in the early years, when the protest movement essentially had a critical character. Slogans like "The freedom of the Gospel, and the pure word of God prevail," were common, often without any specific content about exactly what they meant. Modern Americans should be very sensitized to this sort of thing. We've heard politician after politician refer to the "American people" this, and "American people" that. Of course, we're all American people, so we can all fit ourselves in. It was the same kind of thing here. Who would be against the pure word of God? Not me, of course. That's the kind of generic appeal that was being made in the early years.

In a sense, then, the early evangelical movement, we could say, was somewhat paradoxical. It's more anti-Catholic than it is pro-

Protestant. There was a kind of flattering appeal being made to the laity, the "common man," as it was so often put, to read the Bible and make decisions for themselves, against the oppressive clergy, who had kept the truth from them for centuries. At the same time, though, there was a widespread dispersion of Luther's basic ideas about justification by faith. For example, Joachim Vadian, in a work from 1521 entitled "On the Old and New God, Faith, and Doctrine," echoed Erasmus' view, in the preface his 1516 edition of the New Testament, about the importance of ordinary people reading scripture. They argued that the more one read scripture, the more one understood God. This in turn increases one's faith, and moves one more to love of neighbor. There was an optimism, then, that reading scripture per se would lead not only to religious renewal, but to consensus about that renewal. As we'll see, that optimism was mistaken.

How did a movement like this become popular? How did it become a widespread phenomenon? By what means was it spread? There were three major avenues involved, all of which were important and reinforced one another. I want to first talk about the printed word and published pamphlets; secondly, about visual images in woodcuts; and finally, about the spoken word, including both preaching and word-of-mouth communication.

First of all, then, printed pamphlets. The early Reformation in Germany constitutes the first massive propaganda campaign in print in Western history. The printing press had been invented in the middle of the fifteenth century. It's not until now that the new medium of print shows what it's capable of. The exact publication numbers are not available. Pamphlets have been long destroyed, but one scholar has noted that 5 years prior to 1517, prior to Luther becoming a public figure, some 527 different pamphlets and treatises were published in Germanic lands. In the five years after 1517, the number was over 3000, six times as much. Why? In large measure, because of the early evangelical movement. In addition to those 3000, more than 1000 titles appear in 1524. There were pamphlets dealing with religious and religio-social concerns. They ranged from two all the way up to 80 and more pages. Many of them were reprinted, as Luther's publications were. Some were published in Latin, but the large majority was published in German. Usually they were addressed to that wide, generic figure, the "common man."

Like the American middle class, right? Nobody doesn't belong to the middle class. Nobody is not part of the common man.

An enormous quantity of pamphlets attacked the clergy. They criticized traditional beliefs and practices. They complained about social and economic injustices. They set forth evangelical ideas. This is the first major widespread impact of the printing press. The very notion of addressing theological concerns to ordinary Christians is an astounding break with tradition. Ordinary men, and laymen, were being asked to make up their own minds, to discuss theological issues. It wasn't just for theologians anymore. "You read this too, and decide." Of course, those who were writing the pamphlets thought that the readers would of course have agreed with the viewpoints put forth in them.

Where was censorship in all of this? It was extremely difficult to enforce, in large measure because of that patchwork nature of the cities and territories of the Holy Roman Empire. There were hundreds of different towns and territories. Many pamphlets were printed anonymously; without the name of the printer or the place of publication, it was very difficult to track down who produced them or where they came from. Printing presses themselves were fairly compact pieces of equipment. They could be moved quite easily. The product—the pamphlets—was often very small. They were eminently concealable, and easily transportable. It was all the more important in this era because books were not sold with covers to begin with. You bought the unbound pamphlet or book, and then went to a bookbinder who sold you a cover, if you wished. If you had a small pamphlet, however, and someone came along, you slipped it under your arm and no one knew the difference.

Literacy rates, though, of course, were very low. I made a big point about this in a previous lecture. Maybe five percent in the countryside, or 10 to 30 percent in towns, could read. How were non-literate members of the society reached? In the first instance, the printed word could be read aloud to those who couldn't read themselves. It only took one literate person in a village to spread the news to everyone who cared to listen. Many printed sources mentioned this as well. Pamphlets had words like "The one who reads or hears this" in the first paragraph. This was a sure indication that they were meant to be listened to.

There was more involved, though, than the simple practice of reading aloud, when it came to reaching a wider swath of the population. A second important media through which the Reformation's message was spread, a communication genre of its own, were the single-leaf broadsheets depicting evangelical ideas in a condensed form, satirizing traditional practices, usually with some accompanying text to reinforce the meaning of the image. Many of these contrasted the good, new, pure evangelical with the bad, old, corrupt traditional. They used symbols and images that would be readily understood by people as a part of their visual language, the kinds of symbols and images that they were accustomed to seeing. Recall that late medieval Christianity was an extremely visual religious culture.

I'd like to look briefly at three examples of these woodcuts. First of all, there is Christ and the sheepfold. This was a common theme that existed in several different versions, based on verses taken directly from the Gospel of John, where Jesus says, "I tell you most solemnly, anyone who does not enter the sheepfold through the gate, but gets in some other way, is a thief and a brigand." In the image itself, Catholic monks and nuns are doing exactly that. They're trying to circumvent Christ by not going in through the gate, and are climbing up on the roof, trying to get in by some other way. Meanwhile, Christ, who guards the sheepfold, summons a humble peasant in, located right next to him. In the text below the image, we have Christ, an angel, and the godless crowd, stating their positions. The angel asks the blind, godless crowd why they trust in human doctrines, laws, and their own good works. The angel tells them to search the scriptures and see that only through Christ are they justified. This is a condensed form of Luther's central doctrine. For its part, the crowd tries to defend itself against the angel, affirming the value, vainly, to be sure, of their actions for salvation.

Consider a second image, a much more elaborate one, called "The Distinction Between True and False Religion." Again, subtlety is not the point. Communicating the core of the message is. Here we have a detailed contrast between evangelical truth, and the idolatrous teaching of the Antichrist, in a perfect mirror-image parallel. At the left, we see God the father, benevolent, looking on fondly, surrounded by the angels, who through Christ, the Lamb of God, streams down directly, to whom? Luther preaching from the pulpit. In the foreground, we see the devout early evangelicals, celebrating the two legitimate sacraments, as well as the sacrament of confession; here we have depicted baptism and the Lord's Supper. In the right-hand frame, however, is the punishing God of wrath, surrounded by fire and lightening. In the foreground we see papal indulgences being sold, a fat monk preaching to people clutching their rosaries, a processional in the background, and so forth. There is a sharp, direct contrast between the new, pure, and good, and the old, corrupt, and objectionable.

A final example; these woodcuts could be extremely vulgar. Here's one called "Johannes Cochlaeus: The holy apostle, prophet, murderer, and virgin, born from a papist's bowel movement." Cochlaeus was one of Luther's early Catholic opponents. In the image, the devil, or a demon, defecates into his mouth, filling him with so much crap that he has to defecate himself, which he does all over Luther's books. Other monks down below eagerly receive this, as the demons dance around them. In the lower left, respectable citizens look on in disgust at the image.

The point of these woodcut broadsheets, again, was not to discuss subtle points of theology. It was to get the essential message across. We might be helped if we think of these as the sound-bytes of the reformation. We both know that those 30-second bits, those five-second bits by politicians that make it to the news, are not about subtle points of political policy. Woodcuts were sold in marketplaces and posted in public. There was wide exposure to these woodcuts and images.

We talked about printed pamphlets, we talked about woodcut images; now I want to talk about what was probably the most important of the three forms, the spoken word. Most importantly here, of course, we're talking about preaching, but also about informal word-of-mouth transmission, which was the dominant means of communication in a mostly preliterate society. It's almost impossible to overestimate the importance of preaching in the early Reformation—not only preaching in churches, but also much of it informal and conducted outdoors, when it was disapproved of or suppressed in churches.

We have a congruence here, really, of the medium and the message, the word of God delivered in a verbal medium. It was explained, listened to, and internalized, and, almost always, with criticisms and contrasts over against traditional practices, as in the pamphlet. The

Reformation, in a nutshell, was oriented much more toward the verbal, in contrast to late medieval piety, which was oriented so much toward the visual. This basic distinction and emphasis will persist as a general difference between sixteenth-century Protestantism and Catholicism. It's a distinction we'll also meet in subsequent lectures.

Before we pass to consider the last aspect of this lecture, the reception of the Reformation, I want to just briefly note something about hybrid forms of communication. What do I mean? Sermons which were delivered orally, but afterward printed as pamphlets. Literate people reading aloud to those who couldn't read. Broadsheets that combined an image with an explanatory text. Songs whose text was written down and published. These three forms of communication did not remain separate from one another. They penetrated and helped to compensate for the low literacy levels, especially outside the towns.

Still, for the Reformation to have become a popular movement, it had not only to be spread by preachers, printers, and word-of-mouth, but those who heard the sermons, read the pamphlets, and saw the pictures, heard the message and had to embrace it. Who were those people? How was the message allowed to spread, in defiance of the Edict of Worms, in the first place? With questions like these, we address the social and political history of the early Reformation.

A couple of preliminary comments. Until recently, it was customary to draw a typological distinction between Reformation from "below," and Reformation from "above." That is, there was a difference between the introduction of evangelical ideas and institutions, the basis of popular support and pressure, to which magistrates acquiesced, or the introduction by magistrates, who then tried to get citizens to comply with their own measures. Although the process of the Reformation varied considerably from one city to another, generally speaking this is an overdrawn dichotomy. In most of the towns in Germany and Switzerland, where the Reformation was introduced, it took both a certain critical mass of popular support, and the influence of politically powerful individuals and groups, to introduce change. This was change, moreover, that didn't happen all at once. We know this already in the case of Zwingli's Zurich.

A second important preliminary comment is that in no cases that I know of can we deduce religious affiliation from social standing or occupation. In general, I think this holds as a principle for understanding the intersection between Christianity and social class in the sixteenth century. It's a major finding of much research in the past generation of scholarship, which in many cases has sought precisely to find a tight connection between social class and occupation and religious convictions. Rather, to various degrees, religious differences tended to divide social groups in the sixteenth century. For example, among some of the younger, humanistically-trained scholars and clergy, some opted for the Reformation movement, and others rejected it. Among the German minor nobility, some supported the evangelical movement, and others do not. Duke George of Saxony remained Catholic; Elector Frederick of Saxony supported Luther. One could always find individuals within groups of artisans, whether printers, goldsmiths, weavers, what have you, who did not support the main religious drift of the group.

However—an important however—note that there is no question that there were significant numbers of men, and to some extent, more difficult to determine, of women, from the middle strata of the citizens of the towns; artisans, apprentices, shopkeepers, petty officials, civil servants, who fit the elastic term "the common man," to whom so many of those pamphlets and sermons were addressed, and who wanted the Reformation enough to threaten the fragile peace of the city for it. The magistrates could not ignore them.

As always, there were all sorts of local variations and particularities from city to city in southern Germany and Switzerland in the towns, as they dealt with the early evangelical movement. Nevertheless, we're also able to discern a basic pattern in the way that the Reformation made inroads in the early 1520s. I'd like to close our lecture today by articulating four basic stages.

First of all, there was enthusiasm for Luther's ideas in humanistic circles, as early as the end of 1517 with the *Ninety-Five Theses*. A network, remember, of humanist elites in cities were in contact with one another through written correspondence. Remember, too, that humanism had become the dominant educational paradigm for civic patricians in these cities by the sixteenth century, a way to distinguish themselves by education and culture. There was some overlap between those interested in reformers' ideas, and those with influence in civic government and with a humanist background. Often, they also had had longstanding grievances against the clergy's tax and other privileges, those exemptions that the clergy enjoyed from citizens' duties in the cities.

A second stage began when anticlerical evangelical preachers, who were sympathetic to the new ideas, began proclaiming the Gospel in the towns, denouncing traditional teachings and practices. Pamphlets circulated doing the same. Civic authorities took at this point the minimalist step not to suppress them. This gave preachers and pamphleteers base they needed, and when it caused conflict with the Catholic clergy in the town, as it almost always did, the political authorities often delivered ambiguous preaching edicts that said something like, "All preaching must be according to the Gospel," but again without the content specified, deliberately. They gave the evangelical preachers, then, further space to operate; they thereby put the first pinch on the Catholic clergy. We saw this in the case of Zwingli in Zurich.

A third and decisive stage began when enough people from those middling sorts, as I just described, began to support the preachers and the pamphlet writers, and agitate for change. They were high enough in the social hierarchy to be politically significant, yet low enough to be normally excluded from meaningful political influence. They hassled Catholic clergy, interrupted services, listened to evangelical preachers in large numbers, and demanded changes in preaching and worship, sometimes even engaging in acts of iconoclasm. There was the threat, then, of a fundamental division within the social and political body of the city, between those who were hostile to, and those who were sympathetic to, traditional religion.

Fourth and finally, once again the magistrates were faced with losing control of order, the very basis of their reason for existing in the city in the first place. They acted more decisively. Sometimes they held a disputation between the Catholic and evangelical clergy. In that, the outcome was really already a foregone conclusion, because the dominants already held evangelical convictions. We saw this, too, with the Zurich Disputations. Sometimes they forced the clergy to either accept responsibilities of citizenship, or to leave the city. In general, though, it was an incremental process, step by step, that began to dismantle the old and attempt to establish the new. It was a complex back-and-forth dialectic among humanists, city council members, evangelical preachers, and middling city residents. They moved the process along; reformation from above and below intertwined with one another.

To sum up today's lecture, we've seen that the Reformation in the early 1520s was fundamentally an impatient, forceful, protest movement that criticized and attacked many traditional Catholic practices and institutions. Its message was spread through pamphlets, broadsheets, woodcuts, the spoken word, and hybrid forms of communication. It was established by a back-and-forth combination of popular support and official sanction in the towns of Germany and Switzerland, where it took hold. Try as authorities might, they could not contain it in all its forms. We'll see this in our next lecture, when we talk about the German Peasants' War.

Lecture Eleven
The Peasants' War of 1524–1525

Scope:

The rapid growth of the early evangelical movement fused with longstanding religious, political, and social grievances in the so-called Peasants' War of 1524–1525, the largest mass movement in European history before the French Revolution. In both rural villages and towns, appeals to "the Gospel" were widely understood to imply an end to feudal hierarchy and a call for fraternal equality, as the Reformation message was appropriated in ways sharply at odds with the social and political conservatism of Luther and Zwingli. The radical apocalyptic preacher Thomas Müntzer, from Thuringia in central Germany, was one of the most important leaders of the "Common Man," championing a violent overthrow of the oppressive alliance between secular and ecclesiastical authorities. The suppression of the revolts ended the Reformation as a genuinely mass social movement, stigmatizing anything that seemed like religious radicalism during the rest of the century. Consequently, wherever it was accepted after 1525, the Reformation was always introduced by political authorities in a controlled and domesticated manner.

Outline

I. The Peasants' War of 1524–1525 was a series of regional uprisings that combined longstanding views of village self-determination and late medieval grievances with the extension of a view of reform closer to Zwingli than to Luther.

    A. Central Europe had a long tradition of peasant grievances and revolts, stretching back to the mid-fifteenth century, as peasants resisted efforts of feudal lords to tighten control amidst population growth and economic recovery.

        1. These grievances and revolts centered on the redress of injustices and the preservation of traditional privileges.

        2. The series of *Bundschuh* rebellions between 1493 and 1513 shows that peasants combined grievances with action in the years just before the Reformation.

B. In a certain sense, the Peasants' War radicalized Zwingli's view of reform, contending that society as a whole should be restructured according to God's will to serve the common good.

    1. The Peasants' War went beyond traditional grievances and revolts, because "the Gospel" gave it a stronger, revolutionary imperative.

    2. The Peasants' War went beyond the early Reformation in urban settings, because it involved many more people, entailed greater unrest, extended the meaning of the "Common Man," and called for fundamental social and political restructuring.

II. On the basis of "the Gospel," the Communal Reformation and Peasants' War sought an end to injustices, the restoration of traditional privileges, and the abolition of traditional feudal and ecclesiastical hierarchies.

    A. Common folk from different regions articulated dozens of different complaints and demands in 1524–1525, but the most influential were the *Twelve Articles of the Upper Swabian Peasants* (February 1525).

        1. The *Twelve Articles* were widely distributed in southern and central Germany; more than twenty editions were published within two months.

        2. The *Twelve Articles* moved beyond traditional grievances; they called for an abolition of all feudal obligations and the dismantling of all Church property and organization.

    B. Had the Communal Reformation succeeded in its aims, it would have constituted a true revolution, a radical remaking of the social and political order of society, not merely the restitution of traditional privileges or the redress of grievances.

III. During the Peasants' War, Thomas Müntzer, a radical apocalyptic reformer, called for the violent overthrow of the established ecclesiastical and political order.

    A. Originally sympathetic to Luther, Müntzer broke with him from 1520 on, developing a socially and politically radical theology.

1. Müntzer contrasted the "inner word" of genuine faith produced directly by God through suffering with the "outer word" of false faith based on comfortable privilege and mere scripture study.
2. Müntzer sharply divided the world into the godly, who would usher in God's kingdom, and the godless, who upheld the corrupt social, political, and ecclesiastical order and would be exterminated.

B. Müntzer saw in the remarkable growth and increasing militancy of the Reformation movement after 1523 a sure sign that Christ's Second Coming was imminent.
1. Unlike Luther's passive apocalypticism, Müntzer's active apocalypticism urged peasants to use violent means to help usher in the triumph over the anti-Christian union of ecclesiastical and secular authorities.
2. In his "Sermon to the Princes" (July 1524), Müntzer urged the princes of Saxony to help usher in the new kingdom of righteousness, lest they be overwhelmed and destroyed.

C. In Thuringia, Müntzer urged thousands of underarmed peasants to violent insurrection at the battle of Frankenhausen, promising them that God would protect them.
1. More than 5,000 peasants were killed, with virtually no casualties on the side of the mercenary armies of the combined Catholic and evangelical forces.
2. Müntzer fled, was captured shortly thereafter, and was executed.

IV. The suppression of the "Common Man" in the Peasants' War had profound implications for the future the Protestant Reformation in central Europe.

A. The suppression of the "Common Man" ended the Reformation as a mass social movement with a major impetus "from below."

B. The goals and violent actions of the "Common Man" made any sort of religious radicalism deeply suspect in the eyes of political authorities for the remainder of the sixteenth century and beyond.

C. Political authorities' suspicion of unrest associated with religious change ensured that the implementation of the Reformation, wherever it took place, would occur in a controlled, domesticated manner.

Essential Reading:

Hans-Jürgen Goertz, "Thomas Müntzer," in *Profiles of Radical Reformers: Biographical Sketches from Thomas Müntzer to Paracelsus*, ed. Goertz.

James M. Stayer, *The German Peasants' War and Anabaptist Community of Goods*, chs. 1–2.

George H. Williams, *The Radical Reformation*, 3rd ed., ch. 4.

Supplementary Reading:

Peter Blickle, *The Revolution of 1525: The German Peasants' War from a New Perspective* and *Communal Reformation: The Quest for Salvation in Sixteenth-Century Germany*.

Abraham Friesen, *Thomas Muentzer, A Destroyer of the Godless: The Making of a Sixteenth-Century Religious Revolutionary*.

Questions to Consider:

1. What continuities and discontinuities can be seen between the ideas of Luther and Zwingli on the one hand and the aims and actions of the "Common Man" in the Peasants' War on the other?

2. Why would the failure of the "Common Man" in the Peasants' War have been such a watershed in the social and political history of the Reformation?

Lecture Eleven—Transcript
The Peasants' War of 1524–1525

Welcome to our first lecture dealing with the radical Reformation, with radical Protestantism. You'll recall our basic tripartite division in the first lecture I gave, among Catholicism, magisterial Protestantism, and radical Protestantism. In the previous lecture, we discussed how the early Reformation movement in the towns of Germany during the early 1520s spread; what it was, how it spread, and the process through which it gained momentum and was established in those cities that adopted it. This lecture discusses the most spectacular of ways in which the appeals to the Gospel burst the boundaries of the early magisterial Protestant reformers, such as Luther and Zwingli, and became a manifesto for the radical transformation of society as a whole, that is, in the Peasants' War of 1524 and 1525.

We'll discuss in this lecture, first of all, some of the background and influences on the Peasants' War. Secondly, we'll look at some of the goals of the "attempted revolution" of 1525, as one scholar has referred to it. After that, we'll pass on and consider the radical apocalypticism of an important leader during the Peasants' War, namely Thomas Müntzer. Finally, we'll deal with the suppression of the Peasants' War and some of its very significant consequences.

The German Peasants' War, or the attempted revolution in 1525, was, simply put, the most extensive mass movement in Western European history prior to the French Revolution. That, of course, came at the end of the eighteenth century, and there's no comparing the two in terms of how well each is known. The Peasants' War is much less well known, in part because it was crushed and it didn't achieve its goals. It did not produce significant changes in society as a whole, or in the basic political structure.

The Peasants' War was not a single, organized movement, but rather a series of at least five large-scale rebellions in central Europe, stretching from Alsace, in what is now eastern France, all the way to the east in Austria. Each of the various rebellions had its own local factors and chronology, with the revolt in Austria, for example, not being suppressed until 1526. To a large extent, the Peasants' War was an explosive combination of two things. First of all, it was the long-standing desires of late medieval communities for political self-determination, and grievances about the erosion of traditional privileges at the hands of noble and ecclesiastical landlords. Secondly, it was an extension and radicalization of the vision of reform, closer to Zwingli than to Luther. It was a vision of reform that sought to integrate, if possible, with social and political changes, rather than to separate those two into two distinct domains, as Luther had.

Let's talk about each of these two factors in a bit more detail. Recall that in Lecture Two, I mentioned that a century of relative prosperity for the peasantry, after the Black Death, had been followed by increased pressures on the peasantry of central Europe, beginning around the middle of the fifteenth century, around 1450 or so, after demographic growth picked up again. Landlords clamped down; they imposed new restrictions on peasants concerning taxation, marriage, and the use of common lands, forests, streams, and so forth. For their part, the peasants were within living memory of this better, more prosperous time of previous generations, and they responded to these measures with repeated grievances, demanding that these injustices be corrected, and that their traditional privileges be restored.

When push came to shove, the peasants rose up in rebellion. The Holy Roman Empire saw dozens of peasant rebellions, between the mid-fifteenth century and the Peasants' War of 1524–25. A series of peasant revolts in particular, between 1493 and 1513, took as its unifying symbol the peasant workboot, the "Bundschuh," which was depicted on peasant banners as they went into rebellion. What happened in 1524–25, then, when seen in the context of these earlier peasant rebellions, did not come out of nowhere. Rather, it capped a long tradition of less extensive complaints, of peasant unrest and revolt against the infringements on peasant privileges and customs, particularly with respect to the earlier "golden" century, relatively speaking, of late medieval peasantry.

The second major factor fed into the peasant revolt. Recall that whereas Luther conceived the domains of faith and political authority as two autonomous kingdoms kept separate, lest both become corrupted, Zwingli conceived the two, church and civic authority, as two aspects of one and the same community, to be integrated by and subjugated to the subscriptions of Christian faith. That's the basic distinction between Luther and Zwingli, regarding the relationship of religion to political authority.

The attempted revolution of 1525, the Peasants' War, represented, in a certain respect, the vast extension of a view that was more Zwinglian than Lutheran, about the relationship of Christian truth to the political order; meaning that the political and social aspects of the society should have been made to conform to the Gospel. They should have served the common good in the social and political domains. However, the peasants, and those who sympathized with them, sought to realize this not within the confines of a single city's walls, as was the case in Zwingli's Zurich, for example, but as part of remaking the entire social order. Their notion of the Gospel, as we'll see in a moment, was different than Zwingli's. The Peasants' War of 1524–25 went beyond earlier peasant grievances and revolts, because the appeals to the Gospel gave it a revolutionary imperative. They were not seeking any longer simply to return to traditional privileges, customs, and ways, as earlier, smaller-scale peasant revolts had done. On the basis of a particular approach to the Gospel, they sought to remake together what their society was.

Additionally, and from a slightly different perspective, the Peasants' War extended what we can call the "Communal Reformation." That is, it extended appeals to the "common man" that were so much a part of the popular pamphlets and preaching, the agitation for sweeping change. Here, however, it was embodied on a mass level. It was the early Reformation. The early evangelical movements spilled over town walls and into the countryside, penetrating those small villages and hamlets, where, as you'll recall, the vast majority of the population lived. It produced a mass movement calling for a Christian leveling of society as a whole, in accord with a social and political vision of the common good.

The Peasants' War was different than earlier uprisings, then, because by February of 1525, a widespread series of revolts began involving not only peasants—something of a misnomer, because of the name the German "Peasants' War;" in fact, it also involved those in urban areas that were sympathetic with the peasants, particularly those in the lower reaches of the urban hierarchy. By February of 1525, this series of revolts, where peasants linked arms with sympathetic urban dwellers, aired grievances, and demanded change, represented not merely a righting of injustices, but an entirely new organization of society. What differentiated this revolt from previous ones made it an attempted revolution. More precisely, it involved evangelical ideas, understood with a strong social and political valance. Authorities, and many reformers, would get a whole lot more of the "Common Man" than they bargained for.

What did these groups of peasants and urban sympathizers want in their Communal Reformation? What were their aims and objectives? Literally dozens of different lists of grievances and demands were articulated in 1524 and 1525, by different groups of commoners. Some were more local; others were more widespread. Some were more revolutionary than others as well. Certain of these lists remained very close to the traditional grievances that simply wanted to restore things to the way they were. Among the most important and influential of these grievance lists was *The Twelve Articles of the Upper Swabian Peasants*, published in 1525. It was printed in more than 20 editions within a two-month period. Literally tens of thousands of copies were made, an enormous number. We have hard evidence of how widely distributed these were in southern and central Germany.

This is a summary of *The Twelve Articles'* goals: "Thereafter, not only a righting of the injustices regarding the tithe"—the traditional ecclesiastical tax—"of traditional access to woods and streams for hunting and fishing,"—of what they considered to be arbitrary judicial measures against them—"but also of a new organization based on brotherly love, on fraternal Christian principles, as the fundamental understanding of the Gospel."

It would be a mistake here to separate their social and economic grievances on the one hand, from their religious concerns on the other. Listen to the third of the twelve articles: "Christ redeemed all of us with his precious blood, the shepherd as well as the man of highest station, without exception. Thus, it is provided by the scriptures that we are, and shall be, free." The practices and institutions were inconsistent with the Gospel as they understood it in this way, including serfdom, and all of those traditional feudal obligations that subjected the lower to the higher in the social order were to be abolished. Instead, a series of elected representatives would serve on communal governing committees, displacing both the traditional secular as well as ecclesiastical authorities.

All church organizational property was to be dismantled. Individual congregations would choose their own pastors, with a right to dismissal if they saw fit. This amounted to a radical assault on the entire principle of hierarchy in the social and political order. It was a profoundly subversive and unsettling ambition, given what was accepted in the wider society at the time. Had the goals of the peasants been realized, had they been put into practice, it would have constituted a radical remaking of the entire social, political, and ecclesiastical realms. It would not simply have been a return to the previous status quo of traditional privileges within the parameters of late medieval society. That's a quick summary of the goals of the peasants at their most radical. They denote a radical leveling of institutions, both political and social.

A number of leaders emerged during the Peasants' War at different times and in different regions, who helped with the coordination, the exhortation, and the articulation of such goals. Thuringia is in central Germany. In the Thuringia uprising, the most important and visible leader was a man named Thomas Müntzer. He was a radical apocalyptic preacher, and a severe critic of the evangelical reformers, including Luther especially; he thought that faith had no direct bearing on the righting of social and political injustices. Remember that Luther wanted to keep those spheres distinct.

Müntzer was originally sympathetic to Luther. After about 1520, however, he began to separate and distinguish himself from Luther more and more. He began to develop his own theology, one that was very different than Luther's. Müntzer distinguished fundamentally in regard to the "inner word" of genuine Christian faith. He held that it was produced directly by God in the heart of the believer, and reached only through tribulation and suffering. He distinguished the "inner word" from the "outer word." The "outer word" was of bogus faith, based only on the study of scripture from a position of comfortable privilege. Read in this, the comfort of Wittenberg.

God's omnipotent word could not be confined to the letter of the Bible. It was an active, transforming power that could remake the world, just as it had created it. Müntzer viewed Luther, no less than traditional Catholic priests, as self-indulgent lackeys, princes, and exponents of the outer word only, who grasped nothing of the essence of true Christian faith, and who tried to stand in the way of God's word, even as they claimed to proclaim it.

In addition to the distinction between the inner and outer word, Müntzer sharply divided the world into the godly, those who would soon usher in God's kingdom on earth, and the godless, who upheld the corrupt social, political, and ecclesiastical order, that suppressed

©2001 The Teaching Company.

and oppressed ordinary Christians. According to Müntzer, it was a duty of the godly to destroy the godless in order to realize the real kingdom of God, in anticipation of the imminent end of the world.

It sounds far-fetched, but in the remarkable popular growth and increasing militancy of the Reformation movement after 1523, Müntzer saw sure signs that Christ's second coming was imminent. Who could possibly have foreseen and predicted such events? How else could they have been accounted for within the framework of the time? We've seen that Luther, also, was a strongly apocalyptic thinker, but his apocalypticism differed from Müntzer's. It's here that we ought to distinguish between passive apocalypticism—in the case of Luther, for example, who waited for God to take action—and an active apocalypticism, in the case of Müntzer. His approach was one of initiating action, with a self-understanding of one's self as God's instrument, helping to bring on the apocalypse. This was a distinction between Müntzer and Luther; Müntzer's active, as opposed to Luther's passive, apocalypticism.

Accordingly, in his best-known work, *Sermon to the Princes*, delivered in July of 1524 and then published, Müntzer urged the princes of Saxony to help usher in God's new kingdom of righteousness, to overthrow the ungodly combination of oppressive political authorities and hypocritical ecclesiastical authorities. After the princes ignored his exhortations, Müntzer pressed ahead nonetheless. He became even more strident by the spring of 1525, as the peasant bands grew larger in central Germany. He assured them that they were God's instruments, and that their triumph was imminent.

The culmination, as well as the end, came at the battle of Frankenhausen, in May of 1525. Müntzer led something like 9000 peasants, armed mostly with farm tools, into battle against the cavalry and artillery units of two different German princes. He promised them that they could not be defeated, that God was on their side, and his aims could and would not be thwarted. The outcome? Some 5000 peasants were killed. The total death toll on the other side, of the princes, was in the single digits. It was a complete slaughter. Müntzer himself was captured, and was executed shortly thereafter.

Thomas Müntzer is almost seen, sometimes, as a kind of wild man, as semi-delusional. More charitably, though, we can see behind his words and actions the conviction that Christianity that does not effect concrete change for the oppressed is no Christianity at all. It's simply a prop for the status quo. It's easy to see why, traditionally, Müntzer has appealed to Marxist historians. They interpret him as having expressed a kind of Marxist consciousness behind his conviction, battling against social and political oppression in a theological idiom.

The battle of Frankenhausen was a microcosm of what happened to the Peasants' War in general. The overall rebellion was crushed by princes and lords, both evangelical and Catholic. They employed mercenary armies against woefully overmatched peasants. The peasants are hampered by lack of coordination. Among the different bands, I mentioned that there were five major areas. There were also subgroups in those. There was no effective overall coordination or unification, not to mention any specific agreement on exactly what they wanted. Did they want to restore things? Some were more radical than others, and so forth.

They were also hampered tremendously by their inability to keep fighting forces in the field. Peasants, of course, were tied closely to that agricultural cycle, and had to deal with their crops. When the crops needed attention, there were whole armies leaving the field in order to go tend to those agricultural duties. It was difficult to fight and to lead an effective rebellion on those terms. There was also the fact that they were woefully overmatched, when it came to the military power and what they were up against; that would have been determinative in any case.

What, then, were the consequences of the attempted revolution in 1525, and of the suppression of the Peasants' War? There were three principal results. All of them were important, and all three were related to one another. First of all, the suppression of the Peasants' War marked the end of the Reformation as truly a mass movement, a mass social movement, if one meant by this that there were large numbers of common people agitating for religious change from below. Indications of this included not just the suppression itself, but the publication statistics of the huge number of pamphlets, which I mentioned in our previous lecture, peaked. There were over 1000 titles in 1524. They dropped off precipitously after 1525.

The Peasants' War effectively stigmatized anything within the Reformation that smacked of social radicalism, for the remainder of the century. Many of the reformers were themselves horrified by the

Peasants' War. From their perspective, it was a perversion of the principles of genuine reform. This was mere rebelliousness, selfishness masquerading as religious sincerity. Remember Luther's social and political conservatism, his sharp separation between matters of faith and secular authority, and his deference to established political authority. Nowhere is this deferential conception of Luther more dramatically expressed than in a pamphlet he wrote in mid-1525. It was titled *Against the Murdering, Thieving Hordes of Peasants*. Again, there's not a lot of subtlety in that title.

Luther was sympathetic to the problems faced by ordinary Christians. He certainly saw himself as the spokesman and champion for the "common man." He urged princes and magistrates to help them ease the material conditions in which they lived. Open rebellion against political authorities crossed an absolutely fundamental line, for him. It was a direct contradiction to that specific verse, the passage in Paul's Letter to the Romans: "The powers that be are of God, are instituted by God." In this pamphlet written by Luther, *Against the Murdering, Thieving Hordes of Peasants*, he not only justified the suppression of the peasants, but adamantly insisted on cutting them down. He said to the princes, "This is your sacred duty in your roles as God's legitimate protectors of political stability and social order."

Luther, Zwingli, and other magisterial reformers, Protestants who upheld the political authority of the magistrates in principle, did not want their reforms associated with the rebelliousness of the peasants. We'll see in Lecture Fifteen that this is exactly what their Catholic opponents accused them of. Rather, they bent over backwards to distinguish their political deference and respect for authority from the subversiveness of those involved in the Peasants' War. In other words, the real Reformation was not about rebellion against political authority. It was about justification by faith alone. It was about being freed from ecclesiastical tyranny, not from the social order that God himself had established.

That was the first major result and consequence of the Peasants' War. It was the end of the Communal Reformation as truly a mass social movement. There was a corollary to this, from the side of secular authorities. The second consequence was that the magnitude and the threat of the Peasants' War had the effect of powerfully reinforcing secular authority's already strongly conservative sensibilities. It was conservative, in the sense of preserving things the way they were. Even more than in the early 1520s, authorities became extremely sensitive to any religious message that even suggested social unsettling, or even hinted at social leveling or disobedience. In subsequent decades, they pointed to the peasants' revolt as an example of what could happen if religious reform got out of hand. "Remember the war of 1525." That was exactly what people said, and then, "Oh, no. The Gospel, the Gospel." "If you look at what they were really doing, it's just like that now." It becomes a touchstone for the remainder of the sixteenth century. We'll see that in subsequent lectures.

The third important consequence of the suppression of the Peasants' War was correlative to that kind of hypersensitivity to religious radicalism and subversiveness. The Peasants' War assured that the implementation of the Reformation would proceed in a controlled, domesticated, carefully monitored way, whatever form it assumed. There would be no out-of-control popular agitation, nothing implemented against the wishes, and outside the boundaries, of what political authorities wanted and permitted. To this extent, there was much to be said for the idea that with the defeat of the peasants in 1525, the Reformation in central Europe was no longer a movement that threatened to unsettle or remake the basic hierarchical structure of society, or to unhinge the traditional exercise of political authority.

After 1525, it was the political authorities, then, who more than ever had the upper hand in the long-standing tensions between religious and political authorities. Far from upsetting the established order, then, the long-term influence of the suppression of the Peasants' War was to solidify that order all the more. It made authorities extraordinarily sensitive to anything that looked like political radicalism.

In summary, then, the Peasants' War was both the culmination of and the transformation of decades of peasant grievances, and lesser revolts in Germany. From the middle of the fifteenth through the "Bundschuh" rebellions of the end of the fifteenth and early sixteenth centuries, it culminated in the peasants' revolt itself. It also represented, as I argued, the vast extension, and transformation, again, to society as a whole of a sort of Zwinglian vision of reform, not in a narrow sense of repeating Zwingli's exact views, but in the sense of a view of the Gospel that tried to integrate social and political concerns with religious prescription.Unlike the earlier revolts, however, the Peasants' War at its most radical was genuinely revolutionary, because it marked a fundamental assault on social, political, and ecclesiastical hierarchy as such, energized by the appeal to the Gospel in the early evangelical movement.

The most famous leader of the Peasants' War, as we saw and talked about, was Thomas Müntzer, a radical apocalyptic thinker. He called for an extermination of the godless by the godly, on the basis of his distinction between the "inner word" and "outer word." He and the peasants, in the end, were entirely overmatched, and were the ones who were exterminated, however.

The suppression of the Peasants' War ended the Reformation as a communal mass movement from below, and its agitations for change that fundamentally threatened to remake the social and political order. It also sensitized political authorities to all hints of religious radicalism, throughout the rest of the sixteenth century, and ensured that the Reformation would only be implemented in a controlled manner, wherever it was conducted.

Nevertheless, failure of the transformation of society as a whole did not mean an end to the radical Reformation, nor did it stamp out certain aspirations of the peasants. There were other ways to reject political authority, and to attempt to be Christian. In our next lecture, we will talk about certain of those transformations, and ways in which the suppression of the Peasants' War gave rise to something else; the transformation and reapplication of certain of the peasants' aims, by the earliest Anabaptists, the subject for our following lecture.

Lecture Twelve
The Emergence of Early Anabaptism

Scope:

"Anabaptism" is an umbrella designation for the groups in the radical Reformation that rejected infant baptism in favor of adult commitment as the basis for becoming a Christian and forming a Christian community. Anabaptism first emerged out of disputes about the tithe, religious images, and baptism in Zurich between 1523 and 1525. In the area around Zurich and beyond, early Anabaptism overlapped with the unrest of the Peasants' War, and several Anabaptist leaders briefly introduced Anabaptism as the official religion of a few small towns. The suppression of the peasants influenced Anabaptists to become more self-consciously separatist, continuing some of the aims of the "Common Man" in a much more circumscribed form. The most important early Anabaptist groups were the Swiss Brethren, the South German/Austrian Anabaptists, and the Hutterites, all of whom were severely persecuted in the wake of the Peasants' War.

Outline

I. Anabaptism, the most important strand in the radical Reformation, was based on the view that only a self-conscious, informed commitment to Christ could be the foundation for becoming a Christian.

    A. Anabaptism (specifically the Swiss Brethren) first emerged in Zurich in 1523–1525 out of disputes between Conrad Grebel, Felix Mantz, and others with Zwingli concerning the tithe, images in churches, and finally, the nature of baptism and its relationship to faith.

        1. The earliest Anabaptists argued from the principle of justification by faith alone that infants should not be baptized, because they did not have faith. The Bible contains no explicit mandate for infant baptism.

        2. Grebel and others were disgusted by Zwingli's willingness to let the city council dictate the pace of reform.

        3. The Zurich city council, working together with Zwingli, declared that all infants should be baptized (January

1525), after which the first adult baptisms took place in defiance of the law.

B. The rejection of infant baptism repudiated the sacrament by which people were traditionally understood to become Christians and to be initiated into their local communities.

C. From the outset, Grebel's and Mantz's Anabaptism was radically pacifist and insisted on the direct, explicit following of Christ in discipleship.

    1. Anabaptist discipleship might be seen as one outgrowth of the emphasis on the imitation of Christ in late medieval Christianity.

    2. Early Anabaptist leaders in general were critical of Luther, Zwingli, and other reformers for emphasizing justification by faith alone at the expense of transforming the actual behavior of Christians.

II. Early Anabaptism overlapped chronologically and geographically with the unrest of the Peasants' War, in which some Anabaptists and future Anabaptists were involved.

A. Traditionally, scholars understood the violence of the Peasants' War and Anabaptist pacifism as entirely distinct from each other, but more recent scholarship has shown elements that they held in common.

    1. Grebel and Müntzer disagreed about armed resistance but shared a disdain for the traditional use of the ecclesiastical tithe.

    2. Many Anabaptists were sympathetic to the aims of the "Common Man" to drastically remake the social, political, and ecclesiastical order.

B. As Anabaptism spread during the early months of 1525, it overlapped with the peasant revolts around Zurich and beyond.

    1. In several communities, Anabaptist leaders, among them Balthasar Hubmaier, led short-lived attempts at "civic Anabaptism" and endorsed civic alliances with the peasants.

    2. Numerous people who later became Anabaptists were participants in the Peasants' War. Not all early Swiss Anabaptists held the pacifistic views of Grebel and Mantz.

III. The suppression of the "Common Man" in the Peasants' War influenced Anabaptism, leaving separatism as the only means to preserve certain of its goals in a restricted form.

   A. When the Peasants' War ended in defeat, Anabaptists concluded that if the world rejects truth, then truth must reject the world.

   B. If society as a whole could not be remade according to Christian principles of fraternal love, equality, and justice, then separatist communities of committed Christians could endeavor to do so on a small scale.

IV. The most important early Anabaptist groups were the Swiss Brethren, the South German/Austrian Anabaptists, and the Hutterites, all of whom were severely persecuted and imbued with a mentality of suffering and martyrdom in the years after the Peasants' War.

   A. Michael Sattler's seven *Schleitheim Articles* (February 1527) articulated the strongly separatist pacifism that would mold the Swiss Brethren in subsequent decades.

      1. The separatist rejection of the larger society alarmed political authorities, whether Catholic or Protestant, in the wake of the Peasants' War.

      2. The separatism of the Swiss Brethren persists today in North America among the Amish, who are historical descendants of the Swiss Brethren.

   B. The South German/Austrian Anabaptists were part of a short-lived movement indebted to the apocalyptic legacy of Thomas Müntzer and the Peasants' War.

      1. South German Anabaptist leaders, such as Hans Hut, dropped Müntzer's revolutionary violence but retained his apocalyptic expectations.

      2. After Hut's death in 1528, a relative lack of leadership, combined with severe persecution, largely undermined this branch of Anabaptism by the early 1530s.

   C. Jacob Hutter, an Austrian by birth and upbringing, established an important Anabaptist community in the early 1530s in Moravia, before his own execution in 1536.

      1. Most of the Hutterites were Austrian Anabaptists seeking refuge in Moravia from persecution under Ferdinand I.

2. The Hutterites, unlike the Swiss Brethren, practiced communal ownership of goods, based in part on the Acts of the Apostles.

Essential Reading:

C. Arnold Snyder, *Anabaptist History and Theology: An Introduction*, chs. 4–6, 8.

James M. Stayer, *The German Peasants' War and Anabaptist Community of Goods*, ch. 3.

George H. Williams, *The Radical Reformation*, chs. 6–8, 16.

Supplementary Reading:

Werner O. Packull, *Hutterite Beginnings: Communitarian Experiments during the Reformation*.

C. Arnold Snyder, *The Life and Thought of Michael Sattler*.

James M. Stayer, *Anabaptists and the Sword*.

Questions to Consider:

1. How do Anabaptist views about Christian life and reform differ from those of Luther, Zwingli, and Erasmus?

2. In what ways do the aims of the Communal Reformation and early Anabaptism prefigure modern concerns for social justice?

Lecture Twelve—Transcript
The Emergence of Early Anabaptism

Our last lecture explored the aspirations and the defeat of the Communal Reformation and the Peasants' War of 1524–25. This was our first look at radical Protestantism. Radical Protestants, you'll recall, in one way or another, rejected both Roman Catholicism and the various forms of magisterial Protestantism. This lecture, the twelfth in the course, introduces the most important cluster of groups within radical Protestantism, namely, the Anabaptists. Specifically, we'll meet three early German-speaking Anabaptist groups in this lecture. All of them first emerged in the 1520s. They were the Swiss Brethren, the South German and Austrian Anabaptists, and finally, the Hutterites, who are really an outgrowth of Austrian Anabaptism.

The lecture's concern is to show not only how Anabaptism emerged out of the early evangelical movement, and the disagreements with magisterial reformers, but also to explore the relationship to the Peasants' War of early Anabaptism, and the ways in which Anabaptism was affected by the suppression of the attempted revolution of 1524 and 1525.

The structure of the lecture is organized as follows. First of all, I'll tell you something about the theological core of early Anabaptism in Germanic areas. Secondly, I'll talk about the relationship of Anabaptists to the Peasants' War. After that, we'll explore the impact of the suppression of the Peasants' War of 1525 on Anabaptism, and then, finally, we'll conclude with an overview of the Swiss Brethren, the South German and Austrian Anabaptists, and the Hutterites.

To begin, then, it's important to understand that Anabaptism comes out of the same early 1520s protest movement sparked by Luther, and first played out in the towns of Germany and Switzerland. Indeed, Anabaptism first arose, as I alluded to in Lecture Nine, among Zwingli's own fellow reformers. Among the most important were Conrad Grebel and Felix Mantz, in the Swiss city of Zurich, between 1523 and 1525. The latter date, 1525, is the official beginning of Anabaptism proper, if we go by the date when the first adult baptisms were conducted. The earliest Swiss Anabaptists in Zurich, then, were colleagues of Zwingli's, who, like him, were convinced that scripture alone was the norm for all belief and practice.

From this conviction of *sola scriptura*, however, they drew different conclusions, beginning as early as 1523, when they thought that Zwingli was selling out to magistrates by not opposing the traditional use of the tithe, and by agreeing to the magistrates' timetable for the removal of images and the end to the Mass in churches. "Why," they asked, "should the imperatives of God's word make concessions to worldly city politicians?" The key disagreement that surfaced, however, between Conrad Grebel and Felix Mantz on the one hand, and Zwingli on the other, concerns the implications of the central evangelical doctrine of justification by faith alone. These were differences that cut right to the core of what it was to be a Christian.

If human beings were saved by faith alone, and precognizant infants did not have faith, what sense did infant baptism make? Shouldn't baptism instead be the sign of those who, having first made a faith commitment, only then went on to receive baptism? The Anabaptists started to interpret New Testament passages pertaining to the relationship between faith and baptism in a different way than magisterial reformers. For example, the Gospel of Mark, Chapter 16, Verse 16, refers to the "one who believes and is baptized; with that, one shall be saved." They took this as implying a sequential relationship between them. That is, one must first have faith, and only then should one be baptized. The New Testament, after all, shows Christ and his apostles preaching to and baptizing those adults who accept the good news of the Gospel, not organizing a campaign for infant baptism.

This was the view of Grebel, Mantz, and others in Zurich, over against Zwingli, beginning in 1524. They had the added trump that no explicit mandate for baptism could be found in scripture. Where did this leave Zwingli's and Luther's precious principle of scripture alone? Who really was being closer to the letter of the Bible? Zwingli was compelled to argue for infant baptism on the basis of analogy to the Jewish practice of circumcision; that is, a practice of initiation carried out on infants, in the Jewish community. There must be something parallel in the Christian community. For Zwingli, that was infant baptism; but again, no explicit mandate for infant baptism exists in scripture.

What was the big deal? Why did the issue matter so much? Infants, adults, whatever. Not quite. Recall first of all that baptism is understood as a prerequisite for the possibility of salvation because of Christ's directives in the New Testament, and reinforced by many centuries of tradition. More specifically, in a society where everyone was baptized as an infant, the sacrament also doubled as a rite of passage into the community. To refuse to have one's child baptized was repudiation of the community. It was taken as a defiant gesture against it, a deliberate snub to community authority. Remember, for Zwingli, membership in the Church and citizenship were two sides of the same coin. For him, you could not opt out of one, and still be a part of the other. *Col. 2:1~*

Hence, the Swiss Brethren, the earliest Anabaptists in the city of Zurich, held that there must first have been what they called an "inner baptism" in the mature believer that brought faith, as a result and sign of which he then sought the outer baptism of water, as sign of his commitment to follow Christ. Traditional infant baptism, whether it was practiced by Catholics or magisterial Protestants, was for them nothing more than the superstitious pouring of water on an unthinking being, like getting a rock wet. They described it in that banal a language. Hence, the necessity instead of baptizing adults. The term "Anabaptism" means "rebaptism." It's a term of opprobrium, of insult, used by the enemies of Anabaptists. For them, of course, this was not a rebaptism at all. It was a first baptism that took the place of what never really was a baptism to begin with at all, the infant baptism, wrongly believed in by Protestants and Catholics. The first adult baptisms, then, took place in the city of Zurich, in January of 1525, in defiance of the city's new law that declared that all infants must be baptized. I referred to that in passing, in Lecture Nine, when we were talking about Zwingli and the Reformation in Zurich.

Another central characteristic of the Grebel and Mantz circle was their radical non-resistance, their pacifism, which they also argued was mandated directly in the New Testament. The basis of a passage, for example, is Matthew, Chapter 5, Verse 39: "If anyone strikes you on the right cheek, offer him the other as well."

They took this to be a straightforward, if admittedly very difficult and demanding, requirement for being a Christian, period. It was part of Christian discipleship, following Christ correctly.

In a certain perspective, this Anabaptist notion of discipleship, of following Christ literally and directly, should be set in the late medieval perspective of the deliberate imitation of Christ, by the voluntarily devout. Early Anabaptist leaders were, essentially, doing away with any convenient distinction in ordinary and extraordinary Christians between run-of-the-mill ordinary believers and the voluntarily devout, who were seeking Christ above and beyond, with all kinds of voluntary acts of piety. They were proposing a Christianity in which all were held to a high and exacting standard.

Related to this demand of following Christ directly, literally, was that early Anabaptists took their understanding of justification by faith alone in a different direction than magisterial Protestant reformers. For them, this was merely the interior aspect of a phenomenon that had to have an exterior manifestation. It was part of an uncompromising vision of Christian life as a radical imitation of Christ, of "*Nach Folga*," the German term, a literal "following after" of the savior in discipleship. Only those who accepted this could become Anabaptists; that is, they could become genuine Christians. Accordingly, early Anabaptists criticized Luther, Zwingli, and the other magisterial Protestant reformers for preaching what to them was a kind of "cheap and easy" Christianity. It let people off the hook with its insistence on justification by faith alone, without radical commitment to amendment of life and a concrete following of Christ. The magisterial reformers, for their part, of course, said, "Oh, no, here comes Catholicism again. You're insisting that good works are an integral part to earning your salvation. No, no, it's justification by faith alone." You see the way in which these sorts of controversies got started.

To pass now to a consideration of the relationship between Anabaptism in the early years and the Peasants' War. Traditionally, scholars distinguished sharply between the militancy of the Peasants' War, and the pacifism of early Anabaptism, such as that exemplified in Grebel and Mantz. This is a distinction that, on the surface, certainly seems to make a great deal of sense. More recent scholarship, however, pursuing the fact of the Peasants' War and the origins of Anabaptism overlapped chronologically, and, to a large extent, geographically, have discerned interesting ways in which they shared certain elements in common. For example, even at the opposite extremes of the two movements, Thomas Müntzer, whom we talked about in our previous lecture, and Conrad Grebel, the early leader of Swiss Anabaptism in Zurich, certainly disagreed about the legitimacy of armed resistance. Both opposed the traditional use of the tithe, however, the customary annual ecclesiastical tax. They both also rejected traditional Catholicism, and the magisterial reformers, Luther, Zwingli, and so forth, whom they thought stopped far short of genuine Christian reform, albeit in different ways.

Moreover, recent research has turned up numerous examples of early Anabaptists or future Anabaptists who were sympathetic to the aims of the "common man," as articulated in the Communal Reformation and the Peasants' War. The endeavor to produce Christian reform would fundamentally alter the social structures and the political institutions of society.

One manifestation of the overlap between the two movements, the concern for the "common man" in the Peasants' War and early Anabaptism, was a very short-lived yet significant movement, significant for what it illustrates; namely, civic Anabaptism. That is, the attempt to make Anabaptism the official form of Christianity of a specific town, analogous, for example, to the adoption of Zwinglian Protestantism in Zurich, or in other Swiss cities. Anabaptism spread to smaller towns around Zurich in the early months of 1525. At the same time, the peasants' revolt swept over the region. Balthasar Hubmaier, one of the most important early Anabaptist leaders, and its most theologically sophisticated advocate, had earned a doctorate in theology—by an ironic twist, under the direction of Johannes Eck, Luther's theological opponent. Eck was the doctoral advisor of Balthasar Hubmaier in Ingolstadt. After Hubmaier had been baptized himself, and accepted adult baptism in an Anabaptist fashion, he himself baptized around 300 citizens in the small town of Waldshut, during Easter season, the spring of 1525. The majority of the town's citizens accepted baptism, and Anabaptist terms, including most members of the city council. Waldshut, then, became an Anabaptist town for a very short period of time. At the same time, it was offering active support and supplies to the troops aiding the rebellious peasants.

This is a different view of the Gospel than that radical non-resistance, that pacifism, of Grebel and Mantz in Zurich. There was an overlap, with the concern of the peasants and their program for social justice, so we must conclude that there were different strands within early Anabaptism, in this region, regarding the legitimacy of resistance and the support of violent activity. The example of Waldshut, then, under Hubmaier, shows that it was not inconceivable that Anabaptism could have, and in some cases did, become the established religion of towns, provided that enough adults voluntarily accepted it, consistent with Anabaptist principles. This phase of "civic Anabaptism" was very short-lived indeed. It essentially came to an end later in the year, in 1525, when the Peasants' War was crushed. Hubmaier himself actually went and tried a similar experiment in a town called Michelsberg just over the border in Moravia; that too, came to an end in late 1527.

Contrary to the intuitively obvious contrast between the violence of the Peasants' War and the pacifism of early Anabaptism, recent research has shown that numerous Anabaptists or future Anabaptists were directly involved in the Peasants' War in some capacity or other. It turns out that one can't draw an absolutely sharp distinction between the subversive violence of one, and the nonresistant pacifism of the other, placing individuals clearly in one camp or the other. This makes sense if we see both as emerging from within, out of that wider rubric, concern for the "common man," in the early Reformation movement. We can go further than this, though, and note the particular impact that the suppression of the Peasants' War had on early Anabaptism, both the Swiss Brethren, and the South German/Austrian Anabaptists.

Fundamentally, the suppression strongly stimulated Anabaptist separatism. "If the world so violently rejects the truth, then truth must reject the world." What could the aspirations of the common man, to create a just social and political order based on those Gospel principles of brotherly love, be construed as, other than truth? Anabaptists held that the proper course of action, then, was to reject the world, and to withdraw from active participation in it as much as possible. This expressed their understanding of the strong contrast between following Christ and belonging to the ways of the world in John's Gospel. Again, it seems absolutely confirmed by what they saw around them. Between 70,000 and 100,000 peasants were killed in the suppression of the peasants' revolt. What was that, if not a rejection of the truth? *p 159 5,000 killed*

If society as a whole couldn't be remade along Christian lines of love and justice, that didn't mean the principles were wrong, only that the world could not accept them. What else did Jesus himself say? He foretold that exactly this would be the case, and look what happened to him. He was crucified. Their realization of those principles had to be on a much smaller scale, however. It couldn't transform society as a whole, but it could be realized among separatist communities of committed Christians. They withdrew from the wider society, in order to live Christian life as it ought to be lived.

In this sense, then, the earliest Anabaptist communities of the Swiss Brethren, the South German/Austrian Anabaptists, and the Hutterites all carried on in their respective ways certain aspirations and part of the legacy of the Peasants' War, albeit in a transformed way. Let's turn, then, to the impact that the suppression of the Peasants' War had on the early Anabaptists in the later 1520s and the early 1530s, among the Swiss Brethren, the South German and Austrian Anabaptists, and the Hutterites.

Before looking at each of these in turn, we should note something that affected all of them profoundly. In the wake of the Peasants' War, shaken by its scale and aims that hyper-sensitized all Catholic and Protestant authorities to attempts at religious radicalism, those authorities understandably clamped down on Anabaptists severely. In the decade between 1525 and 1535, several hundred Anabaptists were executed in Germanic lands. On the Anabaptists' side, for their part, this persecution added to their separatism, this pervasive expectation of suffering and martyrdom. This was what Christ's disciples expected at the hands of the world, just as Jesus himself had been branded as a criminal, and endured a humiliating death, and just as the peasants had been slaughtered in tens of thousands two years before. Let's take a quick look, then, at how each of these three groups dealt with the suppression of the Peasants' War, and the transforming effect that it had on each of them.

First of all, the Swiss Brethren, the Anabaptist movement that grew out of the disagreements with Zwingli and Zurich, was marked by a hardening of the separatist impulse, the result of the destruction of the peasants. Again, "if the world rejects truth, truth should reject the world." This principle is crystallized in a new way in an important watershed within the early Swiss Brethren, in February of 1527, with the *Schleitheim Articles,* written by the former Benedictine monk, Michael Sattler. They were produced at a meeting of several Swiss Anabaptist leaders, and in seven concise main points the *Schleitheim Articles* comprised a deliberate rejection of established political institutions, and of the very possibility of those institutions being Christian. Remember, there were 70,000 to 100,000 peasants killed. This was not a time when one was disposed to think that secular political authorities were capable of being Christian. The *Schleitheim Articles* rejected the very possibility of genuine Christians taking oaths to secular governments, as well as retaliating violence with violence; radical pacifism.

Look at it from the perspective of the other side. This was hardly conducive to inspiring confidence on the part of Catholic or Protestant authorities, in a society where oaths constituted an indispensable means of swearing allegiance, of declaring one's word in law courts. This looked for all the world like the same rejection of legitimate institutions that was the hallmark of the peasants in 1525.

With so much of the world topsy-turvy, compared to what it had been before 1520, with so much of it threatened with flux as never before, could authorities have afforded to believe the Brethren's professed claims of pacifism? Could they have afforded to permit their rejection of community norms and authority, by spurning infant baptism? Could they have trusted that the Brethren's separatism would be, and would remain, benign, rather than providing all sorts of opportunities for conspiracy, for hatching new kinds of rebellions, and rejection? The separatism of the Swiss Brethren echoes today, in North America, among the Amish, who are directly descended from them. It persists in the continuing attitude among the Amish of distrust of, and non-reliance on, secular governments. This persists, also, to the present day. For example, there is the Amish detachment from mandated public school education. They knew what home schooling was long before it became trendy.

From the Swiss Brethren, then, to the South German and Austrian Anabaptists. This group preserved more of the legacy of the Peasants' War than did the Swiss Brethren. Their most important early leaders, as well, were influenced by Thomas Müntzer. For example, Hans Hut did not attempt to carry on the cause of the revolution per se, the way that Müntzer had advocated. Rather, he kept apocalyptic expectations fresh; these were more passive than active apocalyptic expectations. You recall that distinction from the previous lecture.

According to Hut, Müntzer had just gotten the date wrong. It was going to be 1528, rather than 1525, that the end would come. He emphasized also, as Müntzer had done, the necessity of Christian suffering as a mark of true Christianity, in imitation of Jesus. There's something close, here, to late medieval emphasis on Christ's passion, of that identificative understanding of how to become more like Christ through an affinity with his passion. Hut also carried on an extensive ministry as an itinerant missionary in southern Germany and Austria ,prior to his own death in 1527. He baptized hundreds of men and women into Anabaptist Christianity. This branch of Anabaptism was less stable than the Swiss Brethren, in large measure because of the severe persecution that they faced from Catholic authorities in Bavaria and Austria. In addition, they suffered from a lack of leadership and clear direction after the death of Hut, before he could live long enough to see the failure of his apocalyptic expectations.

Refugees from among the South German and Austrian Anabaptists, however, went east to parts of Moravia and Bohemia, where they were less persecuted, and peopled the new Communitarian Anabaptism under Jacob Hutter. This group was called the Hutterites. The Hutterites were born as an outgrowth of persecuted Austrian Anabaptism. To that extent, they, too, were affected by the long wake, the long shadow of the Peasants' War. Jacob Hutter himself was a hatmaker, not a trained theologian, from the mountains of Austria. He became an Anabaptist in the late 1520s. He began leading treks of Anabaptist refugees from the persecution under Ferdinand I of Austria east to Moravia, where certain nobles were more amenable to the Hutterites living on their lands.

Perhaps the most distinctive feature of the Hutterites was their insistence on communal ownership of goods. There was the abolition of private property in the ordinary sense. This set them apart from the Swiss Brethren, for example. They based this practice, in part, on the strapped material circumstances in which they as refugees found themselves. In addition, however, this practice was also based quite deliberately and self-consciously on the Acts of the Apostles in the New Testament, the second and fourth chapters of which both allude to the earliest Christians not holding private property; rather, they possessed all goods in common. Their insistence on communal ownership of goods remained a point that not only distinguished them, but also divided the Hutterites from other Anabaptist groups, who were quite critical of this practice. Jacob Hutter himself was hunted down almost constantly between 1529, when he started leading his refugee treks, and his final apprehension in late 1535. It's really quite remarkable that he managed to elude the Habsburg Austrian authorities for as long as he did. After his apprehension, he was interrogated, tortured, and finally burned in the marketplace at Innsbruck in 1536. In meeting martyrdom, Hutter shared the death that befell so many of the other early Anabaptist leaders, vulnerable in the wake of the Peasants' War, facing authorities hyper-sensitized to any sort of religious radicalism and rejection of social and political norms. Other Anabaptist leaders, too, met their deaths, men like Felix Mantz, Michael Sattler, and Balthasar Hubmaier, among others.

To sum up this lecture, then, we have seen how Anabaptism emerged in disagreements with magisterial reformers about baptism and about the nature of being Christian. We have seen how it shared a wider concern for the common man in the Communal Reformation, and how it overlapped with the Peasants' War of 1524–25. We have seen its theological concerns, distinctions from, and relationships to what was going on in a wider context, and finally the emergence of distinctive new forms of Christianity, ones that shared with magisterial reformers the insistence on the Bible alone, but that drew back from infant baptism, and rejected the idea that anything less than an external commitment to following Christ could be a true form of Christianity.

From the suppression of the peasants and their supporters, early Anabaptists drew the conclusion that their objectives could only hope to be realized on a small scale, among select groups of committed separatist Christians. Three early groups of Anabaptists who did this in Germanic regions included the Swiss Brethren, the South German and Austrian Anabaptists, and the Hutterites. In the course up to this point, we've been exploring the Reformation proper. We've remained confined largely to central Europe. We talked about Luther, about Zwingli, the early evangelical movement, the Peasants' War, and now, early Anabaptism, all within the geographical framework of central Europe, Germany, and Switzerland. The early Reformation, however, didn't remain confined to the Holy Roman Empire. One of the distinctive things, and an important emphasis in recent research, has been the importance of setting the German Reformation more broadly in a European context. In our next lecture, we'll start to break out of our cramped central European confines, and carry ourselves outside of central Europe. We'll look at the spread of early Protestantism to France, England, and the Low Countries.

Maps

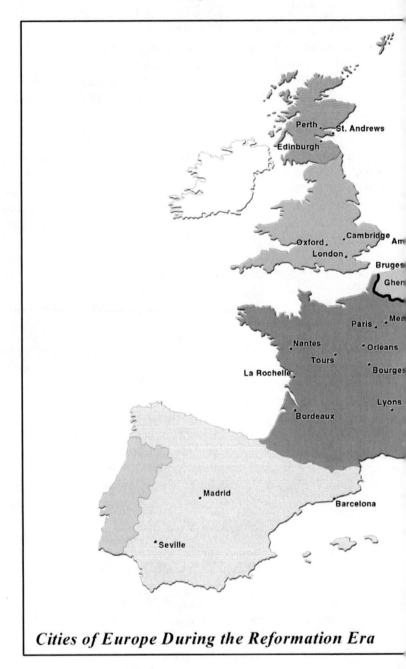

Cities of Europe During the Reformation Era

Emden
Hamburg
Deventer
Münster
rp
Cologne
Eisleben
Wittenberg
Marburg
Erfurt
Leipzig
Frankfurt
Strasbourg
Prague
asel
Augsburg
Vienna
ern
Zurich
Trent
Milan
Venice
Genoa
Florence
Rome
Naples

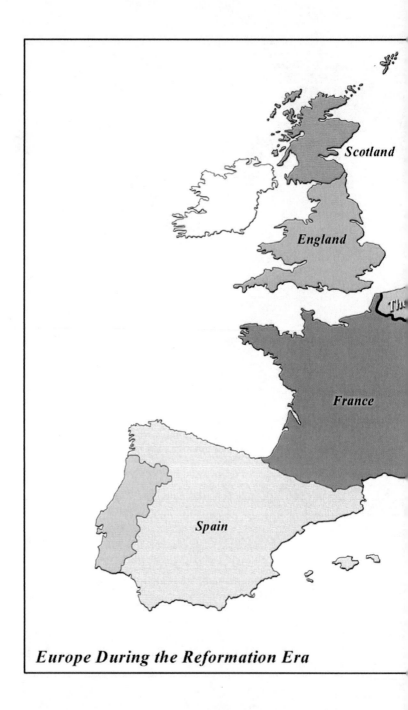

Europe During the Reformation Era

©2001 The Teaching Company.

Timeline

1497 ....The Oratory of Divine Love is founded in Genoa.

1503 ....Erasmus's *Handbook of a Christian Soldier* is published.

1505 ....Martin Luther joins Observant Augustinians in Erfurt and is ordained a priest two years later.

1511 ....Luther moves to Wittenberg University.

1513 ....One in a series of German peasant revolts before the Peasants' War of 1524–1525.

1516 ....Erasmus's *New Testament* published.

1517 ....In Wittenberg, Luther posts his *Ninety-five Theses*, which are immediately published.

1519 ....Huldrych Zwingli begins preaching in Zurich (January). Johann Eck pushes Luther toward *sola scriptura* at the Leipzig Disputation (June–July). Charles V is elected Holy Roman Emperor (June).

1520 ....Leo X's bull *Exsurge domine* threatens Luther with excommunication (June). Luther publishes his three important early treatises (August, October, November).

1521 ....Leo X excommunicates Luther (January) who refuses to recant at the Diet of Worms (April); Charles V condemns him in the Edict of Worms (May). Henry VIII publishes his *Defense of the Seven Sacraments* against Luther; Leo X grants Henry VIII the title "Defender of the Faith."

1522 ....The Augustinian monastery in Antwerp is suppressed for Lutheran heresy. Luther completes his German translation of the *New Testament* and returns to Wittenberg after his period of hiding in the Wartburg castle.

1523 ....The First (January) and Second (October) Zurich Disputations begin the formal acceptance of Zwingli's Protestantism and dismantling of Catholicism by the Zurich city council. Two of the Antwerp Augustinians refuse to recant and become the first of Luther's followers to be executed for heresy, in Brussels (July). Bishop Guillaume Briçonnet presides over reforming initiatives in his diocese of Meaux, in northern France. Clement VII becomes pope after the brief pontificate of Adrian VI.

1524 ....The Peasants' War begins in Germany. Erasmus publishes his *Freedom of the Will*. Five Swiss cantons reject Zwingli's reforms and affirm Catholicism. Over 1,000 German Reformation pamphlets are published during the year, the high tide of printed propaganda for the early Reformation.

1525 ....The first adult baptisms in Zurich defy city law and mark the beginning of the Swiss Brethren (January). The Peasants' War continues and by the fall, is largely defeated. Thomas Müntzer is executed for his role in the Peasants' War. In Switzerland, the first Anabaptists are executed. Luther publishes his *Bondage of the Will* in response to Erasmus's *Freedom of the Will*. In France, the Meaux circle is broken up in the absence of Francis I.

1526 ....The publication of William Tyndale's English translation of the *New Testament* is completed at Worms in Germany and soon begins to be smuggled into England.

1527 ....Imperial troops sack Rome. Michael Sattler's *Schleitheim Articles* articulate the emergent separatist pacifism of the Swiss Brethren.

1528 ....Matteo da Bascio founds the Capuchin order, a reform of the Franciscans, in Italy. The Swiss city of Bern accepts Zwinglian reforms.

1529 ....Luther and Zwingli disagree on the correct understanding of the Lord's Supper at the Marburg Colloquy. Protestant princes and cities protest imperial constraints at the second Diet of Speyer. The city of Basel accepts Zwinglian reforms.

1530 ....Articulation of the Lutheran Augsburg Confession after the imperial Diet of Augsburg. Melchior Hoffman brings Anabaptism to the Low Countries via Emden.

1531 ....Zwingli is killed on the battlefield at Kappel. The Schmalkaldic League is formed as a defensive Protestant political and military alliance in Germany. The first Dutch Anabaptists are executed; Melchior Hoffman declares a moratorium on adult baptisms.

1532 .... The submission of the English clergy to Henry VIII, which prompts Thomas More's resignation as Lord Chancellor.

1533 .... In England, all ecclesiastical appeals to Rome are outlawed, Thomas Cranmer is appointed Archbishop of Canterbury, and Henry VIII secretly marries Anne Boleyn. Adult baptisms resume and their number proliferates rapidly in the Netherlands.

1534 .... The Anabaptist Kingdom of Münster is established. The Act of Supremacy declares that the king is supreme head of the Church in England. Ignatius Loyola gathers his first followers in Paris. The Affair of the Placards leads to intensified measures against heresy in France. Paul III becomes pope.

1535 .... The Anabaptist Kingdom of Münster is crushed. Thomas More, John Fisher, and several Roman Catholic priests and monks are executed for refusing the English oath of supremacy. The Ursulines, a female Catholic religious order, is established by Angela Merici.

1536 .... Calvin publishes the first edition (in Latin) of his *Institutes*, and he arrives in Geneva for the first time.

The suppression and dissolution of the English monasteries begins. Menno Simons is baptized. Erasmus dies.

1537 ....The papally commissioned *Concilium de emendanda ecclesia* denounces ecclesiastical abuses and urges reforms in the Catholic Church.

1538 ....Calvin is exiled from Geneva and moves to Strasbourg. The shrine of Thomas (Becket) of Canterbury is destroyed in England.

1539 ....*The Act of the Six Articles* in England sharply reiterates Henry VIII's hostility to Protestantism.

1540 ....The Jesuits receive formal papal approval by Paul III in Rome.

1541 ....Lutheran and Catholic theologians agree on a formula of justification at the Diet of Regensburg but remain divided on other doctrines. Calvin returns to Geneva after three years in Strasbourg, first publishes his *Institutes* in French, and Geneva accepts his *Ecclesiastical Ordinances*.

1542 ....The Roman Inquisition is established in response to concern about the spread of heresy in Italy.

1544 ....The Peace of Crépy between Charles V and Francis I enables both rulers to devote attention to the suppression of heresy. The Ursulines receive formal papal approval from Paul III. The Jesuits establish their first college in Germany.

1545 ....The Council of Trent opens late in the year.

1546 ....Charles V reorganizes the Inquisition in the Low Countries. Luther dies.

1547 ....Charles V defeats Protestant forces in Germany's Schmalkaldic War. After the death of Henry VIII, a Protestant regime begins in England under the boy-king Edward VI, while English Catholic exiles flee to the Continent. After the death of Francis I, Henry II establishes the *chambre ardente* in France. The Council of Trent is suspended.

1548 ....Charles V imposes the Augsburg Interim on German Lutherans, which helps precipitate a split between Philippist and "Genuine" (Gnesio-) Lutherans.

1549 ....Reforming measures with a more clearly Reformed Protestant character begin in England. The Jesuit Francis Xavier becomes the first Catholic missionary to Japan.

1550 ....Charles V issues the "Bloody Placard," the century's most comprehensive anti-heresy legislation, in the Netherlands.

1551 ....The Council of Trent reconvenes in March and meets until April 1552. Henry II issues the Edict of Chateaubriand, France's most extensive anti-heresy edict.

1552	Thomas Cranmer's *Book of Common Prayer* is published in England. The German College, under Jesuit control, is established in Rome to train parish priests for Germany.
1553	After the death of Edward VI, Mary Tudor becomes queen of England and restores Roman Catholicism.
1554	Mary Tudor weds Philip II of Spain and Reginald Pole returns from Italy to become Archbishop of Canterbury; Protestant exiles flee England for the Continent.
1555	The Peace of Augsburg establishes that territorial princes shall choose whether Catholicism or Lutheranism shall prevail in their territories. The first organized Calvinist churches are established in France (Paris) and the Low Countries (Antwerp). The execution of unrepentant Protestants begins in England. Mennonites and Waterlanders begin their split over banning and shunning. Paul IV becomes pope.
1556	Charles V abdicates as Holy Roman Emperor and retires to a Spanish monastery. Ignatius Loyola dies.
1558	In Geneva, John Knox publishes his *First Blast*, along with other treatises. Mary Tudor dies and Elizabeth I becomes queen of England.
1559	Under Elizabeth, Protestantism is reintroduced to England. John Knox returns to Scotland, where he leads a Protestant rebellion. Henry II of

France dies and is succeeded by Francis II. The first national synod of French Huguenots is held in Paris. Pius IV becomes pope.

1560 .... Francis II of France dies. English military intervention in Scotland against France enables Scotland's adoption of Protestantism by the Reformation Parliament.

1561 .... French Catholics and Huguenots fail to reach any settlement at the Colloquy of Poissy. Mary Stuart returns from France to Scotland. Frederick III of the Palatinate becomes the first German prince to convert from Lutheranism to Calvinism.

1562 .... The Massacre of Vassy inaugurates the French Wars of Religion. The Council of Trent reconvenes to conclude its work.

1563 .... The Council of Trent comes to a close. The *Heidelberg Catechism* is published.

1564 .... The Tridentine canons and decrees receive formal papal approval. Calvin dies.

1565 .... Carlo Borromeo begins his work as Archbishop of Milan.

1566 .... In the Low Countries, collective pressure forces the Compromise of the Nobility, a mitigation of anti-heresy measures, which opens the way for the Iconoclastic Fury. Pius V becomes pope.

1567 .... The Duke of Alva arrives in the Netherlands to punish the Dutch iconoclasts through the Council of Troubles. In Scotland, Mary Stuart abdicates the throne. The separation between Frisian and Flemish Mennonites is completed in the Netherlands.

1568 ....The harsh measures of Alva's Council of Troubles provoke the beginning of the Dutch Revolt against Spain, under the leadership of William of Orange. William Allen establishes the English seminary at Douai to train priests for work in England, in anticipation of the country's eventual return to Catholicism.

1571 ....Emden hosts an important synod of Dutch Calvinist refugees.

1572 ....The Dutch Calvinist Sea Beggars lead an offensive that progressively takes Holland from Spanish control. Catholics kill several thousand Huguenots in France's St. Bartholomew's Day massacres. Gregory XIII becomes pope.

1574 ....Henry III becomes king of France. The first English Catholic missionary priests arrive from the Continent.

1576 ....Unpaid Spanish soldiers mutiny and wreak destruction in Antwerp.

1577 ....The Formula of Concord reconciles most Philippist and "Genuine" Lutherans.

1578 ....Gregory XIII reestablishes the English College in Rome for the purpose of training English missionary priests.

1579 .... The Union of Utrecht establishes the northern provinces of the Low Countries as the Dutch Republic.

1581 .... The Dutch Act of Abjuration formally repudiates the authority of Philip II in the Dutch Republic.

1582 .... The Jesuit missionary Matteo Ricci enters China. The Catholic mission begins in Holland.

1584 .... The death of the Duke of Anjou leaves the Huguenot Henry de Navarre as next in line to the French throne, which reinvigorates the Catholic League. William of Orange is assassinated in Delft.

1585 .... Alessandro Farnese consolidates control of the southern Netherlands for Spain.

1588 .... At Henry III's behest, the French Guises are assassinated.

1589 .... As a retaliation for the murder of the Guises, Henry III is assassinated in France, leaving Henry de Navarre as heir to the throne.

1593 .... Henry de Navarre converts to Catholicism and assumes the French throne as Henry IV.

1598 .... The Edict of Nantes concludes the French Wars of Religion and establishes restricted toleration of Huguenots in France.

1603 .... With the death of Elizabeth I, the English crown passes from the

Tudor to the Stuart line and James I (= James VI of Scotland).

1608 ....To counter aggressive Catholicism in the Holy Roman Empire, the Protestant Union is formed under the leadership of Frederick IV of the Palatinate.

1609 ....In response to the establishment of the Protestant Union, the Catholic League takes shape under the leadership of Maximilian of Bavaria. The first Jesuit Reductions are established in South America.

1618 ....The Defenestration of Prague initiates the Thirty Years' War. In the Dutch Republic, the Synod of Dort resolves the dispute between Calvinism and Arminianism in favor of the former.

1620 ....Catholic forces win a decisive victory under Johann Tilly in the Battle of the White Mountain.

1622 ....Gregory XV endeavors to centralize Catholic missionary efforts by creating the Sacred Congregation for the Propagation of the Faith.

1629 ....In France, the Huguenots lose La Rochelle, their final military stronghold. The Edict of Restitution signals the high water mark of the Counter-Reformation in the Thirty Years' War. Charles I begins his eleven years of "personal rule" in England.

1631 ....Protestant forces win a major victory under Gustavus Adolphus at the Battle of Breitenfeld.

1632	Gustavus Adolphus dies.
1635	The Peace of Prague concludes the Swedish phase of the Thirty Years' War.
1640	The Short Parliament is held and the Long Parliament begins in England.
1642	The first civil war, between royalists and parliamentarians, begins in England.
1646	A Presbyterian church order is established in England after the parliamentarian victory in the first civil war.
1648	The Peace of Westphalia ends the Thirty Years' War and establishes the enduring religio-political divisions of Europe.
1649	Charles I is executed by order of the Rump Parliament; England is proclaimed a Republic.
1654	In his role as Lord Protector of England, Oliver Cromwell establishes a tolerant and inclusive state church.
1660	The English monarchy and the Church of England are restored to their prerevolutionary forms.
1685	Louis XIV revokes the Edict of Nantes, ending toleration for Huguenots in France.

Glossary

Anabaptism: The general term used to designate those Christian groups in the radical Reformation who rejected infant baptism in favor of adult understanding and commitment as a prerequisite for becoming a Christian and for baptism. The most important Anabaptist groups were the Swiss Brethren, the South German/Austrian Anabaptists, the Hutterites, and the Mennonites.

anticlericalism: Critical or hostile attitudes or practices directed against members of the clergy, whether Catholic priests or, after the Protestant Reformation was established, Protestant ministers. Anticlericalism might be subdivided by the specific target of criticism (e.g., antipapalism, antimonasticism), and it was variously directed against clerical abuses, clerical privileges, or both.

apocalypticism: The term used to describe the anticipation of the imminent end of the world, which in Christian teaching, includes the second coming of Christ, the resurrection of the dead, and the Last Judgment by Christ.

apostolic succession: The Christian notion that Christ's apostles, who received their authority from him, pass it in turn to their successors, thus preserving his authority in the Church. In Roman Catholicism, these successors are understood to be the Church's bishops.

banning and shunning: The Anabaptist disciplinary practice of excluding a baptized member of the community from fellowship because of some moral or other infraction, followed by the group's collective refusal to have any contact with the excluded member.

baptism: The sacrament of initiation into the Christian community practiced by Catholics, Protestants, and Anabaptists (although not by certain other radical Protestants). Magisterial Protestants, like Catholics, baptized infants, a practice Anabaptists rejected in favor of baptizing only adults who had self-consciously committed to becoming Christians.

Calvinism: The branch of Reformed Protestantism that takes its name from John Calvin, the French refugee reformer of Geneva, whence it spread to have a significant influence in France, England, Scotland, Germany, and the Low Countries. Calvinism, characterized by its theological rigor, liturgical austerity, and aspiration to create godly polities, was the most dynamic form of Protestantism in the second half of the sixteenth century.

canonization: In Roman Catholicism, the official papal recognition of a holy man or woman as a saint, that is, an advocate with God in heaven for the supplications and prayers of living Christians.

Catholic reform: The collective designation for those aspects of late medieval and early modern Catholicism primarily concerned with the internal self-renewal and reform of Catholic devotion, practice, and institutions, rather than with opposition to heresy or reaction to the Protestant Reformation.

Church Fathers: The leading Christian theologians of the second through the sixth centuries, the publication and study of whose Greek and Latin writings were central to the Christian humanists' desire to reform the Church through erudition and education. The writings of the Church Fathers, above all Augustine, played an important role in early modern Christian theology; Protestant and Catholic theologians disputed the correct interpretation of their writings.

Communal Reformation: English translation of the German term *Gemeindereformation*, used to designate the German Reformation movement in the early 1520s through the end of the Peasants' War, when it was a genuinely popular social movement with a broad demographic base in both the towns and rural areas of southern and central Germany.

conciliarism: In the domain of ecclesiology, the late medieval position holding that ultimate authority in the Church reposes with church councils rather than with the papacy. Conciliarism reached its apogee in the early fifteenth century and waned from the mid-fifteenth century, although it remained important well into the Reformation era.

confessionalization: The process in the Reformation era whereby secular and ecclesiastical authorities worked together in the effort to create well-informed, conscientious Christians who had specific confessional identities (Lutheran, Calvinist, Roman Catholic) and would also be well-disciplined, obedient political subjects.

confraternities: In late medieval and early modern Catholic Europe, the most important collective lay religious institutions, variously constituted mutual aid societies organized for the spiritual and social well-being of their members.

consistory: The principal institution responsible for the exercise of moral and religious discipline in Calvinist Geneva, and wherever Calvinism took full root according to the Genevan model. The consistory was composed of the local Calvinist church's pastors and elders.

conventicles: Secret, underground gatherings of like-minded Christians in contexts of persecution, for purposes of worship, conversation, scripture study, and mutual encouragement and support.

Counter-Reformation: The collective term for those aspects of early modern Catholicism concerned primarily to oppose, denounce, and undo the Protestant and radical Reformations.

diocese: The principal geographical and administrative subdivisions of Latin Christendom in the Middle Ages and of Catholic Europe (and Protestant England) in the Reformation era, overseen by a bishop. Dioceses were subdivided into parishes.

episcopacy: The office of bishop in the Roman Catholic Church, the Church of England, and the Lutheran churches of some countries. The ecclesiological significance of the episcopacy was rejected in Reformed Protestantism and the radical Reformation.

Eucharist: The celebratory ritual meal of thanksgiving in collective Christian worship that is based on the Last Supper of Jesus with his apostles. It can also refer specifically to the consecrated bread and wine consumed during this meal. The Eucharist, or Lord's Supper, was one of the most disputed areas of Christian theology and liturgy in the Reformation era.

excommunication: The formal expulsion of a baptized Christian from the community of the Roman Catholic Church and, therefore, from the reception of the sacraments, after due warning and exhortation to rectify the offense or condition for which excommunication is threatened. Excommunication was appropriated in various forms by Protestant groups in the Reformation era (e.g., banning and shunning among Anabaptists).

heresy: The deliberate holding of erroneous Christian doctrines, as defined by orthodox authorities. Because orthodoxy was disputed in the Reformation era, heresy was also disputed. Heresy is not to be confused with unbelief; only a baptized Christian can be a heretic.

humanism: In the Renaissance, the movement to recover and teach the language, literature, rhetoric, poetry, and history of the ancient Greek and Roman classics to instill virtue and good government. Christian humanism adapted this program to the reform of the Church through the recovery and teaching of the Church Fathers' writings and the Bible in their original languages.

iconoclasm: The violent or controlled destruction of religious images or works of art. In the Reformation era, Protestant iconoclasm was frequently directed against Catholic religious art, both inside and outside churches.

idolatry: In Christianity, the worship of anything that is not God. In the Reformation era, Protestants who rejected the real presence of Christ in the Eucharist and Catholic ideas about religious images and relics accused Catholics of idolatry in venerating the Eucharist, religious images, and saints' relics.

indulgence: In the late Middle Ages and the Reformation era, in Catholic teaching, the Church's complete or partial remission of the purgatorial punishment for sins by a person making a proper confession and fulfilling the conditions stipulated by an authorized cleric for attaining the indulgence. Luther's dissatisfaction with the abuse of indulgences lay behind his *Ninety-five Theses.*

Inquisition: An ecclesiastical tribunal in the Catholic Church specially designated to inquire into and suppress heresy. Not a monolithic institution, the principal inquisitions in late medieval and early modern Europe were the medieval (established in the thirteenth century), the Spanish (est. 1478), and the Roman (est. 1542).

justification by faith alone: The phrase describing the central doctrinal assertion of Protestantism that human beings are made acceptable to God strictly through trust in Christ as their savior, a trust produced in them entirely by God's grace. Thus, humans contribute nothing whatsoever to their own salvation. The doctrine was formally condemned by the Council of Trent, which insisted that human beings cooperate with God's grace in the process of salvation.

liturgy: Collective Christian worship according to some regular, established pattern or procedure. Liturgical forms varied widely across the various traditions of early modern Christianity.

Lord's Supper: A general name for the celebratory ritual meal of thanksgiving in collective Christian worship that is based on the Last Supper of Jesus with his apostles. (See also **Eucharist**.)

Lutheranism: The branch of Protestantism that takes its name from Martin Luther, as distinct from Reformed Protestantism or radical Protestantism. Lutheranism, which remained theologically, liturgically, and aesthetically closer to Roman Catholicism than did Reformed Protestantism, became the official form of Christianity in many German territories and in the Scandinavian countries.

magisterial Protestantism: Those forms of Protestantism that were introduced with the sanction, support, and/or coercion of secular magistrates, whether in cities, territories, or nations. Magisterial Protestantism includes Lutheranism and Reformed Protestantism and excludes the radical Reformation. In this course, "Protestantism" is generally used as shorthand for "magisterial Protestantism."

mendicants: Literally "beggars," the term refers to the regular clergy who originally begged alms for their survival as itinerant preachers and ministers, chiefly the members of the Franciscan and Dominican orders, but also including the Carmelites and Augustinians. Synonymous with "mendicant friars" or "friars."

papacy: The office of pope in the Roman Catholic Church, the highest office in its hierarchical structure. Rejection of the papacy and its authority was the only tenet shared by all Protestants in the Reformation era.

parish: A geographical and administrative subdivision of a diocese in Catholic Europe, overseen by a parish priest (or by a minister in those areas of Protestant Europe that retained parishes as geographical and administrative designations).

penance: In one sense, a synonym for the sacrament of confession in the Roman Catholic Church; the term can also refer to the activities done to fulfill the penalties stipulated for the forgiveness of sins according to the sacrament, as well as to the state of being contrite for, repentant about, one's sins. Protestants rejected the Catholic meanings linked to the sacrament of penance but generally emphasized the importance of repentance as a condition for amendment of life.

Petrine supremacy: The Catholic teaching that links Peter's preeminence among the apostles to the understanding of him as the first pope and, thus, to the succession of popes that began with Peter and derives its authority from Christ. Hence, the papal see of Rome is called the "See of St. Peter."

predestination: The Christian teaching, importantly influenced by Augustine in the Reformation era, that human beings are destined for salvation or damnation as the result of God's will, independent of their own choices or actions. Among the major traditions in early modern Christianity, the doctrine was emphasized and elaborated most by Calvin and Calvinist theologians.

Protestantism: The broadest designation of all those Christian groups in Latin Christendom who, in the Reformation era, rejected the authority of the Roman Catholic Church. The distinction between magisterial Protestantism and radical Protestantism comprises its fundamental subdivision. In this course, "Protestantism" is generally used as shorthand for "magisterial Protestantism."

providence: The Christian teaching that God actively orders and governs all things and events in his creation, often despite appearances to the contrary. Belief in God's providence was fundamental to virtually all Christians in the Reformation era.

radical Reformation: Those forms of Protestantism that rejected Christianity as it was introduced and supported by secular authorities. Anabaptists are the most significant subgroup in the radical Reformation.

Reformed Protestantism: Along with Lutheranism, one of the two major traditions in magisterial Protestantism. Although Calvinism and Zwinglianism are its two most important subtraditions, Reformed Protestantism is an umbrella designation that is bigger than either.

regulars: As distinguished from mendicants and secular clergy, these were cloistered monks or nuns in Roman Catholicism who belonged to religious orders that followed a monastic "rule" (*regula*). The rule theoretically kept them apart from the wider world, pursuing lives of prayer, work, and contemplation. Among the most important were the Benedictines, Cistercians, and Carthusians.

resistance theory: Protestant political thought that developed in Lutheranism and Calvinism in the sixteenth century concerning the conditions and identities of those who might legitimately resist and/or oppose an ungodly (i.e., Catholic) ruler.

Roman Catholicism: The early modern Christian tradition that was institutionally continuous with medieval Latin Christianity, the authority of which was repudiated, in various ways and to various degrees, by all Protestant groups in the Reformation era.

royal supremacy: The English law enacted in 1534 by Parliament at Henry VIII's behest that made the sovereign the supreme head of the Church in England. The royal supremacy emerged from Henry VIII's desire to have his marriage to Katherine of Aragon annulled so that he could wed his mistress, Anne Boleyn.

sacraments: In Catholicism, specifically designated sacred rituals that confer God's grace on the recipient. The Fourth Lateran Council (1215) enumerated seven: baptism, confession (penance), communion (Eucharist), confirmation, marriage, holy orders, and extreme unction. Most Protestants accepted only baptism and communion, although different reformers and groups understood these two in widely divergent ways. The correct understanding of the sacraments was bitterly contested among different Christian groups in the Reformation era.

saints: In Roman Catholicism, holy men and women whose presence in heaven has been attested after their deaths by miracles they have worked, who have been officially canonized, and who can intercede with God on behalf of ordinary men and women. Protestants rejected saints' intercessory role but sometimes adopted the term to refer to living members of their own group.

secular clergy: As distinguished from the mendicants and the regular clergy, these were members of the clergy serving in the world (*saeculum*), most often as ordinary parish priests or at lower clerical ranks. They were not members of a religious order and were under the direct authority of a bishop.

sola fide: A Latin phrase meaning "by faith alone," this popular slogan of the Protestant Reformation expressed in a condensed form the assertion that Christians were saved by God solely on the basis of faith, imparted wholly by God's grace, and not as the result of any effort or action whatsoever on their own part. Good works were part of Christian love and directed toward one's fellow human beings, but contributed nothing to one's salvation. The Council of Trent formally condemned this teaching as heretical.

sola scriptura: A Latin phrase meaning "by scripture alone," this popular slogan of the Protestant Reformation articulated in a compressed way the claim that the Bible alone, not the papacy, church councils, or ecclesiastical tradition in general, is the sole authority for Christian faith and life. The Council of Trent formally condemned this teaching as heretical.

spirituali: The collective name for the elite, humanistic, reform-minded group of Italian prelates in Italy in the 1530s and 1540s who were sympathetic to the doctrine of justification by faith alone but did not reject papal authority. The Council of Trent's condemnation of justification by faith alone forced them to choose between the two commitments.

transubstantiation: In Catholic teaching, the dogma that with the priest's words of consecration in the Mass, the appearance of the bread and wine remain, but their substance is miraculously changed into the body and blood of Christ, following his own words to his apostles at the Last Supper ("This is my body"). Protestants rejected the dogma of transubstantiation, although Lutherans retained the teaching of Christ's real presence in the Eucharist.

Biographical Notes

Carlo Borromeo (1538–1584): Archbishop of Milan from 1565 until his death in 1584, where his diligent reforming activities epitomized the ideal of the pastorally minded, post-Tridentine Catholic bishop. He held regular provincial councils and diocesan synods, carried out systematic visitations of parishes and monasteries, established and supported a major diocesan seminary for the training of priests, and promoted the schools of Christian doctrine, all in accordance with the decrees of the Council of Trent. His zeal provoked conflict with civil authorities in Milan, though he eventually won their support. Borromeo became the model for other post-Tridentine bishops. He was formally canonized as a saint in 1610.

John Calvin (1509–1564): The leading reformer and theologian in the second generation of the Protestant Reformation, he was born in France but became the resident exile religious leader in Geneva, Switzerland, after his conversion to Protestantism. Trained as a humanist and a lawyer, his uncompromising reforms led to his exile from Geneva in 1538; he spent three years in Strasbourg before being invited back to Geneva in 1541, where he remained until his death. Calvin's *Institutes of the Christian Religion*, first published in 1536 and revised several times until it reached its final form in 1559, is the single most important Protestant theological work of the Reformation era. Calvinism became the most dynamic, influential form of Protestantism in Europe in the second half of the sixteenth century.

Charles V (1500–1558): As the Holy Roman Emperor from 1519 until 1556, he was probably the most important political figure in the early decades of the Reformation era. A staunch defender of Catholicism and opponent of Protestantism, he ruled over vast territories either directly or indirectly, including Spain, the Low Countries, Austria, northern Italy, most of central Europe, and parts of eastern Europe. He issued the Edict of Worms that condemned Luther in 1521, defeated the allied Protestant forces in the Schmalkaldic War of 1547, and imposed the Augsburg Interim on Lutheran towns and territories before concluding the Peace of Augsburg in 1555. His chief political rival was Francis I of France, with whom he was frequently at war until Francis's death in 1547.

Elizabeth I (1533–1603): Daughter of Henry VIII and Anne Boleyn, she was the queen of England from 1558 until 1603 and restored Protestantism to England. The sheer longevity of her reign, in contrast to those of her predecessors Edward VI and Mary, was probably the most important factor in transforming England into a Protestant country by the 1580s. Elizabeth pursued a moderate, pragmatic Protestantism that emphasized obedience and sought to avoid the violence that religious differences were provoking on the Continent.

Erasmus (c. 1466–1536): The leading Christian humanist of the early sixteenth century, he sought the gradual renewal of Christendom based on the fusion of classical and biblical erudition, education, and piety in the "philosophy of Christ." His prodigious literary output included dozens of scholarly, satirical, instructional, and moral works. Erasmus produced editions of many of the Greek and Latin Church Fathers, as well as an edition of the *New Testament* in the original Greek with his own Latin translation (1516). Other important works included his *Handbook of the Christian Soldier* (1503) and *Praise of Folly* (1511). He criticized clerical ignorance, immorality, and greed; ridiculed lay "superstition"; and rejected scholastic theology. Although originally supportive of Luther, Erasmus's very different views and approach to theology came to a head in their famous debate over the role of free will in Christian salvation in 1524–1525.

Francis I (1494–1547): The French king who patronized humanism and humanist reform but opposed Protestantism, particularly after the Affair of the Placards in 1534. During the 1520s, his implicit distinction between elite, educated reform and disruptive, seditious heresy shielded the reforming measures under Guillaume Briçonnet, the bishop of Meaux. The later years of his reign saw a sharp increase in executions for heresy in France. Francis's chief political rivals throughout his reign were Charles V and Henry VIII.

Henry IV (de Navarre) (1553–1610): The French king whose conversion from Calvinism to Catholicism in 1593 helped bring an end to the French Wars of Religion with the Edict of Nantes in 1598. The son of Jeanne de Navarre and Antoine de Bourbon, Henry, a committed Protestant and Huguenot military leader in the Wars of Religion, became the next in line to the throne after the death of the Duke of Anjou in 1584. This precipitated opposition from the militant Catholic League, which rejected in principle the notion of a Protestant king, and ushered in the violent religio-political clashes of the later 1580s and early 1590s. When Henry III was assassinated in 1589, Henry de Navarre became a king without a crown, one not secured until he agreed to convert. Despite adopting Catholicism, during the rest of his reign, Henry's continued protection and toleration of Protestants, both at his court and further afield, enabled France to recover somewhat from its religious civil wars.

Henry VIII (1491–1547): The English king at whose behest the country severed its longstanding institutional links to the Roman Catholic Church and created a separate national church under royal control. Before the late 1520s and his desire to have his marriage to Katherine of Aragon annulled, Henry was a stalwart defender of Catholic orthodoxy. In 1521, he published a treatise against Luther and earned the title "Defender of the Faith" from Pope Leo X. Clement VII's refusal to grant the annulment precipitated a series of parliamentary acts between 1532 and 1534 that created an English church separate from Roman jurisdiction and subject to the English monarch as "supreme head." Despite repudiating Rome, Henry remained hostile to Protestantism, an antagonism evinced late in his reign, especially after the Six Articles Act of 1539. In the later 1530s, he oversaw the dissolution of all the English monasteries, the vast holdings of which were taken by the crown and quickly sold to fund war.

Melchior Hoffman (1495?–1543): The peripatetic radical Protestant prophet and preacher who brought Anabaptism to the Low Countries when he went to Emden in 1530. He prophesied the end of the world for 1533, with Strasbourg as the New Jerusalem, where godly magistrates would destroy the godless. All those who had been (re)baptized would be saved. Hoffman's first Dutch converts in Emden became the nucleus of the Melchiorite Anabaptist movement in the Netherlands, which grew exponentially and was transformed after 1533, most dramatically by those who became Münsterites. Hoffman returned to Strasbourg, where he was imprisoned for his Anabaptism, and died in obscurity.

John Knox (c. 1514–1572): An impassioned, uncompromising Calvinist reformer who played a leading role in the Scottish Reformation, he converted to Protestantism sometime in the early 1540s. He first became a public figure in 1547, when he preached his first sermon, then spent two years as a prisoner on a French galley ship. After his release, he went to England, where he preached and ministered, then fled to the Continent and Geneva as one of the Marian exiles in 1554. Deeply impressed by Calvin and Geneva, he returned to Scotland for several months in 1555–1556, then again in 1559, when he provoked the uprisings that intersected with a series of political events to produce the Scottish parliament's adoption of Protestantism in 1560. Knox wrote several treatises in 1558 that contributed to Calvinist political resistance theory, as well as a lengthy account of the Reformation in Scotland.

Jan van Leiden (1509–1536): The self-proclaimed prophet-king and ruler of the Anabaptist Kingdom of Münster in 1534–1535, he had been a tailor and unsuccessful trader before his baptism by Jan Matthijs in late 1533. Sent by Matthijs as an apostolic missionary to Münster in April 1534, after the Anabaptist takeover of the city and Matthijs's death, Jan van Leiden became the city's ruler and brutally dispatched anyone who opposed him. Under van Leiden, the "New Jerusalem" practiced communal ownership of goods and polygamy, both of which scandalized European contemporaries. After a siege finally broke the regime in late June 1535, Jan was executed in early 1536.

Ignatius Loyola (1491?–1556): The founder of the Society of Jesus (the Jesuits), the most important Catholic religious order of the Reformation era. While convalescing from battle injuries in 1521, Ignatius underwent the first in a series of conversion experiences that led him to make a pilgrimage to Jerusalem, to learn Latin, then to study theology in Paris. There, in 1534, he gathered around him a circle of six students, including Francis Xavier and Diego Laínez, who became the core of the earliest Jesuits. Prevented from going to Jerusalem by war, they instead went to Rome, where the new order received papal approval in 1540. In Rome, Ignatius established the Jesuit Roman College in 1551 and oversaw the rapid numerical and geographical expansion of the early order, which included over 1,000 members at the time of his death. He modeled his *Spiritual Exercises* on his own conversion, and it became the central text in Jesuit spirituality; through the society's members, the text exercised a widespread influence in Catholic Europe.

Martin Luther (1483–1546): The first and most influential reformer and publicist in the first generation of Protestantism, Luther came to reject papal and conciliar authority in favor of the Bible as the sole norm for Christian faith and life. After his early education and university education at the University of Erfurt in central Germany, Luther entered the Observant Augustinian order in 1505, was ordained a priest in 1507, and began teaching at the University of Wittenberg in 1511. Riddled with anxiety about his sinfulness, he eventually found deliverance in the teaching and experience of salvation by "faith alone," which emerged between 1513 and 1519. In 1517, he posted his famous *Ninety-five Theses,* protesting against indulgences. He was then driven to more and more radical statements in the course of debates with theological adversaries between 1518 and 1521, when he defied both Pope Leo X and Emperor Charles V. He sharply rejected the militancy of the peasants in 1525, remaining traditional and conservative in his social and political views. Luther's writings, including his translation of the Bible into German, plus hundreds of pamphlets, treatises, songs, and letters, had an enormous influence on the early Protestant Reformation and the consolidation of Lutheranism in Germany.

Thomas Müntzer (c. 1490–1525): A radical apocalyptic and militant reformer from central Germany who preached violent revolution during the Peasants' War of 1525. Originally sympathetic to Luther, Müntzer progressively moved away from and ridiculed him as a panderer to princes. He understood the rising tide of peasant and urban agitation in the early 1520s as a sign of the coming apocalypse, in which God would destroy the ungodly alliance of oppressive rulers and sycophantic priests and ministers. After a stint as a minister and preacher in the small Thuringian town of Allstedt, Müntzer became increasingly involved in the cause of the peasants. In May 1525, he led several thousand woefully underarmed peasants into battle at Frankenhausen, where they were slaughtered. Shortly thereafter, he was captured and executed. In subsequent years, his legacy endured in an attenuated manner among certain central and south German Anabaptists.

Philip II (1527–1598): The Spanish king and son of Charles V, he was the most powerful ruler in Europe in the second half of the sixteenth century, overseeing a worldwide empire as a result of Spanish colonization (the Philippines are named after him). A devout Catholic and zealous opponent of Protestantism, his refusal to mitigate the anti-heresy measures in the Low Countries precipitated the Iconoclastic Fury of 1566, the Dutch Revolt, and the Spanish loss of the northern Netherlands. Despite his Catholic convictions, Philip was concerned to maintain royal control over many aspects of the Spanish church, as well as over the Spanish Inquisition.

Menno Simons (c. 1496–1561): The most influential Dutch Anabaptist leader in the wake of the Anabaptist Kingdom of Münster, especially after the early 1540s. Menno was a parish priest in Friesland who became an Anabaptist after finding no basis for infant baptism in either the Bible or in any of the early Protestant reformers. Like other Anabaptist leaders in German-speaking regions, he stressed the importance of adult commitment and moral rectitude as a prerequisite for being Christian. He renounced his position as parish priest in early 1536, was (re)baptized, and lived most of his career as a reformer in the relative safety of north Germany in order to avoid persecution. He remained fundamentally oriented toward the Low Countries, where his followers, eventually known as Mennonites, were more numerous than any other Protestant group until the explosive growth of Dutch Calvinism in the 1560s.

Teresa of Avila (1515–1582): The Spanish founder of the Discalced Carmelites and the most remarkable female Christian writer of the sixteenth century. She entered the well-to-do Carmelite convent in Avila in 1535, where she remained for twenty-seven years. She began pursuing religious life seriously in 1538 and became increasingly involved in mystical prayer after 1555. Disrupting the tradition of aristocratic patronage of the Carmelite monastery in Avila in 1562, she established a new house based on strict poverty and rigorous adherence to the rule of the order. Fourteen more houses were established by the time of her death. Her initiatives and mystical experiences provoked controversy, and she was asked to justify herself to her confessors. Teresa's extensive literary output, including her autobiography and *The Interior Castle*, rank among the great works of early modern Catholicism. She was canonized in 1622.

William of Orange (1533–1584): The Dutch nobleman around whom resistance to Spain coalesced beginning in 1568, which led to the formation of an independent Dutch nation. Although dependent on Calvinist anti-Catholic sentiment and action, William himself sought to maintain a unified, political, anti-Spanish focus to the rebellion, across the northern and southern provinces of the Low

Countries. This position proved untenable, with anti-Spanish Calvinism predominating in the new United Provinces of the north and Catholicism and Spanish control prevailing in the south. William was assassinated in 1584. He is justifiably regarded as the "father of his country."

Huldrych Zwingli (1484–1531): The Protestant reformer whose influence was responsible for the abolition of Catholicism and the adoption of Protestantism in the Swiss city of Zurich between 1523 and 1525. Educated in part at the universities of Basel and Vienna, Zwingli was ordained a priest in 1506 and was deeply influenced by Christian humanism; he held Erasmus in high regard. He was appointed preacher in Zurich in 1519. Zwingli considered the civic government and church as two aspects of one and the same Christian community, both of which should be organized based on biblical teachings. His sharp disagreement with Luther over the nature of the Lord's Supper found dramatic expression in the Marburg Colloquy of 1529, preventing a political alliance between Zwinglian and Lutheran cities and setting the Lutheran and Reformed Protestant traditions on divergent paths.

Bibliography

Handbooks, Reference Works, and Introductory Anthologies

Brady, Thomas A., Jr., Heiko A. Oberman, and James D. Tracy, editors. *Handbook of European History, 1400–1600: Late Middle Ages, Renaissance, and Reformation*, 2 vols. (1994; Grand Rapids, Mich., 1996). Excellent collection of forty substantive articles written by leading experts covering the political, social, economic, institutional, cultural, and religious territory of the fifteenth and sixteenth centuries.

Goertz, Hans-Jürgen, editor. *Profiles of Radical Reformers: Biographical Sketches from Thomas Müntzer to Paracelsus* (Kitchener, Ont., 1982). Concise life-and-thought overviews of twenty-one of the leading radical Protestant reformers.

Greengrass, Mark, editor. *The Longman Companion to the European Reformation, c. 1500–1618* (London and New York, 1998). Useful compilation of chronologies, ruling dynasties and family trees, biographical sketches, and maps pertaining to early modern Christianity, especially the Protestant Reformation.

Hillerbrand, Hans, editor. *The Oxford Encyclopedia of the Reformation*, 4 vols. (Oxford and New York, 1996). Outstanding reference work with entries covering significant persons, events, movements, and ideas related to the Reformation. Stronger on Protestantism and radical Protestantism than on Catholicism.

Pettegree, Andrew, editor. *The Early Reformation in Europe* (Cambridge, 1992). Ten articles, each on a different country or region, cover the varied course of the Protestant Reformation from the 1520s through the 1550s.

———, editor. *The Reformation World* (London and New York, 2000). Excellent state-of-the-field collection of thirty articles on the Protestant Reformation, covering all of Europe, from the pre-Reformation Church into the seventeenth century.

Prestwich, Menna, editor. *International Calvinism, 1541–1715* (Oxford, 1985). First-rate collection of articles on Calvinism in Geneva, France, the Netherlands, Germany, east central Europe, England, Scotland, and colonial North America.

Scribner, Bob, Roy Porter, and Mikuláš Teich, editors. *The Reformation in National Context* (Cambridge, 1994). Thirteen articles provide good introductory overviews of the Protestant Reformation in its divergent national contexts.

Single-Author Surveys and Syntheses

Bireley, Robert. *The Refashioning of Catholicism, 1450–1700* (Washington, D.C., 1999). Lucid, concise treatment of early modern Catholicism; successful in sympathetically reconstructing its embeddedness in other early modern political and cultural realities.

Cameron, Euan. *The European Reformation* (Oxford, 1991). The best recent synthesis on the Protestant Reformation in an international context. Very well written; exceptionally lucid on late medieval Christianity and the theology of the reformers.

Delumeau, Jean. *Catholicism between Luther and Voltaire: A New View of the Counter-Reformation* (London, 1977). Now somewhat dated but influential for its long-term view of the transformation of Catholicism in the early modern period.

Hsia, R. Po-chia. *The World of Catholic Renewal, 1540–1770* (Cambridge, 1998). Good introduction to early modern Catholicism, beginning with the Council of Trent. Devoted mostly to the later sixteenth and seventeenth centuries.

Lindberg, Carter. *The European Reformations* (Cambridge, Mass., 1996). Older style, confessionalist Protestant treatment of the era, despite the plural in the title.

Mullett, Michael A. *The Catholic Reformation* (London and New York, 1999). Dense survey of early modern Catholicism, stressing the medieval roots of Catholic reform and renewal.

Snyder, C. Arnold. *Anabaptist History and Theology: An Introduction* (Kitchener, Ont., 1996). Clear, comprehensive, highly accessible survey of all the main branches of Anabaptism. Best one-volume introduction available.

Williams, George H. *The Radical Reformation*, 3rd ed. (Kirksville, Mo., 1992). Encyclopedic, comprehensive, yet historiographically dated work covering rationalist and spiritualist radical Protestants, as well as all branches of Anabaptism, in both western and eastern Europe. First published in 1962.

Books and Articles

Arthur, Anthony. *The Tailor King: The Rise and Fall of the Anabaptist Kingdom of Münster* (New York, 1999). Vividly written, popular narrative of Jan van Leiden and the Münsterite kingdom.

Asch, Ronald G. *The Thirty Years' War: The Holy Roman Empire and Europe, 1618–1648* (New York, 1997). Most recent survey in English on the Thirty Years' War.

Bagchi, David V. N. *Luther's Earliest Opponents: Catholic Controversialists, 1518–25* (Minneapolis, 1991). Very fine, careful, analytical study of a topic previously neglected in English-language scholarship: the character and extent of early Catholic opposition to Luther.

Bainton, Roland. *Here I Stand: A Life of Martin Luther* (New York, 1950). Classic, popular, highly readable biography of Luther.

Benedict, Philip. *Rouen during the Wars of Religion* (Cambridge, 1981). One of the best local studies of the French Wars of Religion in English.

————. *"Un roi, une loi, deux fois:* Parameters for the History of Catholic-Reformed Co-existence in France, 1555–1685." In *Tolerance and Intolerance in the European Reformation,* ed. Ole Peter Grell and Bob Scribner (Cambridge, 1996). Insightful discussion of the relationship between Catholics and Huguenots in France from the Wars of Religion through the revocation of the Edict of Nantes.

Blickle, Peter. *Communal Reformation: The Quest for Salvation in Sixteenth-Century Germany* (Atlantic Highlands, N.J., 1992). Important analysis of the connections between the early German urban Reformation and the Peasants' War under the rubric "communal Reformation," extending the analytical framework of his *Revolution of 1525.*

————. *The Revolution of 1525: The German Peasants' War from a New Perspective* (Baltimore and London, 1981). Sophisticated interpretation of the Peasants' War in the context of late medieval economic and social tensions, arguing that the peasant leaders' take on the Reformation message led them to aspire to genuine social and political revolution rather than mere rebellion.

Bonney, Richard. *The European Dynastic States, 1494–1660* (Oxford, 1991). Dense, comprehensive overview of both the important institutions and the chronological development of early modern European states.

Boxer, Charles R. *The Church Militant and Iberian Expansion, 1440–1770* (Baltimore, 1978). Concise, useful overview of the relationship between Spanish and Portuguese Catholic missions and colonization.

Brady, Thomas A., Jr. "In Search of the Godly City: The Domestication of Religion in the German Urban Reformation." In *The German People and the Reformation,* ed. R. Po-chia Hsia (Ithaca, N.Y., 1989). Superb synthetic article analyzing the process by which, beginning in the 1520s, German cities introduced the Reformation without subverting the social and political status quo.

————. *The Politics of the Reformation in Germany: Jacob Sturm (1489–1553) of Strasbourg* (Atlantic Highlands, N.J., 1997). Lucid, crisp account that uses the humanist magistrate Sturm as a prism on the course of the Reformation in Strasbourg and in the Empire more broadly up to the Peace of Augsburg.

————. *Turning Swiss: Cities and Empire, 1450–1550* (Cambridge, 1985). Argues that the southwestern German cities in the early Reformation looked to the independent cities of the Swiss Confederation as political models.

Brigden, Susan. *London and the Reformation* (Oxford, 1989). Extraordinarily learned, deeply researched, and carefully written narrative of the Reformation in England's only true city in the Reformation era.

Calvin, John. *Institutes of the Christian Religion*, 2 vols. Translated by Ford Lewis Battles, edited by John T. McNeill (Philadelphia, 1960). Standard English edition of Calvin's most important systematic theological work.

Canons and Decrees of the Council of Trent. Translated by H. J. Schroeder (Rockford, Ill., 1992). English translation of all the official pronouncements of the Council of Trent.

Cochrane, Eric. *Italy 1530–1630* (London and New York, 1988). Synthesis of Italian history in the century after the High Renaissance, including an excellent chapter on Catholic reform and the Council of Trent.

Collinson, Patrick. *The Elizabethan Puritan Movement* (1967; Oxford, 1990). Classic, extraordinarily thorough narrative of the emergence, consolidation, and decline of Elizabethan puritanism as an identifiable movement.

Davis, Natalie Zemon. *Society and Culture in Early Modern France* (Stanford, 1975). Important, extremely influential collection of articles dealing with aspects of the social, cultural, and religious history of sixteenth-century France.

Dickens, A. G. *The English Reformation*, 2nd ed. (University Park, Pa., 1989). Classic, traditional narrative of the English Reformation, first published in 1964, emphasizing the problems in the late medieval Church, the importance of Lollardy, and grassroots support for Protestantism. Criticized by much recent scholarship.

Diefendorf, Barbara. *Beneath the Cross: Catholics and Huguenots in Sixteenth-Century Paris* (New York, 1991). Valuable, insightful study on Catholic-Huguenot relations in Paris in the years prior to and including the St. Bartholomew's Day massacre.

Ditchfield, Simon. *Liturgy, Sanctity and History in Tridentine Italy: Pietro Maria Campi and the Preservation of the Particular* (Cambridge, 1995). Superb, carefully researched study about the relationships among Catholic hagiography, worship, devotion, and historical writing in the late sixteenth and seventeenth centuries.

Donaldson, Gordon. *The Scottish Reformation* (1960; Cambridge, 1979). Remains the best place to start for a narrative account of the Reformation in Scotland.

Duffy, Eamon. *The Stripping of the Altars: Traditional Religion in England, c. 1400–c. 1580* (New Haven, 1992). A monumental reinterpretation of the Protestant Reformation in England, viewed from the perspective of what was destroyed rather than created. Exceptionally sympathetic, penetrating reconstruction of late medieval Catholicism.

Duke, Alastair. *Reformation and Revolt in the Low Countries* (London and Ronceverte, 1990). Valuable collection of essays on the Dutch Reformation and Dutch Revolt by one of the leading experts in the field.

Dures, Alan. *English Catholicism, 1558–1642: Continuity and Change* (Harlow, Essex, 1983). Concise introductory overview on the survival and character of English Catholicism between the death of Mary Tudor and the English Revolution.

Eck, Johann. *Enchiridion of Commonplaces against Luther and Other Enemies of the Church*. Edited and translated by Ford Lewis Battles (Grand Rapids, Mich., 1979). English translation of an important early Catholic work against the teachings of the early Protestant reformers.

Edwards, Mark U., Jr. *Printing, Propaganda, and Martin Luther* (Berkeley, 1994). Shows not only the importance of printed pamphlets and broadsheets to early German Reformation propaganda, but also the extent to which Luther's writings dominated it.

Erasmus, Desiderius, and Martin Luther. *Discourse on Free Will.* Translated and edited by Ernst F. Winter (New York, 1961). Selections from Erasmus's *Freedom of the Will* (1524) and Luther's *Bondage of the Will* (1525), sufficient to give the reader a clear sense of their differences.

Evennett, H. Outram. *The Spirit of the Counter Reformation.* Edited by John Bossy (Notre Dame, Ind., 1970). Classic, sensitive treatment of Catholic spirituality and institutions in the sixteenth century, based on lectures delivered in 1951.

Forster, Marc R. *The Counter-Reformation in the Villages: Religion and Reform in the Bishopric of Speyer* (Ithaca, N.Y., 1992). Valuable local study that challenges one-way, top-down version of the way in which Tridentine Catholicism was implemented.

Friesen, Abraham. *Thomas Muentzer, A Destroyer of the Godless: The Making of a Sixteenth-Century Religious Revolutionary* (Berkeley, 1990). Study of Müntzer's theology and reforming career that attempts to show the influence on him of Eusebius, Augustine, and Tauler.

Gregory, Brad S. *Salvation at Stake: Christian Martyrdom in Early Modern Europe* (Cambridge, Mass., 1999). Cross-confessional, multi-perspectival analysis of Protestant, Anabaptist, and Catholic martyrdom in the Reformation era and its importance for understanding religious sensibilities and the formation of distinct confessional traditions.

Haigh, Christopher. *English Reformations: Religion, Politics, and Society under the Tudors* (Oxford, 1993). Important recent revisionist narrative of the English Reformation, emphasizing political contingency and the slow, incomplete Protestantization of England by the early seventeenth century.

Hill, Christopher. *The World Turned Upside Down: Radical Ideas During the English Revolution* (1972; New York, 1991). Classic, sympathetic study of the numerous radical religious and political groups that emerged in England during the 1640s and 1650s.

Hirst, Derek. *Authority and Conflict: England, 1603–1658* (Cambridge, Mass., 1986). Excellent narrative history of early Stuart England and the English Revolution, emphasizing the relationship between politics and religion.

Holt, Mack P. *The French Wars of Religion, 1562–1629* (Cambridge, 1996). Narrative overview of the religious wars in France, notable for including the conflicts of the 1620s and for the scholarly presence of the social history of the Reformation.

Höpfl, Harro. *The Christian Polity of John Calvin* (Cambridge, 1982). Brilliant analysis of how changes in context shaped Calvin's political thought in successive versions of the *Institutes.*

Hsia, R. Po-chia. "Münster and the Anabaptists." In *The German People and the Reformation,* ed. Hsia (Ithaca, N.Y., 1989). Good interpretive article about the Anabaptist Kingdom of Münster.

———. *Social Discipline in the Reformation: Central Europe, 1550–1750* (London, 1989). Valuable synthesis dealing with Lutheran, Calvinist, and Catholic confessionalization in Germany that takes a comparative, long-term perspective.

Huppert, George. *After the Black Death: A Social History of Early Modern Europe,* 2nd ed. (Bloomington, Ind., 1998). Good introduction to basic social conditions and structures of late medieval and early modern Europe.

Israel, Jonathan I. *The Dutch Republic: Its Rise, Greatness, and Fall 1477–1806* (Oxford, 1995). Massive, detailed history on all aspects of the northern Netherlands, with excellent chapters on the Dutch Reformation, Dutch Revolt, and religion in the seventeenth century.

Jedin, Hubert. "Catholic Reformation or Counter-Reformation?" In *The Counter-Reformation: The Essential Readings,* ed. David M. Luebke (Malden, Mass., 1999). Classic essay, first published in German in 1946, that distinguished between Catholic Reform and Counter-Reformation.

———. *A History of the Council of Trent,* vols. 1–2 (St. Louis, 1957). English translation of the first two of four volumes (through 1547) of the magisterial history of the Council of Trent.

Kaplan, Benjamin J. *Calvinists and Libertines: Confession and Community in Utrecht, 1578–1620* (Oxford, 1995). Excellent study of side-by-side, competing Protestant communities in the Dutch city of Utrecht, one stricter than the other.

Kingdon, Robert M. *Geneva and the Coming of the Wars of Religion in France, 1555–1563* (Geneva, 1956). Classic, influential study on the importance of Geneva for the early Calvinist churches in France.

Knecht, R. J. *The French Wars of Religion, 1559–1598* (New York, 1989). Succinct, useful overview that appends a number of key documents in translation.

Lindley, Keith, editor. *The English Civil War and Revolution: A Sourcebook* (New York, 1998). Selection of primary documents pertinent to the politics and religion of the English Revolution.

Luther, Martin. *Martin Luther's Basic Theological Writings.* Edited by Timothy F. Lull (Minneapolis, 1989). Good one-volume selection of Luther's most important pamphlets and treatises, drawn from the standard American edition of Luther's collected works.

MacCormack, Sabine. "'The Heart Has Its Reasons': Predicaments of Missionary Christianity in Early Colonial Peru." In *The Counter-Reformation: The Essential Readings,* ed. David M. Luebke (Malden, Mass., 1999). Excellent article concerning different missionary approaches and their pitfalls in early modern Peru.

MacCulloch, Diarmaid. *The Later Reformation in England, 1547–1603* (Houndmills, Basingstoke, 1990). The best introduction to English Protestantism in the reigns of Edward VI and Elizabeth.

McConica, James K. *Erasmus* (Oxford, 1991). Concise, incisive account of Erasmus's intellectual formation, important writings, and influence as a Christian humanist.

McGinness, Frederick J. *Right Thinking and Sacred Oratory in Counter-Reformation Rome* (Princeton, 1995). Fine study on the image of Rome as the center of the Catholic world in the decades after the Council of Trent, concentrating especially on preaching.

Moeller, Bernd. *Imperial Cities and the Reformation* (Ithaca, N.Y., 1972). Includes the enormously influential title essay about the fit between late medieval urban ideology and the Reformation.

———. "Religious Life in Germany on the Eve of the Reformation." In *Pre-Reformation Germany*, ed. and trans. Gerald Strauss (London, 1972). Classic article arguing for the vitality of Catholic belief and practice on the eve of the Reformation in Germany.

Monter, William. *Calvin's Geneva* (New York, 1967). Remains an excellent introduction to the city and its institutions in the time of Calvin.

Nauert, Charles. *Humanism and the Culture of Renaissance Europe* (Cambridge, 1995). Broad, synthetic introduction to Renaissance humanism in general and its place in wider European society and culture, both in Italy and north of the Alps.

Oakley, Francis. *The Western Church in the Later Middle Ages* (Ithaca, N.Y., 1979). Fine, well-written survey on the late medieval Church, its institutions, intellectual traditions, and spiritual traditions.

Oberman, Heiko A. *Luther: Man between God and the Devil* (New Haven, 1989). Superb, penetrating evocation of Luther's theology and experience in context, eschewing modern distortions. Best single-volume study of Luther available in English.

Olin, John C., editor. *The Catholic Reformation: Savonarola to Ignatius Loyola. Reform in the Church, 1495–1540* (New York, 1969). Collection of English sources pertinent to Catholic Reform up to the founding of the Society of Jesus.

O'Malley, John. *The First Jesuits* (Cambridge, Mass., 1993). Masterful, deeply learned synthesis of the character and ministries of the Society of Jesus from 1540 up to the early 1560s.

Pabel, Hilmar, editor. *Erasmus' Vision of the Church* (Kirksville, Mo., 1995). Collection of essays by leading Erasmus scholars on the Christian humanist's views on ecclesiology and reform.

Packull, Werner. *Hutterite Beginnings: Communitarian Experiments in the Reformation* (Baltimore, 1995). Deeply researched, careful study of early German-speaking Anabaptism, including but not limited to Jakob Huter and the Hutterites.

Parker, Geoffrey. *The Dutch Revolt* (Ithaca, N.Y., 1977). Outstanding, concise narrative of the Dutch Revolt from the antecedents in the 1550s to the consolidation in the early seventeenth century, concentrating especially on 1564 to 1589.

———, editor. *The Thirty Years' War* (London and New York, 1997). Collection of detailed articles concentrating on political and diplomatic history.

Pettegree, Andrew. *Emden and the Dutch Revolt: Exile and the Development of Reformed Protestantism* (Oxford, 1992). Well-researched study on the importance of Emden for Calvinism in the Netherlands, emphasizing its role as a destination for refugees and a center of printing.

Potter, G. R. *Zwingli* (Cambridge, 1976). Standard, comprehensive biography of Zwingli in English.

Rabb, Theodore K. *The Struggle for Stability in Early Modern Europe* (1975; Oxford, 1986). Classic, elegant essay on Europe's seventeenth-century crisis and its resolution, emphasizing the centrality of the Thirty Years' War.

Reardon, Bernard M. G. *Religious Thought in the Reformation*, 2nd ed. (London and New York, 1995). Probably the best one-volume introduction to the theology of the major Protestant reformers. Just one chapter each on radical Protestantism and Catholicism.

Rex, Richard. *Henry VIII and the English Reformation* (Houndmills, 1993). Lucid, analytical approach to the Henrician Reformation, notable for treatment of its impact on traditional religious practices.

Richardson, R.C. *The Debate on the English Revolution*, 3rd ed. (New York, 1998). Excellent orientation to historians' debates over the nature of the English Revolution.

Ross, Andrew C. *A Vision Betrayed: The Jesuits in Japan and China, 1542–1742* (Edinburgh, 1994). Good overview of the missionary successes and disappointments of the Society of Jesus in Asia.

Scribner, Robert W. *For the Sake of Simple Folk: Popular Propaganda for the German Reformation*, 2nd ed. (Oxford, 1994). Influential, sophisticated analysis of early Reformation iconography in the context of the period's visual culture.

Simons, Menno. *The Complete Writings of Menno Simons*. Translated by Leonard Verduin, edited by J. C. Wenger (Scottdale, Pa., 1956). Standard English translation of the writings of the most important Dutch Anabaptist leader.

Skinner, Quentin. *The Foundations of Modern Political Thought*, 2 vols. (Cambridge, 1978). Valuable synthesis of Renaissance (vol. 1) and Reformation (vol. 2) political thought in its relationship to political events in the fifteenth and sixteenth centuries.

Smith, Alan G. R. *The Emergence of a Nation State: The Commonwealth of England, 1529–1660*, 2nd ed. (1997). Detailed, synthetic overview of England's political, social, economic, cultural, and religious history from the Henrician Reformation to the Restoration.

Snyder, C. Arnold. *The Life and Thought of Michael Sattler* (Scottdale, Pa., 1984). Excellent analysis of an early central Swiss Brethren leader and author of the *Schleitheim Articles*, important for suggesting ties between Sattler's Anabaptist thought and his years as a Benedictine monk.

Spence, Jonathan. *The Memory Palace of Matteo Ricci* (1984; New York, 1994). Brilliant, beautifully written story of Jesuit missionary Matteo Ricci in China that skillfully meshes European and Asian cultural history.

Stayer, James M. *Anabaptists and the Sword*, 2nd ed. (Lawrence, Kans., 1976). Classic study of Anabaptist attitudes toward temporal authority and the use of governmental coercion by a master historian of the Radical Reformation.

———. *The German Peasants' War and Anabaptist Community of Goods* (Montreal and Kingston, 1991). A collection of interrelated essays, especially important for showing connections between the German Peasants' War and early Anabaptism.

Stephens, W. P. *Zwingli: An Introduction to His Thought* (Oxford, 1992). Clear, useful introduction to Zwingli's theology, arranged thematically.

Stone, Lawrence. *The Causes of the English Revolution, 1529–1642* (1972; London and New York, 1996). Concise, elegant essay on the long-term, middle-term, and short-term causes of the English Revolution; still valuable despite being criticized by more recent scholarship.

Strauss, Gerald. *Luther's House of Learning: Indoctrination of the Young in the German Reformation* (Baltimore, 1978). Very important and influential study of the theory, practice, and substantial failure of Lutheran catechetical and educational instruction in Germany.

Swanson, R. N. *Religion and Devotion in Europe, c. 1215–c. 1515* (Cambridge, 1995). Best one-volume overview in English of Catholic institutions, beliefs, practices, and offices between the Fourth Lateran Council and the Reformation.

ten Doornkat Koolman, Jacobus. *Dirk Philips: Friend and Colleague of Menno Simons, 1504–1568.* Edited by C. Arnold Snyder (Kitchener, Ont., 1998). Translated from the Dutch original (1964), a dated but informationally useful study of an important Mennonite writer and leader.

Tracy, James D. "With and Without the Counter-Reformation: The Catholic Church in the Spanish Netherlands and the Dutch Republic, 1580–1650." *Catholic Historical Review* 71 (1985). Valuable overview of four decades of scholarship on Dutch Catholicism in the northern and southern Netherlands.

Wendel, François. *Calvin: Origins and Development of His Religious Thought* (Durham, N.C., 1987). Probably the best one-volume introduction and overview of Calvin's theology; balanced and incisive.

Notes

Notes